Fake News in Digital Cultures

Fake News in Digital Cultures: Technology, Populism and Digital Misinformation

BY

ROB COVER
RMIT University, Australia

ASHLEIGH HAW
University of Melbourne, Australia

AND

JAY DANIEL THOMPSON
RMIT University, Australia

emerald
PUBLISHING

United Kingdom – North America – Japan – India – Malaysia – China

Emerald Publishing Limited
Emerald Publishing, Floor 5, Northspring, 21-23 Wellington Street, Leeds LS1 4DL.

First edition 2022

Reprints and permissions service
Contact: www.copyright.com

British Library Cataloguing in Publication Data
A catalogue record for this book is available from the British Library

ISBN: 978-1-80117-877-8 (Print)
ISBN: 978-1-80117-876-1 (Online)
ISBN: 978-1-80117-878-5 (Epub)
ISBN: 978-1-80117-879-2 (Paperback)

INVESTOR IN PEOPLE

Rob dedicates this book to the late Ashton Taylor, cousin and former student, whose journalism and blogging on health disinformation scandals played an important role in highlighting the material impact of false hope on Australians with chronic illnesses.

Ashleigh dedicates this book to her father, Rex Haw, whose tireless career in journalism and unwaivering dedication to purveying information that informs democracy has led to many fruitful discussions about the core issues of this book.

Jay dedicates this book to the late Janet Malcolm, whose elegant prose and commitment to journalistic ethics has inspired generations of media writers.

Contents

Acknowledgements

The thinking, research and discourse underpinning this book has benefitted from many valuable conversations with peers, students, research participants and friends in many settings around the world.

The authors wish to acknowledge the staff, students and colleagues at RMIT University and the University of Melbourne for their support and for providing time to develop this work.

Great conversations with colleagues and peers are key in forming new ideas, approaches and ways of thinking differently about an everyday topic. We owe a debt of gratitude to many people, including particularly Linda Brennan, Benedetta Brevini, Mark Davis, Karen Farquharson, Catherine Gomes, Catharine Lumby, Denis Muller, Christy Newman, Lukas Parker, Tinonee Pym, Kurt Sengul, Verity Trott, Lisa Waller, John Weldon, Scott Wright and Charlotte Young.

We also thank Rex and Fiona Haw, Peter and Trish Thompson, Dean Tunbridge and Jeff Williams.

Chapter One

Introduction: Digital Cultures and Fake News

What is Fake News?

In its current, contemporary form, fake news emerged as a concept, a topic and a social issue in the mid-2010s. There has, of course, been a long-standing concept of false communication, lies, propaganda and media bias, extending back centuries and related often to the key emergent media and communication forms of the day. However, the circulation today of fake news as online material – either as deliberate disinformation or accidentally believed and shared as misinformation – is widely recognised as having a serious and problematic impact on how we perceive politics and politicians. It is also understood as affecting the capacity to distribute accurate health information (particularly since the COVID-19 pandemic), the capability of 'real' journalists to perform the task of objective reporting and re-circulating newsworthy content, and the ability of public figures, celebrities and everyday individuals to maintain reputation and control public narratives about their lives, work and activities. Questions about the current and future meaning of truth, post-truth, facts, journalistic practices and news routines are increasingly debated not only by professionals, scholars and practitioners, but by politicians, artists, everyday readers and viewers of news, and others.

If we were to ask a random person on the street what they thought about fake news, there are considerable odds they would have a strong opinion and most would probably express their concern about the quality of information in an era in which disinformation, misinformation and falsehood circulate purporting to be news. If we were to ask a political agent at any time over the past five years, they will more likely express their concern that the circulation of fake news in the form of deliberate disinformation has substantially complexified the practices needed for proper political messaging during an election period. And if we ask people in health communication or social welfare at any time since the start of 2020, they will undoubtedly explain that both deliberate disinformation dressed up as news stories and *misinformation* (the re-circulation of inaccurate ideas by those who have been misled by such fake news) have made it more difficult to get results from health communication, including gaining compliance with the life-saving social distancing and mask-wearing practices needed globally during the

Fake News in Digital Cultures: Technology, Populism and Digital Misinformation, 1–15
Copyright © 2022 by Rob Cover, Ashleigh Haw and Jay Daniel Thompson
Published under exclusive licence by Emerald Publishing Limited
doi:10.1108/978-1-80117-876-120221001

COVID-19 pandemic, with faith in institutional health communicators, and in garnering traction with vaccination regimes. In that sense, fake news is not just a matter of communication becoming more complex in the twenty-first century, or of the extra labour demanded of communication professionals to ensure factual communication, but has an impact on the everyday lives of ordinary communicators – where social participation, identity and belonging is grounded in cultural relationalities that are grounded in communication.

In the twenty-first century, fake news can be described as follows: deceptive content circulated primarily through digital networks, created deliberately to shape a particular public viewpoint or perception of a topic. It is broadly understood as text (including audio or video) which purports to be news but is intentionally and verifiably false, aiming to mislead readers and viewers (Allcott & Gentzkow, 2017, p. 213). It generally relies on a kind of 'trickery' whereby those deliberately circulating fake news for nefarious purposes do so by dressing up information in a form that might appear to be news (for example, adopting the tone, style, newsworthiness and pyramiding functions of recognisable news) and with embellishments that make it appear to be from a credible news source (for example, a website that has an address, or URL, very closely matching that of a recognised news site, or the deliberate use of banners, headers and logos of credible news sites).

An important example is news which has circulated through social media purporting to be from a credible source. In October 2016, a viral story circulated that claimed anti-Trump protesters attending his pre-election rallies were being paid by the Democratic Party. A user would click a link circulating on social media that contained the headline 'Donald Trump Protester Speaks Out: I Was Paid $3,500 To Protest Trump's Rally'. Clicking the link would take the user to a web page purporting to be that of the United States' *American Broadcasting Company* (ABC). The page had the logo, look and feel of an ABC news story, but was not news published by them. The giveaway? A URL that, at first glance, is similar to ABC's website but not actually the correct URL. A discerning reader might notice the site, but we doubt that many people necessarily check a browser's address bar unless there is a particular reason. Good security software aligned with a computer browser might pick up on a known fake news site and alert the reader. But for a very large number of digital citizens, a false story may be taken in as fact. A portion of the electorate may be led to believe that the recognised Democrats were using underhand tactics to destabilise Donald Trump's election campaign. Others may believe that the genuine protest movement and dissent against Donald Trump was smaller than otherwise known (Keller, 2016). Ultimately, however, those who were misled were *potentially* at risk of casting votes or forming attitudes that were improperly influenced not by a distillation of fact but by the purely non-factual lie.

We discuss the definitions of fake news and its relationships with disinformation, misinformation, propaganda, deep-fakes and concepts of truth and democracy in the next chapter. It is helpful here to briefly to drill down a little further into some of the key concepts, and what these might mean for apprehending and addressing fake news as a social problem. That is, to recognise fake news as a serious social issue, we are obliged to consider not only its meanings and effects but to draw on cultural studies' collective tools to make sense of its origins and formation in historical, philosophical, social and cultural knowledge frameworks. This means that, at times, fake news is a vague concept, sometimes it is a catch-all for anything disliked, sometimes it is used to discredit genuine factual communication, and other times its definitions are too simplistic to be of any use in finding solutions. Mara (2019) defines fake news as a news story that has been released through recognised media that is either greatly exaggerated or outrightly untrue (4), arguing that the unknowable capacity for a tweet to go viral and thereby be circulated and reinforced through that circulation globally is a key factor in the production and persistence of fake news. Conversely, Brian McNair (2017) understands the meaning of fake news not through the destabilising movement of its false content but as an expression of 'a wider crisis of trust in elites, including political and mainstream media elites, whose members are struggling to maintain their traditional roles in our liberal democracies' (p. x). In looking to the ways in which fake news is the emanation of alternative political practices, McNair is interested in defining it through its concomitant impact that further embeds and sustains distrust, both produced through and reinforcing political and social crises that mark the twenty-first century.

At other times, however, fake news might be understood to be news that comes from a credible news source but is a mistake gone viral. This is not the same as news where a factual error (of the kind for which we expect a later correction by the publication) has crept in. Rather, it is where a mistake is made based on the circulation of a falsehood and re-circulated by a credible media source. For example, on New Year's Eve of 2016, BBCNewsUKI tweeted a post which read: 'BREAKING: Buckingham Palace announces the death of Queen Elizabeth II at the age of 90. Circumstances are unknown. More to follow'. The tweet is obviously believable: 90 years is not an unexpected age for a death. Those in the know would realise, of course, that an announcement from Buckingham Palace would give some details of the circumstances, but most would also know that BBC are likely to be the first principal media to communicate the story. The BBCNewsUKI account was fake (Taylor, 2016). But a different story had happened earlier – in June 2015 a BBC journalist had accidentally tweeted 'Queen Elizabeth has DIED. @BBCWorld'. The tweets were quickly retracted with an apology; later reports stated the BBC had been carrying out a rehearsal for announcing the Queen's death and the journalist had mistakenly posted it as if real news (Winchester, 2015). Naturally, the tweet was viral before it could be stopped, and it is only by the virality of a retraction and explanation that the public were informed of the facts. While the 2015 incident was an accident and the 2016 incident a fake news hoax, in both cases there is a real risk beyond wounded feelings, upset royal fans or a concerned Buckingham Palace: share markets, valuation of currency, and everyday people's travel and business plans are usually instantly affected by the news of the death of a major figure, world leader or, in this case, a head of state.

· In this opening chapter, we begin by discussing some of the first-level definitions of fake news before building on them in more detail in later chapters. We provide the theoretical framework for understanding the emergence of fake news, not as an alien concept that has infiltrated our forms of communication, but as arising out of cultural formations that were already in play. We present a run-down of the later chapters and address the core arguments of this book: that to apprehend and make sense of fake news, we need to consider it from a range of perspectives that account for how changes to cultural and communication practices, developments and uptake of digital communication methods, shifts in the understanding of truth and meaning, and frameworks that encourage conspiratorial thinking and negative attitudes towards minorities all come together to play a role in the rise of fake news as a social problem. It is only by taking it to task as a core element of contemporary culture that we can begin to find ways to remedy fake news and address the future of communication ethics.

Cultural Circulation of Fake News: Disinformation, Misinformation and Risk

In Chapter Two, we present a typology of the different aspects, angles and forms of fake news, although a brief summary of some of these is important to unpack here before we can begin to theorise the cultural conditions that enable the production, circulation and conceptualisation of fake news. If fake news is that which we define as false content dressed up to look like, or be misread as, news, then it is important to make sense of it in terms of the complex meanings and practices that constitute disinformation, misinformation and what has recently begun to be called 'post-truth'.

We differentiate *disinformation* (deliberate false content) from *misinformation* in this book. Misinformation is typically understood as false, inaccurate, or misleading information that is disseminated regardless of whether or not there is an intention to deceive (Lazer et al., 2018). That would include a person on-forwarding disinformation content because the user genuinely believes that content to be true. Where this matters for fake news, however, is in the blurring between legitimate news sources and the *facts* of disinformation and misinformation. As journalistic routines become further stretched by the neoliberal demands in profit-making news enterprises that seek to reduce expenditure and labour costs, journalists who may be investigating misinformation that has circulated via Twitter, for example, have less capacity and time to fact-check, gain alternative interview quotes or otherwise assess the veracity of the content before on-sharing with the brand power of their news masthead. The field of news as the record of fact is dismantled unwittingly not by the fact of disinformation, but by the problem of the rampant circulation of misinformation.

One of our favourite examples of the relationship between disinformation, misinformation and fake news is a piece of content circulated heavily on Facebook in early 2021. In the style of a magazine or feature article, it is content that claims Australian singer Olivia Newton-John is promoting a line of hemp gummies (sugar treats containing cannabidiol or CBD) and is now under attack by pharmaceutical companies looking to close down her alternative medicine. The article, titled 'Big Pharma In Outrage Over Olivia Newton-John Latest Business Venture – She Fires Back With This!' purports to be from *People* magazine, using the well-recognised *People* logo at the top of the web page. The first giveaway that this might be fake news for the discerning reader is that it incongruously is a site page at the URL https://womenclothingbeauty.com/. The article presents information claiming that Newton-John's start-up selling CBD lollies as a pain relief and health supplement has taken off, that as CEO of this company she is struggling to keep up with demand, and the Bayer and Purdue (two major pharmaceutical companies) are 'furious after seeing a massive dip in their sales, calling for Oliva Newton-John to be indicted ...' This fake article goes on with content claiming Newton-John has appeared on television to state she will not be intimidated by these companies. The article then gives a run-down on the alleged health value of hemp gummies (for pain relief, for reducing blood glucose among persons with diabetes, to reduce anxiety, to help quit smoking). Shifting more into advertorial half-way down, the content gives testimonials for Olivia Newton-John's hemp gummies from Hugh Laurie, Colin Firth, the late Sean Connery and Dame Maggie Smith. The bottom of the page contains an advertisement (limited time special offer) for jars of hemp gummies and some Facebook or Twitter style comments feed giving generic endorsements from everyday people.

From the perspective of scholars, of discerning readers, and of people critically engaged in health discourses, this fake news piece is hilarious. From the perspective of engaging with health communication risks, however, it is worrying. How does it work? The content begins as disinformation – a deliberate attempt to trick people into believing a popular, ageing singer has branched out into health supplement development and supply. It relies on a particular kind of discourse that claims adversity between this company and major pharmaceutical companies, primarily to appeal to a particular audience: those who are likely to disavow 'big pharma' and keen to see it punished, fail or make a loss. It uses language to appeal to the existing adherents of non-pharmaceutical health supplements, while relying on celebrity endorsements. It targets an older market (those reasonably more likely to experience arthritic pain, diabetes, etc.) and uses celebrities from a similar age group. Claiming to be a feature from both *People* and *Time* magazines, it covers the celebrity gossip and current affairs readerships. The fake news story was disseminated on Facebook as a paid-for advertisement, relying on Facebook's newsfeed algorithm to send it to particular feeds. This is the point at which it has the potential to become *misinformation* – when with a click one user passes it on to another user, likes it, unwittingly endorsing it, or perhaps in some cases openly recommending it (before ever making a purchase). If the combination of disinformation and misinformed viral on-pushing are successful, the story becomes fake news, recognised by some readers as fake (and perhaps reported to Facebook) but nevertheless read by a portion of readers mistakenly *as if* a real article. If it appeals, if the criteria are right, a problematic health product will be purchased in favour of prescribed medicine. And that puts lives at risk.

Fake News as Cultural Emergence and Cultural Crisis

Fake news has sometimes been described *as if* it is an alien phenomenon that is disrupting our otherwise ordinary, normal or timeless news, information and truth practices. Often associated with the problematic election of Donald Trump to the US presidency, it has also occasionally been assumed that the problem of fake news will go away when Trump, people behind disinformation, and poor practices of dishonesty also go away, and when social networks lift their game in developing tools that will prevent the circulation of non-factual information (effective tools for this purpose do not yet exist, and may never do so given the impact this has not only non-factual content but on opinion, personal stories, viewpoints and other kinds of speech.) While the idea that fake news is something from outside our contemporary culture that can be excised is a very pleasant ideal, this way of thinking utterly neglects the fact that fake news is an emergent problem grounded in contemporary culture – a culture that makes, constitutes and sets the conditions for the rise of contemporary fake news, rather than simply one that is problematically 'infected' by it.

To make sense of this emergence, we can rely on some of the early cultural studies analyses of Raymond Williams (1977) to help make sense of how different new configurations come into being not from outside but from within contemporary culture, how they present new challenges to dominant, ordinary practices that have come to seem 'normal', and how new practices themselves may be either subsumed as part of our dominant norm or even replace the known 'wisdom' of the existing media and information dissemination practices.

Fake news, in a cultural perspective, is not merely a challenge to more ethical practices of information-sharing, networking and disseminating news, nor is it simply a new iteration of propaganda, biased news-writing or hoaxes. Rather, in Raymond Williams' culturalist terminology, it can be understood as the cultural production of a new 'structure of feeling', describing the public consciousness of a particular historical moment in regard to a particular group or setting within a cultural milieu. It is useful to think about this in terms of Williams' (1977) distinctions between the *residual*, the *dominant*, and the *emergent* (pp. 122–125). All three frameworks are part of the broad structure of feeling of a culture, but they function in somewhat different ways.

In the second decade of the twenty-first century, we might argue that there are several extant 'residual' attitudes towards news and information. For Williams, the residual is not 'archaic' or wholly located in the past – we might say that recording information on stone tablets, or using only horseback couriers to share news or even the telegram are archaic, and have absolutely no functional value in contemporary society. Indeed, the infrastructure and knowledge frameworks for these practices are no longer in place. The residual, however, describes certain practices, meanings, values, experiences and ways of being that operate today but cannot be expressed or understood in terms of dominant culture. We could suggest, for example, that community group newsletters that are printed and mailed out are part of the residual practice of news-sharing and dissemination. They exist, they are undertaken by many non-profit groups, they have eschewed the value of digital media for dissemination or sometimes deliberately not taken advantage of its affordances in order to appeal to a particular set of tastes and audience practices.

Likewise, in many cases, community newspapers serving migrant and foreign-language communities play a vital role in the lives of everyday readers

(Cover, 2013) but are not fully assimilable to the contemporary liberal-capitalist profit-making news production environment. Such residual practices continue, for Williams (1977), because the dominant cannot go too far in excluding or eradicating the residual without drawing attention to the hegemonic practices of the dominant (p. 123). For example, local community print media continues to be funded and supported by governments not necessarily because it fits within dominant neoliberal platforms – often it is barely profit-making and supported by grants – but because in letting that part of the media sector disappear there is a greater risk of dissatisfaction with the practices and motivations of 'mainstream' news media. When we see arguments about the utility and significance of the community media sector or, for example, government funding regimes that prop up community media through grants that are not accessible by major media players, we are witnessing the interplay between the residual and the dominant.

Raymond Williams spent less time defining how the dominant cultural structure is constituted, although we might consider this to be the culture of liberal-capitalist media and communication. This is not simply one element or aspect of news in everyday life, but incorporates a range of practices that emerged at different times and co-exist (not always happily) in the everyday lives of readers, journalists, content producers and those who profit from them. An example is the contemporary print newspaper as it emerged in seventeenth century Europe (subsequent to the printing press and in the context of both nationalistic and middle-class developments) and found profit through a mix of sales and advertising. Read on a daily or weekly basis by those who had it delivered, those who purchased it from a location, and those who later read online version on publications' websites became the dominant news practice within the culture of news consumption. This dominance has not, of course, gone unchallenged by news and media dissemination practices that emerged in the 1990s and 2000s, including the rise of the blogosphere, and the production of news content by new actors such as social networks and search engines, and the increasing shift to distribution through feeds rather than the 'pull' mechanism of deliberate site visits. The relative rise of direct publication of news agencies such as Reuters and Associated Press is another challenge.

Finally, the practice of consuming news through social media feeds that rely on a combination of user data and cookies to target specific content to specific groups of readers is another formation that emerged over the past two decades and has come to be normative as part of the dominant landscape or 'matrix' of news media production and consumption practices. Many aspects of this emergence have been, of course, subsumed by savvy corporate news outlets to form part of the transformation of the dominant. In that sense, the dominant incorporates an unhappy, tenuous alliance of products, platforms, company, regulatory practices, readership practices, tastes, appreciations and criticisms – all of which centre on the conversion of content into profit and the adaptation of audiences, readers, viewers and users' attention into a commodity, itself on-sold to advertisers and sponsors.

Importantly, a major part of the dominant structure of feeling includes both trust and distrust of news in its many forms. *Trust* in news sources has been the key element in the dominant culture of news consumption. Among scholars, it incorporates practices of citing news articles as fact in order to underpin an argument, which may mean a temporary suspension of the critical project of news critique. Among other everyday readers, it involves everything from the practice of uncritical reading and belief in the information communication in a news article, to sharing it on social media, discussing the news with friends and family and taking clippings or screenshots of news – that is, the everyday intended use of the dominant media regime.

At the same time, practices of distrust are sometimes more nuanced and include both scholarly and lay criticism of bias, critiques of the entire profit-making news regime, preferences around quality, taste and content, adversarial debates about publishers, criticism of individual journalists. A long and theoretically powerful scholarly critique that understands all communication to be marked by polysemy (multiple meanings, multiple 'truths') has underscored the need for a democratic public to be wary of any perception that a news outlet speaks a monolithic truth. This critique sits alongside the equally important guardedness over any communication understood to benefit an establishment, an inequitable socio-economic status quo, governance regimes, disciplinary practices and other activities that set agendas and promote gate-keeping that has traditionally prevented the equal circulation of alternative viewpoints. Such criticisms have been core approaches to media and communication within the political science, humanities, sociology and cultural studies critique of media, communication and language since the 1970s. Taught in many university courses and debated in ever greater depth among scholars in journal articles, books and at conferences, a critical approach grounded in anti-institutional and anti-establishment thinking is a core element in the academic pursuit of more just, more ethical and more equitable ways of organising society.

The fact that trust and distrust co-exist does not undo the dominant media framework or leave it unstable. Social structures are not marked by a universal one-sided perspective, but by frameworks of debate. However, within that disagreement are the seeds for the emergence of fake news. By this, we don't mean the emergence of individual actors in fake news, whether those who might be producing or sharing it, fake news factory farms, hoaxers or others. What we are talking about is the emergence of the conditions that both constitute fake news and make it an issue. For Williams, the emergence differs from both the residual and the dominant. He describes the emergence as being marked by new articulations that arise not as processes isolated from the dominant but from new configurations of knowledge, meanings, values, practices and relationships. That which is emergent is not necessarily fully oppositional to the dominant, but may include 'elements of some new phase of the dominant culture' as well as those which are depicted as 'substantially alternative' (p. 123). In other words, a new emergent process does not come about in isolation, but *through* the dominant in ways which also leave it open to reincorporation (p. 124) or sometimes to being depicted as an oppositional threat to the dominant and thereby excluded or suppressed (p. 126).

Here we might describe the current phase of everyday capacity to generate fake news which has the look and feel of a real news story but is deliberate disinformation – the capacity to bypass gate-keeping frameworks. Or we might describe the culture of post-truth in which some of the more ludicrous forms of disinformation and misinformation (such as the fakery of anti-vaccination movements or COVID-19 denialism) becomes believable because the already-existing scepticism about establishment media morphs into a new phase. This new phase is marked by the conditions that allow a group of actors to believe they can or should produce alternative content that tricks people into believing their non-evidenced perspective or shapes a readership into adhering to a particular belief or attitude. And it is the emergent conditions that make it possible for such media to be unwittingly circulated by the misinformed as become a *normative* experience of everyday life. Finally, what is emergent is the counter-activity: what is culturally normative is not necessarily hegemonic and without dissent. The fact that fake news starts to become a *talking point* from about 2015 or 2016, that *fact-checking* agencies begin to arise, that government, political, corporate and scholarly actors begin to look for ways to curtail fake news (some to restore an older, dominant framework for news media, others to new, more ethical and as-yet-unforeseen sets of alternatives) points to the fractious, liminal setting in which the emergent fake news framework interacts with the dominant.

At another level, we can understand fake news not merely coming about or emerging due to the crisis in the dominant regime, but also as crisis itself. It marks a shift in how we consume news, produce it and critique it. For scholars such as ourselves, it changes our relationship with institutional and corporate media, which emerges suddenly as an ally against populism, the extremes of white supremacism, the exigencies of anti-health discourses and conspiracy theories, and the anti-establishment arguments that threaten violence. Resulting from the emergence of fake news and the problematic outcomes of disinformation and misinformation, then, corporate media is re-positioned culturally as something to defend as offering a form of security against the violent chaos of untruthful communication. Fake news is crisis not because it necessarily changes our reading and media consumption practice, nor only because it has the capacity to disrupt our ability to make political decisions and everyday decisions of health, life and liveability (Tucker et al., 2018), but because it forces shifts in cultural, social and political relationships, perceptions, attitudes and ways of perceiving communication itself.

The crisis narrative of fake news is perhaps best witnessed when the topic becomes subject to official public inquiries. For example, in the Australian context, the Commonwealth Senate has announced a select committee for the investigation of the future of journalism in Australia incorporating issues related to so-called fake news (Donelly, 2017). As minority senator Nick Xenophon put it, 'If we want the fourth estate to be vibrant and diverse we need to deal with the issues that this inquiry raises, including fake news' (Donelly, 2017). The underlying discourse that motivates such an inquiry is the relationship between, on the one hand, a perception of a threat to *traditional* perspectives of a news industry operating within recognised and codified practices of determining newsworthiness, formal and informal relationships with established institutions, organisations and governments, and recognition by a public that the news content is factual. While the circulation of fiction, the idea of news 'mistakes', and the production of misleading or biased stories is not in any way new (McNair, 2017, pp. 17–18), it is not solely fake news that is the cause of the crisis, but it's very *contemporaneity* that is seen to endanger a normative range (Foucault, 2007, p. 63) that permits a flexible, albeit limited range of perspectives of news in which fake news becomes 'threat' to that established order.

Stuart Hall (1979) argued that, rather than being understood as a rupture that destroys the past, crises are *formative*. He described such productive formation in response to crises this way:

> a new balance of forces, the emergence of new elements, ... new political configurations and 'philosophies', a profound restructuring of ... ideological discourses ... pointing to a new result, a new sort of 'settlement' – 'within certain limits'. (p. 15)

Although intended to describe the operations of populist power blocs, this also quite nicely describes the way in which the *sudden* shift to everydayness is brought about by the advent of a culture or era in which we are encouraged to 'worry' about fake news and in which we bear witness to the regular circulation of disinformation. It produces the space for the emergence of a new set of practices for identity, liveability, mobility and belonging: unknowable and unforeseeable, operating in the liminality of radical change in process. Suddenness drives the representation of the pandemic not as remarkable or novel but as crisis itself.

Liminality, defined as the quality of ambiguity of being located physically, emotionally, culturally or in terms of identity in a space or time of threshold (Turner, 1969), is a useful way of framing the contemporary situation of fake news, particularly in terms of the unknowability as to how it can best be addressed or curtailed. The unknowability that is opened by a cultural rupture is, for Maurizio Lazzarato (2013), an aporia, since rupture emerges from both from within history and from that which is outside history (p. 20). While Lazzarato rightly sees 'crisis' as a *permanent* mode of contemporary western and international politics and history since at least the 1970s, an active cultural product designed to enable neoliberal and biopolitical governance (p. 10), the crisis operates as a *transformative rupture* through that aporia of seen and unseen, knowable and unknowable (Duggan, 2003, p. 87). The form that transformation takes is, then, not something that can be mapped in advance, opening a further space of liminality in which subjectivity loses its ground. What fake news *does* for contemporary practices of news making and news consumption is not yet known – we are only the liminal space of unknowability so far.

About this Book

Many of the above ways of comprehending fake news imply that, sometimes rightly, there is a deliberate actor behind deceptive content as seen in the existence of 'fake news farms' which undertake labour to generate deliberately slanted or false content while in other cases there is a professional, cultural and technological set of practices that accidentally, surreptitiously or without deliberate agency generates misinformation in ways which are taken to be news. However, we argue in this book that what is not yet fully understood in an era of fake news is the array of social, cultural, technological and communicative changes that have occurred to allow fake news in its contemporary form to emerge as both a communication phenomenon and a social problem. That is, the culture of digital interactivity and user-generated content that developed in the 1990s and challenged the gate-keeping labour of traditional communication, political and news-making institutions enables the practice of creating and circulating unverified digital content that purports to be factual. At the same time, and in ways which surprised many adherents of poststructuralist, postmodern and polysemic approaches to discourse, the broad, populist disavowal of evidence, concepts of 'truth' (however problematically defined), and fact-checking verification practices in news-making enabled the idea of news as mere content without referent. Finally, shifting understandings as to how public attitudes are formed, approached, changed and managed through political and communicative practices underpins the culture in which fake news operates and in which the veracity of other communication can be known and apprehended.

This book unpacks the complex and intersecting components of social, cultural, political and technological change that underpin the emergence of fake news. Important here, however, is not merely to bemoan fake news and declare an end to an era of factuality, truth, meaning or justice. Rather, it is to consider some of the ways in which alternative practices of quality journalism are emerging in light of fake news, online hostility, trolling and call-out culture. For example, the development of new news sources that focus on evidence, the realignment of journalistic roles in older news institutions such as the BBC, and the development of fact-checking bureaus in many parts of the world to support quality journalism are underpinned by new technological endeavours designed to help protect users of social media from false news and to alert audiences to deliberate news fakery. What these indicate is a phenomenal public interest in the ethics of journalism, digital content production and digital citizenship in ways which allow 'fake news' to be seen not as a site for the deficit of meaning or the end of factuality, but for the hope, interest and engagement of publics with quality and meaning.

Our work in this book is a starting point to introduce readers to the idea of fake news and to help locate it not as something alien and disruptive to contemporary culture, but as something that emerges from within contemporary social, cultural, digital and audience practices. It is, in that sense, constituted in the array of responses to ongoing shifts in technologies of communication and flows of information. We therefore attempt to investigate some of the ways available for understanding non-verified or non-evidence based news within journalistic routines as well as the use of the term 'fake news' as an accusation against undesirable news sources. We try to make sense of fake news as an emergent phenomenon, to use Raymond Williams' (1977) cultural terms, by which it is the product of social and cultural factors that reflect norms, trends and developments that happen both deliberately and non-voluntarily. We focus often in this book on the fact that fake news emerges through one particular, unexpected utilisation of interactivity and the democratisation of content production, while at the same time recognising that the postmodernisation of meaning and the increasing acceptance among a broader population of polysemy is at least partly responsible for the loss of institutional authority in news production and circulation – both a positive and a negative.

Both digital culture and postmodern polysemy are pivotal to the establishment of an environment in which deliberately false news stories can circulate and in which audiences become increasingly sceptical of news and other digital content in general. We address some of the ways in which attitude – as an orientation towards an object of thought – has shifted in contemporary culture, particularly in relation to competing forms of trust. We engage with the relationship between fake news and contemporary modes of 'call out' culture as a form of digital engagement and digital hostility: public judgement outside of institutions such as courts and traditional quality news outlets that rely on evidence. At heart of this topic is a key ethical question: what role does fake news debates play in sponsoring a more ethical engagement with news, media, content production, digital engagement and audiencehood? To ask this is to move beyond bemoaning the loss of a past news regime that was never quite as honest, democratic, liberal or effective as nostalgia tells us, and to look instead to how a more ethical, democratic digital citizen might emerge from what we learn about fake news if we theorise its emergence (and the cultural conditions that have sustained it) for the past half-decade.

The next chapter begins by cataloguing and further developing some initial definitions, notions and concepts for understanding what constitutes fake news from the perspective of cultural perceptions of truth. Using examples drawn from the US presidential election of 2016, the Brexit referendum of 2016 and recent examples from late 2016 and early 2017 in Australia, the chapter will present an initial typology of fake news: (i) News that appears on websites designed to look like official, well-known news brands (e.g., CNN) and purposely attempting to fool readers into believing they have accessed those sites; (ii) News that does the same but is circulated on social networking sites such as Facebook written in a tone that mirrors journalistic styles; (iii) News stories that are developed for political purposes (such as partisan alt-right, and international stories about Russian intervention in the election) and made viral in mainstream English-language online content; (iv) deliberately false or misleading news stories that are further circulated by mainstream recognised news stories which have not adequately fact-checked before re-circulation; (v) accidental falsehood produced by recognised journalists within the complex – and sometimes failing – processes of news routines intersecting with unclear government and administration practices of disseminating stories and which prove to be non-authorised. The chapter revisits Foucault's writings on truth and ethics to help us map the origins and distinctions of each of the common ways of defining fake news, and spends time considering why a typology of fake news is helpful in clarifying some of the ways in which we benefit by understanding the cultural and political environments of its emergence, including the role 'content overload' plays in condition an anti-institutional audience.

The third chapter begins our attempt to explain fake news as cultural emergence, focussing in this instance on the role of digital cultures, interactivity and user-generated content regimes as a condition for the production and viral circulation of fake news, disinformation and misinformation. Fake news, in this sense, emerges not as a deliberate intent of individual actors seeking to gain political, financial or moral leverage within public debates, but in the context of a digital culture built on interactivity that enabled widespread participation in the production of knowledge and meaning. This form of interactivity began in the era we now refer to as Web 1.0 (c. 1995–2005) in which participation, democratisation of production processes and the engagement with meaning were widely celebrated; it expanded with the further increase in participation in the post-2005 period referred to sometimes as the era of Web 2.0, marked by a massive uptake of internet access globally, broadband speeds, the circulation of image and video alongside text, YouTube, Wikipedia and social media. While it is important to understand the history and development of contemporary digital cultures as providing the context for the emergence of fake news practices, it is also important to unpack the argument so as to avoid mutually exclusive positive/negative arguments in relation to interactivity. This chapter presents the history of digital interactivity in the wider context of shifts from passive audience to active users and the democratisation of news production; it shows how fake news is one among a range of consequences of digital interactivity, thereby helping place our understanding of fake news in its historical, technological and cultural context.

Chapter Four builds on this by focussing on the other side of the coin in the cultural formations that help constitute fake news. Using Raymond Williams' approach to emergent cultures, it is shown here how fake news both builds upon and transforms older cultural forms, including the appropriation of elements of postmodernism (polysemy, poststructuralism, critique) that have been transformed through an anti-institutionalism (including an adversarial relation to traditional major news institutions) and a populism that has marked contemporary responses to the global political establishment, law and pedagogies (including the rise of Donald Trump, Brexit in the UK, anti-immigration sensibilities in Oceania, the disavowal of climate science, 'call out' culture, etc.). The association with an idea of 'alternative facts' has been part of the narrative through which fake news is perceived. Alternative facts emerge, however, not because a White House staffer uttered the phrase to produce an excuse for divergence of views and poor spin management, but because the postmodern and poststructuralist critiques that so usefully undid concepts of universality of meaning and that excluded subjugated voices are now no longer critiques but cultural norms in western communicative practice. This chapter, again, unpacks the conceptual and cultural framework through which polysemy shifts from being a critical tool to a discursive practice. It covers political speech, parody tweets, and responses to fake news. The aim is to untangle the ethical concerns that emerge when critique is utilised to justify non-truthful reporting.

Chapter Five explores one of the more alarming mechanisms of disinformation to emerge in the past few years – the 'deepfake' video. The deepfake is a technologically enhanced false video and audio content that draws on both real and existing images but in reconfigured forms to produce even greater credibility and believability, than textual news and text-based fake news. We address this not as a surreptitious practice, but as something which sits at the intersection between the topics of the previous two chapters – the digital formation of interactivity, and the contemporary framework of postmodern hyperreality and pastiche. The deepfake belongs to and extends the boundaries of fake news, posing a greater threat to the quality and control of evidence, information and communicative norms. Like other aspects of fake news, it is hardly alien to culture; rather, the tools which enable it have been desired and demanded from within culture, making the deepfake inevitable and its enabling tools utilised for purposes other than perhaps those desired from within the tensions of Enlightenment and postmodern cultures.

Chapter Six is an opportunity to make sense of fake news in the context of conspiracy theories. This chapter investigates journalistic reportage of conspiracy theories, with a focus fake news related to health information and the COVID-19 pandemic. It explores the 'mainstreaming' of conspiracy theories via the spread on social media and subsequent reporting in news media, and the ways in which this cross-over allows those theories to be recognised not as 'fake' but as matters of public interest by their proponents. The opaque line between fake news and public interest is unpacked as a cultural form that governs how we are able to think about public communication generally. Secondly, the chapter investigates ethical issues related to the reporting of conspiracy theories and the role of the online commentator as a public health expert. In doing so, it builds on the questions of polysemy, postmodernisation and the ways in which cultural forms produce the idea not of multiplicity but of 'hidden truths' that appeal to disenfranchised subjects.

A key dimension of fake news is its weaponisation of uncertainty in 'troubled times'. Here, the fake news audience is actively produced through the spreading of fear, uncertainty and misinformation. This has been witnessed particularly in public communication that reports on, debates and informs the *Black Lives Matter* movement as a setting of global social consciences in the 2020s. Campaigns of misinformation, deeply embedded hate speech and racism mark the circulation of knowledge, reports and discussions of this emergent movement, particularly in the United States, Europe, Australia and the United Kingdom. In Chapter Seven, we discuss the closely intertwined relationship between fake news and far-right anti-minority discourses, and how this relationship serves to legitimise the vilification of minorities. In doing so, the chapter investigates how fake news emerges in the context of right-wing populist politics, how discourses that harm marginalised people are strategically introduced into the public domain, how these evolve into acceptable and legitimate perspectives, and the implications for public attitudes, policy, democracy and human rights.

One of the common responses to the advent of criticism of fake news is that written content circulated online cannot be 'trusted'. Chapter Eight takes to task the concept of trust in the twenty-first century. Understanding trust to be a relational attitude and orientation towards a source, idea, concept, speaker or ideology, the chapter considers how contemporary audience relationships produced within the tribalisation of attitude, culture and politics operates within an era of digital hostility: that evidence, reporting method, news structure or the intertextual relationship between news stories has dissipated in favour of trust in sources that are known, regardless of the verifiable framework of evidence utilised by those sources. The tribalisation that results reduces the capacity of journalism to participate in framing public sphere debate, since different audiences with different ideological perspectives are increasingly less likely to participate in the consumption of balanced news in the context of fragmented publics, or engage increasingly in dichotomised and adversarial flame wars in online forums. The chapter theorises attitude, trust and audiencehood in the context of a digital culture and in terms of its role in sponsoring the circulation of fake news. It does so through two key case studies drawn from the UK: Brexit (the protracted departure of the UK from the European Union) and Megxit (the highly publicised relinquishment of royal duties by the Duke and Duchess of Sussex).

Fake news does not go unchallenged. There are a plethora of suggested remedies, solutions, policy interventions, proposed regulatory frameworks and pedagogies discussed in scholarship, public sphere discourse and by legislators, politicians and media commentators. Chapter Nine asks what it means to think about the cultural emergence of fake news from the perspective of remedies, and how such remedial thinking is presented without critical engagement as to the compatibilities of different approaches, the ethics of remedying, and the impact of regulation.

The final, conclusive chapter is an opportunity to consider fake news, disinformation and misinformation in the context of ethics. Drawing on Judith Butler's approach to ethics, this chapter argues that while we cannot turn back the clock on the cultural changes that enabled fake news, we are obliged to apprehend it in order to prevent the violence of disinformation and misinformation in its pollution of what we refer to as the media and information ecology. By promoting a critique based on their contingency rather than their dissolution, we promote the *shared* activity of apprehending the violence of fake news as the key necessary pathway to a future of dignity, inclusivity, sustainability and peace.

Chapter Two

What Is Fake News? Defining Truth

Introduction

In January 2021, a sizeable group of pro-Trump protesters stormed the US Capitol building in Washington D.C. They were acting in response to then US President Donald Trump's claims that he had been robbed of victory in the 2020 US election. The protesters included a young woman named Elizabeth, who was interviewed by a TV news reporter shortly after her attempt to enter that building was unsuccessful. The woman was red-eyed and shaken, saying police had sprayed her with mace. When asked why she was demonstrating, Elizabeth responded earnestly: 'It's a revolution!' At first glance, this clip appears to be yet another example of the dangers that have arisen from Trump's dishonesty. The outgoing president addressed the crowd moments before they swarmed the building, repeating the assertion that his electoral triumph had been 'stolen by the fake news media' (AP News, 2021). These claims were supported by the president's personal lawyer, Rudy Giuliani, who spoke to gatherers. The footage could also serve as a caution against placing too much faith in leaders, especially those who expound bombastic, brutish braggadocio that has little basis in fact.

That a disruptive riot should be the outcome of a public belief in false information was well-predicted and the topic of considerable public concern for several years, particularly in relation to the trust by some sectors of the public in non-factual, conspiratorial or inflammatory content distributed online by President Trump. Indeed, before his presidency, he was called out for false or misleading statements based on unfounded claims. For example, Trump had been publicly alleging from as early as 2008 that Barack Obama's presidency was illegitimate, based on the inaccurate claim that he was born outside Hawaii (in addition to the false claim that Obama was a practising Muslim). In an October 2016 rally, Trump told attendees that the murder rate in the United States was 'the highest it's been in 45 years', when in fact they had decreased to the lowest levels in 40 years (Lee, 2016). During the 2016 election, a number of fake Facebook accounts and automated Twitter accounts promoted unfounded allegations that the then Democrat presidential nominee Hillary Clinton was involved in criminal activity, including participation in a paedophile ring (Howard, Woolley, & Calo, 2018, p. 90). It was reported that during that election, 115 fake stories that were pro-Trump were shared on Facebook a total of 30 million times, and 41 pro-Clinton fake stories

Fake News in Digital Cultures: Technology, Populism and Digital Misinformation, 17–27
Copyright © 2022 by Rob Cover, Ashleigh Haw and Jay Daniel Thompson
Published under exclusive licence by Emerald Publishing Limited
doi:10.1108/978-1-80117-876-120221002

were shared a total of 7.6 million times (Allcott & Gentzkow, 2017, p. 212). It has never been possible to determine the extent to which President Trump's electoral success resulted from the circulation of false or misleading online content, since no election is won on a single social or cultural phenomenon and it is unknown the extent to which those who were within the 'reach' of those stories actually believed them and voted on the basis of them. What we do know, however, is that something we now refer to and understand as 'fake news' grew from being a mode of circulating fringe conspiratorial claims in 2008 to a serious element in the media and communication ecology of the 2016 election and beyond.

As the culmination of a presidency during an era of fake news, the Capitol riots are arguably paradigmatic of fake news and the cultural milieu in which this phenomenon has arisen. The dissolution of a concept of truth, the expectation of honesty among elected officials and public speakers, and the framework by which fake news both emerges from and feeds into cultural shifts, disorder, misappropriated perceptions and new ways of perceiving the world are all part of that paradigm. This chapter begins by explaining some of the ways in which fake news has been defined, and the conceptual crossovers between fake news, disinformation, misinformation, propaganda and 'alternative facts'. These phenomena are not new; their most recent incarnations reflect a broader cultural logic commonly referred to as 'post-truth'. By teasing out the overlaps, similarities, conflicts and interpretations across the various definitions, we establish a typology of fake news. Such a typology is important because it clarifies the ways in which the field of fake news is beneficial to understanding social, cultural and political environments in the post-truth era. By looking to the detail, diversity and distinctions and providing greater clarity, we are better positioned to begin to cultivate an ethical response to the rapid and widespread distribution of information that ranges from factually dubious to dangerously misleading. The chapter ends by exploring how these definitions play out (sometimes concurrently) in the media coverage of a prominent case study germane for our times: the utilisation of different aspects of fake news across working together across the Trump presidency and leading, ultimately, to the 2021 Capitol riot.

Truth and Post-truth

This chapter's key contention is that fake news is paradigmatic of 'post-truth'. In order to explicate that point, we need to ask: What is post-truth, exactly? In order to answer that question, it is useful to examine the term 'truth', and its distinction from a word that it is commonly used interchangeably with in everyday parlance: 'fact'. It is also useful to assess the relationship between truth and power, and how this is reconfigured in what might be described as the post-truth condition. Facts encompass those events, procedures and so forth that objectively took place; that are apparently beyond doubt. We write 'apparently' due to the rise of so-called fake news, which will be examined later in the chapter. Truth describes an individual or group experience of a particular reality; how that group or individual perceives the facts that have unfolded.

To illustrate the fact/truth distinction: it is a fact that on 11 September 2001, a plane was flown by Al Qaeda terrorists into the World Trade Center. A truth commonly expounded by politicians, reporters and members of the general public, and supported by evidence, is that this collision destroyed the World Trade Center (Eager & Musso, 2001). There are, however, persistent conspiracy theories which purport a very different truth: that while a plane did indeed hit the building, the building was destroyed by other actors, perhaps members of the United States government or a so-called 'deep state' working behind the scenes (Bell, 2019, and see Chapter Five). Unlike fact, truth is subjective; it refers as much to personal interpretation of what happened as what actually happened. Truth as a concept is also thoroughly enmeshed in, and generative of power relations. That standpoint has been most famously elucidated by Michel Foucault, who argued:

> Truth is a thing of this world: it is produced only by virtue of mul-tiple forms of constraint. And it induces regular effects of power. Each society has its regime of truth, its 'general politics' of truth: that is, the types of discourse which it accepts and makes func-tion as true; the mechanisms and instances which enable one to distinguish true and false statements, the means by which each is sanctioned; the techniques and procedures accorded value in the acquisition of truth; the status of those who are charged with say-ing what counts as true. (Foucault, 1980, p. 131)

Foucault is arguing against the belief that 'truth is … by nature free' (Foucault, 1976, p. 60). According to Foucault, the truth will not necessarily free anyone or anything, and nor is it something that 'just is'. What counts as 'truth', and how this comes to count as 'truth', is constructed and enforced by a range of groups and individuals. 'Truth', or what counts as truth, supports a certain worldview or goal. Such 'Truths' are not always based on facts; indeed, sometimes the truth varies considerably from the available facts.

To illustrate the above points: the 'truth' behind the 9/11 conspiracy described above is that the US government engineered the terrorist attacks as a ruse to go to war. On 20 September 2001, then US-president George W. Bush described ter-rorism as a 'threat to our way of life' (Bush, 2001). This threat might have been a truth for Bush, but it may have resonated less for those whose 'way of life' did not fit the one implicit in the president's rhetoric: that is, a way of life characterised by nationalism and conservatism. Indeed, the references to this way of life being threatened, and Bush' now-infamous (and infamously discredited) assurance that Iraq harboured weapons of mass destruction could be understood as justifica-tion to invade that nation (Hartnett & Stengrim, 2004). This was an invasion that armed forces from Australia and the United Kingdom were deployed towards.

The subjectiveness of truth, its sometimes strained relationship with facts, and the power relations embedded within versions of truth these are all defining components of what has come to be known as post-truth. Journalism scholar Silvio Waisbord (2018a) writes that this term 'captures new conditions for pub-lic communication that signal the impossibility of truth as shared assessments about reality' (p. 19). The four conditions are illustrative of the arguments we raise in addressing the cultural framework of the instability of truth as pivotal in the formation of fake news. The first encompasses upsurges in populism and a growing opposition to 'elites' (Waisbord, 2018a, p. 17). Examples of such populism include Trump in the United States, the far-right minor party One Nation in Australia (Sengul, 2019), and Jai Bolsanaro in Brazil. The second group of conditions that have given rise to post-truth encompass a myriad of advances in online technology that have made it easier to produce and disseminate content of all kinds. These have included advances in webcam (Miller & Sinanan, 2014) and smartphone technology; and a proliferation of social media platforms. That proliferation is itself elucidated through Manuel Castells' (2010) conceptualisation of the 'network society'. He notes that:

> while networks are an old form of organization in the human experience, digital networking technologies, characteristic of the Information Age, powered social and organizational networks in ways that allowed their endless expansion and reconfiguration, overcoming the traditional limitations of networking forms of organization to manage complexity beyond a certain size of the network. (p. xviii)

In a networked mediascape, information can be shared across borders more rapidly than was possible a generation ago, as well as to much larger audiences. While this benefits the sharing of knowledge and the production of a collective intelligence in ways of greater accessibility than were previously known in the history of communication, it does also entail the distinct disadvantage of permitting any user to produce and post factually incorrect content, whether deliberate disinformation for propaganda or conspiratorial purposes (such as anti-vaccination rhetoric, QAnon), or circulating misinformation by sharing content that happens to be false or was based on an error (e.g., the 2009 reports of actor Jeff Goldblum's death).

In addition, the instantaneity of information sharing, whether in the form of a tweet, a private Facebook message or a newspaper headline has very substantial benefits in allowing information, knowledge and social engagement to occur in ways which are very close to real-time despite distance. At the same time, however, instantaneity can have some disadvantages, including reduced time for media gatekeepers (editors, content moderators) to confirm the accuracy of the information (Slavtcheva-Petkova, 2016, p. 1116). Perhaps, more worryingly, such instantaneity produces cultural practices of digital use which see and note headlines, comments, ideas and information in piecemeal ways without the time taken to read through a full piece and make a determined judgement on its veracity through critical literacies. The speed and extensiveness of communication, then, not only makes it difficult to intervene quickly in light of the dissolution of more traditional gate-keeping practices, but shifts the mode of readership from one of slow, daily engagement with news sources to the sensationalist pinging of very frequent en masse updates – the audience is positioned not to be well-equipped for discernment. In this context, a culture of post-truth emerges through and as a result of the complexification of communication in contemporary digital culture.

The third group of conditions encompasses what Megan Boler and Elizabeth Davis (2018) describe as 'a decisive shift in discourses of emotionality in media and politics' (p. 75). Emotions have always circulated at the intersection between politics and communication, however the online mobilisation of affective and emotive relations in an era of online communication has increased very substantially. The seeds for emotive language through spectacle and relationships, loyalties and connections built on non-rational and non-critical approaches were laid in 1980s neoliberal culture and in the scholarly and postmodern critique of rationalist agency. In the case of the former, the shift in advertising culture away from logical argumentation, facts and claims to an emotional appeal using a visual vocabulary, quick cuts and minimised narrative (Pettegrew, 1995, p. 492). Over time and alongside tabloid media and the promotion of popular reporting (Glynn, 2000), this has helped constitute an audience–user relationship with information, communication, content and text that is emotive rather than critical, whereby a concept of truth or fact is less important than the corporeal response to which the public is increasingly positioned (Creed, 1993, p. 13).

The terms post-truth and fake news are sometimes used interchangeably, or with little acknowledgment of a distinction between them. We suggest that fake news is a key manifestation of post-truth; this is what happens to news in the post-truth era. The term news itself refers in the most basic sense to media reporting of current events and phenomena. Although the content we commonly understand as news is an artificial construct (like all genres of communication), it is recognisable because it aligns with a number of values. These include *timeliness* of the content that is being reported, *relevance* to a particular audience, determined in geographic, social identity, career demarcation or other context, and often *conflict and adversity* represented by the two-sidedness of a disagreement and primary and secondary definers providing evidence on each side of that disagreement (Harcup & O'Neill, 2017, p. 1472). News outlets themselves play an integral role in deciding the newsworthiness of an event, phenomenon or occurrence and about what readers will and will not be informed. Between the determination of what counts as news, the capacity to decide what readers will know, view and hear about, and which matters become the topic of public debate, the genre and routines of news production continue to inform. Together, this is known as agenda-setting, and is a crucial aspect of any mediascape. Traditional Western models of news reportage have maintained that reportage should be objective, neutral in tone, and simply report 'the facts' (Harrison, 2018; Martine & DeMaeyer, 2019). More partisan-oriented news services, of course, have become increasingly biased over time, eschewing objectivity and neutrality as a general practice and relying more on opinion than reportage. Waisbord (2018b), for example, has argued that we are witnessing a 'gap between journalism wedded to scientific realism and belief communities embedded in partisan, ideological, and religious epistemologies' (p. 1871). In fact, what we might be witnessing is an increasing approach to journalism that is unabashedly wedded to those epistemologies.

In many ways, then, fake news replicates news agenda-setting principles by mimicking the genre and participating in the decidability of inclusion and exclusion, albeit in most cases not merely biased but wholly untruthful. In that sense, fake news itself is an active participant in news agenda-setting. A 2018 study reveals that fake news 'take[s] cues from the partisan media when it came to stories that mentioned the economy, education, environment, international relations, religion, taxes, and unemployment' (Vargo, Guo, & Amazeen, 2018, p. 2043), meaning that not only does it imitate news, but reproduces some of the more biased news practices already at play. This is another way of saying that fake news does not appear on the scene in such a way as to allow us to identify a 'real' news that is *always* neutral, factual, objective and in the public interest. Rather, it emerges at the far end of a continuum of news and content production practices that have increasingly and problematically introduced bias, intent, exclusion and distortion and taken those practices to their logical extreme.

Towards a Typology of Fake News

Establishing a typology of fake news is valuable in providing the tools by which it can better be understood, apprehended and – if possible – remedied. As with all terms and concepts, the meaning it has depends on context and on the reading formations or discourses by which meanings are activated (Bennett, 1983, p. 218). In that sense, the term morphs and changes, making it more difficult to address. We will give some background here on a few of the key meanings and uses of the term and the related concepts: *disinformation, misinformation, democracy,* and *insult.*

Disinformation is broadly defined as false or misleading information that has been circulated deliberately to deceive, often with a political, social or personal goal as its intended outcome (Pacepa & Rychlak, 2013). The concept itself emerged in the early-to-mid twentieth century to describe activities of intelligence agencies (especially those of the United Kingdom, United States and Soviet Union) to mislead rival countries about their strengths, goals or intentions, or to discredit their rival countries' leadership among their own populace, and was often deployed through rumours across spy networks, false flag information, forged documents and other falsifications (Samier, 2014, p. 176). The term, however, did not enter everyday speech until the 1980s during the Reagan administration in the United States, subsequent to a campaign of disinformation to destabilise the Ghaddafi regime in Libya (Biagi, 2014).

In the most contemporary setting, suggestions, assumptions and some evidence indicate that the intelligence agencies of various nations may be involved in disinformational activities, but the production and dissemination of disinformation is no longer conducted through spy networks passing on deliberately false information. Rather, it targets political figures and the highly politicised appointments of officials through disinformation constructed by influence networks sharing stories made up to look like truth, news, gossip, revelation or in the language of fact, and disseminated on Twitter. In some cases, these have been known to emerge first in the English-speaking world from Twitter accounts – undoubtedly false identities – linked to, among others, Russian accounts operating as trolls (de Haldevang, 2018). In other cases, bots (software designed to mimic human actions and share information in forums and through social networks) have been designed to send out enough conflicting information to make people *confused* about a social or political issue. An excellent example of fake news that originates in disinformation is found in the case of smear campaigns against Dr Christine Blasey Ford who made sexual assault allegations against the then Supreme Court nominee Brett Kavanaugh. During the media coverage, social networks were flooded with illicit disinformation both supporting and disavowing Dr Ford's claims, creating substantial difficulties for the public to understand key issues. In one important example, a purportedly anti-Kavanaugh tweet was re-tweeted over 11,000 times containing a link to a *Wall Street Journal* article that did not exist, thereby innovating around the more regular practices involved in converting disinformation into fake news (de Haldevang, 2018).

While the disinformation was problematic for the claims made by Dr Ford and, indeed, is the sort of confusion that makes other claims by women about sexual assault more complex and more difficult to be recognised publicly (Bartlett, Clarke, & Cover, 2019), the extent to which disinformation has any real impact on political decisions, affiliations, and voting patterns is not determined, and claims on a causative link tend to rely on assumptions rather than facts of a media effect on voters and citizens (Turner, 2012). This does not mean that deliberate disinformation designed to have an impact on voters or to gain a political outcome is not significant or does not have an impact – the collateral damage on reputations and the potential for defamation without a clear source by which to extract an apology, clarity or penalty is a serious problem for practices of remedying and penalising defamation, and for regulation mechanisms designed to protect individuals from the harm of certain kinds of speech.

While national intelligence interests may retain a role in disinformation, the field is also understood to have been entered by private interests, including the activities of 'fake news farms' that produce and disseminate viral disinformation, potentially for hire and/or to support commercial and political rather than state interests or personal financial interests by benefitting from the production of content that feeds into existing dissent (LePrince-Ringuet, 2018). There are many examples, some of which we address in later chapters, in which the purpose of fake news has been to create spectacle and interest to draw online users to a monetised website – the content of the fake news is not what matters, it is the act of distributing something which confirms some views, alarms some readers and otherwise generates the kind of curiosity to encourage a user to pursue a link. In some cases, of course, it is difficult to discern the motivation for fake news, and whether the disseminating content or the 'clickability' of a link is the key issue.

The most well-known case of disinformational fake news farms was identified in an investigation by *BuzzFeed* in late 2016. Their investigators discovered that more than one hundred new websites were registered to addressed in the small Balkan town of Veles, Macedonia, all of which had relatively generic Americanised domain names and all of which published 'aggressively pro-Trump content aimed at conservatives and Trump supporters in the US' (Silverman & Alexander, 2016). Much of the information was found to be untrue, false, misleading or plagiarised from right-wing sites in the United States, but written or re-written in the form of news and blog posts. According to the investigation, the motivation behind the production of false content on these sites was that the monetised clicks create a profit from minimal labour in the production of that content. According to *BuzzFeed*, the problem is not merely the content but how it competes favourably in dissemination, circulation and re-posting in contrast to existing and recognised quality journalism. For example, a deliberately fake story that claimed then US presidential candidate Hillary Clinton had stated in 2013 that she was keen to see Donald Trump run for president because she felt he was 'honest and can't be bought', garnered 480,000 shares, reactions, and comments on Facebook, while a *New York Times* exclusive revealing Donald Trump's USD $916 million loss in 1995 generated only 175,000 reactions or shares on Facebook in over a month. Here, disinformation, as deliberate falsehoods circulated for nefarious purposes competes very significantly for the attention of an electorate, a populace or a group of users and, through drawing on its sensationalist approach and the capacity to generate outrage or anger, gains a readership that the more staid and factual quality press cannot. We discuss more about the role of sensationalism and outrage in setting the conditions for fake news in Chapter Three.

Misinformation, on the other hand, encompasses information that is incorrect, but that is not necessarily published and disseminated with the aim of misleading and deceiving. That is, misinformation is typically understood as false, inaccurate, or misleading information that is disseminated regardless of whether or not there is an intention to deceive (Lazer et al., 2018). That would include, for example, a person on-forwarding the disinformational content about Clinton supporting Trump, because that user genuinely believed that Clinton said so. That user may believe this for two reasons: the disinformation is dressed up as news, and the user may be pre-disposed for a range of political, social, economic or relational reasons to wish to see Clinton disparaged as a flip-flopper. Although the meaning of misinformation is traditionally broad, it is most often associated today with the unwitting circulation of inaccurate, incorrect or de-contextualised information through social networks that creates false beliefs about topics of importance (Stawicki, Firstenberg, & Papadimos, 2020). Obviously, there is a relationship between those who communicate disinformation and those who spread misinformation, whereby those who seek to communicate disinformation rely on the affordances of digital–cultural practices of users who, within the framework of contemporary instantaneity, re-tweet, re-post and re-share information without critical engagement, thought, fact-checking or capability (Papacharissi, 2015, p. 44). For those users in their networks who do not engage with formal news sources, credible informants or scholarly investigation practices, the trust in their friends' shared misinformation can create a problematic belief system, change an attitude or have a negative impact on clear decision-making.

A further key concept in making sense of fake news as a concept and form of speech or articulation is its definition as antithetical to democracy and as a force which disrupts democracy. Broadly, fake news is often discussed in contemporary journalism and opinion writing as being in an adversarial relationship with to *democracy* (e.g., Chakhoyan, 2018; Slavtcheva-Petkova, 2016). Although democracy can be thought of in terms of being a 'fugitive condition that persistently defies realization' (Lloyd, 2007, p. 129), a representative liberal democracy as the standard western model of contemporary governance is premised on the idea that citizens should be able to participate to the fullest extent within civic life and electoral processes, without fear of violence or retribution. It is perceived as a vulnerable object of effect: threatened on the one hand by institutionalised neoliberalism, its gestures to democratic processes and its autocratic corporate cultures (Duggan, 2003) and, on the other hand, as under attack from contemporary populism, which operates as both a demand for more democracy contra neoliberal and left-liberal establishments, and also a curtailment of democracy in the call for more exclusionary, anti-diversity and persecutory politics (Anselmi, 2018). The effective decentralisation of journalism as a key arbiter of truth and authority, and the concomitant rise of fake news as an everyday experience, then, presents a *laissez-faire* framework through which content circulates. Waisbord (2018b) suggests this in arguing that although journalism has held a key role as an arbiter of truth in democratic frameworks, the dissolution of truth as key and guaranteed framework of news, despite bias, points to the always-present shakiness of democracy itself.

Finally, we cannot have a workable typology of fake news without a reference to its use as insult and as offence. Understanding the issues of fake news involves taking into account how the term itself became available for use as an insult or accusation to discredit factually-sourced ethically-sound reporting. Arguably, this began with former US President Donald Trump who, dissatisfied with the critical coverage of news services such as the *New York Times* and *CNN* referred to their pieces regularly and persistently over his term in office as 'fake news' (Jamieson, 2017). This began in January 2017, when President Trump refused to allow Jim Acosta, a senior White House correspondent from *CNN* to ask a question, sparking a tirade of accusations and insults that changed the meaning of fake news from one based on the circulation of disinformation and misinformation to one that demonstrates adversity to recognised journalism (Subedar, 2018). When Acosta attempted to put a question to the then president-elect, Trump stated: 'Not you. Your organization is terrible'. Acosta responded, saying: 'Since you're attacking us, can you give us a question? Mr President-elect, since you're attacking our news organization, can you give us a chance?'. And the president-elect's response was: 'I'm not going to give you a question. You are fake news'.

This began a trend in which Donald Trump referred persistently and regularly to any non-supportive media outlet as fake news, a term he used particularly during his large rallies, as well as in the context of COVID-19 reporting. By July 2017, Trump had referred to recognised media outlets or media reports as fake news on at least 34 occasions. These included references to *the New York Times, the Washington Post, CNN,* and 'mainstream media' generally (Britzky, 2017). Similar weaponisation of the term fake news has been observed in Australia. For instance, in their analysis of Australian political statements following the 2016 US Election, Farhall, Carson, Wright, Gibbons, and Lukamto (2019) found that conservatives routinely referenced 'fake news' to discredit political rivals. Egelhofer and Lecheler (2019) closely examined this kind of weaponisation and in turn, proposed that fake news – in addition to being understood as a *genre* of communication encompassing the sharing of disinformation in the public sphere – can also be conceptualised as a label that is strategically deployed in order to delegitimise factual media content.

In most cases, the Trumpian use of the term fake news operates as an *insult* designed to deflect attention away from key issues or the controversy that was building early in his presidency, but also as a way of discrediting factual information among his followers and adherents (Maley, 2017). An insult is usually understood as a form of verbal aggression or violence, and it works upon the object of its expression by shaping 'the relation one has to others and to the world' (Eribon, 2004, p. 15). As a performative utterance, an insult draws on and sustains an accusatory perspective and reshapes it as a verdict or judgement that both assimilates the object to a recognisably marginalised category and simultaneously reduces the subject to that injurious statement. In the case of Trump's violence towards evidence-based media, his insults position serious journalism as non-serious, underlining and sustaining public assumptions that it is not to be trusted. Referring to a news service as fake news fits in with a particular formation of contemporary populism and the theatrics of insult, but it has a more serious effect: it exacerbates the conditions by which fake news circulates as *meaningful content* to readers who become even more distrusting of recognised news services and established media outlets.

In addition, the deployment of the fake news label as a means of insulting recognised, left-leaning liberal news media both buys into and further promotes an adversarial framework for different news services, depending on ordinary political and partisan bias. We could take note, for example of President Trump's melodramatic tweets about news (prior to his Twitter account being terminated in February 2021), which includes this example from 1 June 2020:

> The Lamestream Media is doing everything within their power to foment hatred and anarchy. As long as everybody understands what they are doing, that they are FAKE NEWS and truly bad people with a sick agenda, we can easily work through them to GREATNESS!

The highly emotive, polarised, 'us versus them' language deployed in social media arguments between Trump supporters and detractors is redolent of the 'culture wars' rhetoric of right-leaning media commentators, whether they are discussing Trump or any number of contentious issues social, political and cultural issues (Davis, 2019a). This language sets up a conflict between two highly polarised sides (e.g., left-wing versus right-wing; elite versus oppressed). This language also flouts liberal-humanist norms of rational speech that has formed part of the perception of democracy and public sphere civil debate and reciprocity (Davis, 2019b, p. 366). The ad hominem attacks that underline the adversity at play are often directed not only to those news services being labelled as fake news, but to the journalists who labour inside those organisations and media processes.

The Interplay of Fake News Types: The 2021 Capitol Riots

Just as fake news was deployed by Trump and his media supporters as an insult across his term as president, his presidency was marked by fake news about him, his decisions and his policies. One study found 115 pro-Trump items of false, disinformational or misleading content that have been categorised as fake news shared on Facebook 30 million times (Allcott & Gentzkow, 2017, p. 212). A CBNC study found that 4 of Trump's 10 most popular tweets during his presidency contained falsehoods relating to the 2020 election (Rattner, 2021). Arguably, the danger of fake news is demonstrated in the fact that its deployment in support of Trump's populist presidency and its utilisation to discredit more recognised, establishment media, resulted in the 2021 Capitol riots in which 5 lives were lost and 53 arrests were made. Protesting the outcome of the most recent US election, which Donald Trump claimed he lost illegitimately, the protesters included a man in a furry, horned cap wielding a placard that read: 'Q sent me'. 'Q' is a reference to QAnon, an internet conspiracy theory based on the premise that President Trump has been trying to save the world from a cabal of elite, blood-drinking paedophiles. This, of course, is a story grounded in conspiracy theories but one which circulates through fake news' disinformation and, subsequently, misinformation flows.

In one respect, these riots were a predictable denouement to a presidency that has most aptly been described as a 'linguistic emergency' (McIntosh, 2020, p. 1). This emergency is suggested in how Trump weaponised the term fake news to discredit opponents, and indeed anybody who said anything that contradicted his pronouncements. Fake news was the top two-word phrase used in the tweets posted during his presidency (Rattner, 2021). At a rally immediately preceding the riots, Trump was quoted as saying:

> All of us here today do not want to see our election victory stolen
> by emboldened radical-left Democrats, which is what they're doing.
> And stolen by the fake news media. (cited in Naylor, 2021)

Trump was referring to the November 2020 presidential election, which he lost to Joe Biden (Democratic Party). We suggest that Trump's deployment of the term fake news both as a rhetorical weapon and as the substance of his own rhetoric played crucial roles in giving rise to the Capitol riots.

This chapter has argued that fake news is a prominent example of the phenomenon commonly referred to as post-truth. Post-truth is characterised chiefly by a blurring of the dividing lines between fact and fiction, thereby ramping up the subjectiveness of the term truth. What we have tried to demonstrate in this chapter is that, contrary to seeing fake news as just one phenomenon, it is in the interplay between the different aspects, components and formations of fake news – disinformation, misinformation, its use against democracy, and its deployment as an insult – that destabilisation of social order arises. There are, at times, good reason for anti-government protest, for the critique of established institutions, and for questioning fact, evidence and truth. The violence of the Capitol riots and the situation of contemporary US politics and governance has, however, demonstrated the need for such questioning to be grounded in evidence, rational and critical investigation, and considered interrogation, rather than by misleading the public in ways which result in death, violence and disorder of a kind that has no value to the project of democracy.

Chapter Three

The Cultural Emergence of Fake News I: Digital Cultures, Interactive Practices and Artificial Feeds

Introduction

Although false or misleading communication has been an identified and recognised element of written communication or spoken utterance across the long duration of 'news' as a genre of public sphere media, the contemporary idea of 'fake news' has emerged in the past half-decade as something which is constituted within and through issues of public anxiety, opening heated debate on questions related to truth and media responsibility, media literacies and of the capabilities of audiences to recognise factuality from deliberate falsehood. It has also been a concept invoked in recent debates on populist electoral outcomes and provoked arguments for political intervention in the context of fake news' role in providing misleading coverage in parliamentary electoral cycles. This re-emergence of concerns about the veracity of media and digital communication has become situated at the very heart of public debates about social engagement and politics, intersecting other social phenomena such as the COVID-19 pandemic of 2020, the surge in interest in the Black Lives Matter movement, and is mentioned in virtually every public discussion about political communication today.

Some nascent research work has commenced to help develop ways in which journalism studies, digital media studies, political science and education can address fake news. However, there are yet to be studies on how digital communication practices have been active in producing the conditions for fake news to become both widespread and a topic of concern. In the case of the latter, these knowledge frameworks relate to audience practices associated with (1) communication forms, such as digital, networked and interactive media cultures, and (2) the embedding in contemporary western societies of a permanent critique of concepts of absolute truth. The question invoked here is this: as a form of mass communication that emerged in traditional, one-way, gate-kept and agenda-oriented frameworks that pre-date digital media and 'everyday' user-generation of content, is journalism (and its integrity) based on enlightenment-era notions of truth and factuality both incompatible with contemporary communication

Fake News in Digital Cultures: Technology, Populism and Digital Misinformation, 29–43
Copyright © 2022 by Rob Cover, Ashleigh Haw and Jay Daniel Thompson
Published under exclusive licence by Emerald Publishing Limited
doi:10.1108/978-1-80117-876-120221003

cultures, and under explicit challenge from various agents and forces that engage in fake news for sometimes nefarious purposes.

In the study of fake news' cultural origins, there lies a key question about digital culture as providing both the capability of actors with ill-intent to circulate false information in ways that appear believable, and digital culture's role in setting at least some of the conditions for the contemporary populist zeitgeist of distrust in established institutions. Simultaneously, of course, both the advent of digital, interactive culture and the demand by new actors to enter the field of news production are, themselves, both effects of long-term cultural shifts that called for the democratisation of the capacity to speak and be heard. In these contexts, it is perhaps best to understand the circulation of fake news as part of a contemporary 'structure of feeling' that incorporates the form which digital culture has taken, the populist anti-establishment movement, the emanation of call-out culture's interest in dealing with criminal issues through online vigilantism (Bartlett, Clarke, & Cover, 2019), the simultaneity of progressive communicative sharing, online practices of ethical and mutual care, as well as performances of digital hostility and trolling (Jane, 2015; Lumsden & Morgan, 2017), cynical data mining (Lovink & Rossiter, 2018, p. 4) and unscrupulous practices of digital surveillance, etc. In other words, while there was a lot to celebrate about the democratic potential of early Web 1.0 internet and Web 2.0 high-speed sharing and visual communication (Green, 2008, p. 2), there has also been a cultural practice of mourning the lost democratic and ethical potentiality that the increasingly widespread use and multiplicity of uses of digital communication tools have produced.

If we are to think about fake news not as that which circulates through benign digital communication channels, nor as that which is caused by digital culture, but as that which emerges in the interplay of dominant and emergent aspects of digital media's contemporaneity and sociality, then we might think about how to frame motivations that take advantage of this social setting. We could, for example, suggest that there appear to be three motivations for the production of fake news: (1) a political motivation, for example, supporters of extreme or populist parties in Western democracies producing stories that discredit rival candidates during an election period; (2) an economic motivation, for example, disseminating stories on Facebook that are outrageous enough to encourage readers to click on a YouTube link and thereby create value for that YouTube user's page or via services such as Google AdSense (Dewey, 2016); or (3) a more obscure motivation in simply attempting to create trouble for trouble's own pleasure, with neither political nor economic gain at the centre of the cause. By suggesting that there are motivations is not to say that there is a conscious attempt to create, instil and use fake news, but it is also to distance ourselves from any idea that fake news comes about 'automatically' as a result of digital culture. It is to argue, instead, that the very motivations themselves are not only enabled but emerge alongside the social and technological changes that make digital cultures possible, and that those changes provide the conditions by which the contemporary form of fake news emerges as both phenomenon and as social problem demanding a response.

In this chapter, we demonstrate some of the ways in which contemporary digital cultures are responsible for the emergence of an environment in which fake news emerges. Everyday cultural practices of digital communication are central to contemporary life, communication sensibilities, and frameworks of identity, and they can no longer be separated from a concept of 'traditional media' (such as broadcast) or 'real life' (such as real friends versus Facebook friends) in simple ways. Rather, digital communication is central to the contemporary structure of feeling in which global citizenship is conducted within communicative frames (Cover, 2016). Contemporary digital culture is founded on several ideas, including firstly the Web 1.0 conceptualisation of knowledge, data and information as that which is readily available online through simple searches for networked texts. What this produces is a glut of information and data that, unlike an era of published books operating as a variable repository of textuality, requires both training and labour to interpret information's veracity, quality and meaning. Secondly, digital culture is built on the idea of interactivity as a framework for contemporary public sphere engagement. It is the democratisation of content generation – in contrast to earlier technical restrictions to publishing or communicating in the public sphere, it permits ordinary subjects without gate-keeping to (i) comment and reply directly to other authors, (ii) create and distribute their own content, (iii) change, add to, delete and manipulate other existing content, and (iv) communicate directly and conversationally, all across an array of platforms, devices, frameworks of time and spatial locations (McMillan, 2002), in ways which have radically changed older notions of sender–message–receiver and the concepts of author and audience (Cover, 2006).

We argue that the changing nature of the cultural formation of digital communication, alongside the postmodernisation of contemporary culture (as an audience position that disaggregates concepts of 'truth' from utterances leading to a dissolution of 'ethical communication') plays a substantial role in establishing the conditions by which fake news, disinformation, misinformation, anti-democratic messaging and deep-fake imagery emerge as an issue at the present time. Important here is that the broad fields of media, digital cultures and journalism research have generally celebrated both digital cultures of the democratisation of media participation and production and, simultaneously, utilised and furthered the work of postmodern and post-structuralist accounts that disavow the possibility of universal truth regimes and the articulation of 'true facts'.

Indeed, the emergence of fake news opens the ethical requirement of a critique not of individual actors engaging in the production of falsified content alone, but in the role the outcomes of digital cultures have made in providing the tools for media dissemination (search engines, Twitter, social networking, photoshopping, everyday audio-visual communication, visual manipulation, etc.) that have been powerful enough to rival the traditional journalistic forms and their role in gate-keeping public sphere communication. This is, of course, in addition to the way in which critique of facts undoes the possibility of a return to journalism as a space of veracity or a site warranting engagement to ensure truthful and ethical communication. In other words, are there grounds now for concerns over the ways in which the tools of digital interactivity and postmodern critique have produced negative consequences with the power to upset or undo liberal democratic communication?

We address in this chapter the first of two frameworks of the cultural conditions that foster the emergence of an environment in which fake news could grow – the everyday digital. We discuss firstly the concept of digital culture as the setting for fake news' emergence, before a broader discussion of the historical and contemporary framework of interactivity, user-generated content distribution and practices of sharing as enabling the circulation of untrue content dressed up as news. This is followed by some further detail on how the dissolution of gate-keeping by traditional media institutions and editorial practices has likewise created an environment of ease for fake news' distribution. We end this chapter with a short discussion of the digital conditions that help make fake news believable to its target and unintended audiences: the growth of online echo chambers, filter bubbles and tribalised audience clusters. Again, we argue that these are not necessarily the product themselves of digital media but another good example of an older cultural formation that comes to fruition in the context of the digital.

Locating Fake News: Emergences Within Digital Culture

In November 2016, Facebook CEO Mark Zuckerberg wrote to all Facebook users to affirm his organisation's concerns around taking misinformation seriously. This was a pivotal moment in the evolution of fake news as a concept, for it made clear not just the link between contemporary digital communication forms such as social networking, but the centrality of digital media to fake news being framed as 'problem' and 'social issue'. Facebook had been criticised in public sphere debate over the previous few weeks for being the channel through which examples of fake news, deliberate misinformation in the form of news stories purporting to be from recognised sources, had been circulated – sometimes as a deliberate act of putting misinformation about US politicians online; sometimes the result of others unwittingly forwarding and further circulating information they believed to be true. Zuckerberg pointed out that historically Facebook and other social networking sites have needed to rely on community attitudes in order to 'understand what is fake and what is not' (Zuckerberg, 2016). In this context, a public communication framework that has been made more complex in the development of Web 2.0 interactivity towards cloud networking and shifts towards digital hostility and individualised online utility has made it difficult to determine what constitutes news, what constitutes fakery, and what fake news might be.

Among the very first analyses of Donald Trump's presidential victory in November 2016, a number of journalists were critical of digital media cultures and particularly social networking sites as being part of the 'cause' of false and misleading news stories that actively solidified disenchanted voters within a narrow, Trump-led ideological framework (Keller, 2016). A number of commentators pointed not only to the fact that networks enable the dissemination of fake news, but that digital cultures and online practices of readers as being simultaneously 'interactive' (forwarding) but 'inactive' (failing to check sources) as core of the issue (Oremus, 2016). While these accounts tend to privilege the idea that there are individuals who are digital media users that can be labelled as having partial responsibility for the spread of fake news (Allcott & Gentzkow, 2017), a more nuanced understanding of digital interactivity, digital manipulation, and digital dissemination as 'cultural practice' is helpful in explaining the conditions that lead to fake news as both 'possibility' and 'problem'.

We argued in Chapter One that fake news arises within an emergent cultural framework, to use Raymond Williams' (1977) means of framing cultural change. In the 1990s, one could differentiate between the dominant communicative culture marked by one-way broadcast television, cinema, published print newspapers and published print books. Underlying the cultural formation of the dominant is control over publication and dissemination. From the 1990s, however, an emergent, contemporary structure of feeling emerges in the demand and up-take of digital communication, the widespread purchase of home computers and later smart phones, and the strong, nearly-ubiquitous engagement with online communication tools, practices, ways of perceiving, practices of sharing and formations of speech. These serve as the contemporary structure of feeling (or zeitgeist), marked by a multiplicity of affective feeling towards digital media and its impacts. What emerged was not only subsumed by the dominant neoliberal culture of marketising content in its more traditional forms, but actively re-framed the dominant's forms of communication, dissemination and engagement.

If we are to think about dominant media practices in terms of constituting something we consider 'real life' (including traditional print and broadcast media), and the emergent as built on 'virtual' (everything engaged with through digital means), then we are being overly simplistic about the present state, form and cultural frameworks of the competing, overlapping and mutually supportive dominant and emergent cultures. The distinction between the real and the so-called virtual or digital has not only eroded over time, but was never fully meaningful in the first place. John Urry makes the valid point that the dichotomies of 'real/unreal, face-to-face/life on the screen, immobile/mobile, community/virtual and presence/absence' are no longer helpful (Urry, 2007, pp. 180–181), and we can certainly argue that even for those who eschew digital media, contemporary social participation does not occur outside of the context of digitality. Indeed, this false dichotomy that is occasionally articulated as a generational difference (young people who are 'always online' while older people struggle to login to their email accounts) which again was never more than a misleading stereotype. There is no longer any real point in assuming that some people prefer traditional media while, say, younger persons are engaging in identity practices in online contexts, nor is it valuable to assume that one has a particular reading practice in watching the news on television and recognising oneself or one's identity category in news stories without this being markedly influenced by the practices of utilising digital media in non-news contexts (and when one sits in front of the television with a tablet device in hand and the hand of one's partner in the other, this influence across the networked fabric of traditional and digital and corporeal occurs simultaneously). Digital media is now so closely integrated into contemporary cultural practices that its very use has been for at least a decade not innovative and exciting but banal and mundane everyday activities (Buckingham, 2008, p. 14). Unfortunately, assumptions about this dichotomy continue to be used as a means of over-simplifying the problem of fake news – as if by some nostalgic return to older institutional controls, having something that mirrors print dissemination, or encouraging people to see what has been 'lost' in cultural 'change', we can eradicate fake news.

Understanding social networking's role in what constitutes the quality of information is to take into account some of the ways in which social networking activities, as digital communication tools par excellence, are integrated into the cultural fabric of everyday culture, subjectivity, identity and relationality. This is not to suggest that social networking practices are hegemonic, but that broadly speaking contemporary western subjectivity is not performed without social net-working as the site that acts performatively to constitute identity, relationality and belonging (Cover, 2016). In serving as a key conveyor of information through various, complex, algorithm-directed flows of content, both 'official' and user-generated, while being wholly integrated into communication cultures, social net-working shapes the perception of the everyday, self-identity, norms of belonging and frameworks that govern behaviour, performance and being.

To put this back into the context of fake news, the contemporary fruition of interactive and participatory desires that emerges over time in the development of digital networked cultures, and culminates today in the mass participation in social networks actively enables a number of the social, cultural, economic and technological conditions of fake news. Firstly, the ability of anyone to produce outside of gate-keeper networks, as we discuss in more detail in the two follow-ing sections, enables actors with potentially nefarious or scurrilous motivations to produce deliberately false and misleading content. Secondly, the instantaneity of sharing, responding, and the capacity for repetition and permanency enabled by digital tools (Papacharissi, 2015, p. 44) provides the conditions by which users who may be misled by fake news operate reactively rather than critically. This may include, for example, the unthinking hitting of the share button that further circu-lates fake news not because the user agrees with it, but because the corporeal prac-tice of sharing information that is vaguely recognised as relevant is the cultural form of online engagement. Thirdly, the digital framework of communication that is marked by a comparable loss of civility in interaction (Dorlin, 2016, p. 236) is one in which an etiquette of honesty, objectivity and a sense of truth underly-ing published communication is further eroded in favour of practices of emotive engagement with spectacle – a matter we discuss in more detail in the next chapter, but which here can be said to be inseparable from the contemporary forms digital culture has taken. To reiterate, while we do not disavow the benefits and advan-tages of digital communication, nor do we suggest digital media should be blamed for the rise of fake news, it remains that the conditions that enable the emergence of fake news as both phenomenon and social issue are grounded in the cultural changes that both produce and are affected by contemporary digital culture.

The Digital Culture of Interactivity, Co-creativity and Democracy

If we are to investigate the available ways of understanding fake news' emergence in the context of digital cultures, then there is enormous value in paying attention to the formative effect of contemporary online platforms and practices, including social networking's genealogical inheritance from early interactivity, participa-tory culture and user-generated content distribution of the internet and World

Wide Web to today's capabilities to upload, share, comment, distribute, narrow-cast, blog and otherwise articulate ourselves – with a multiplicity of motivations and desires – online to very wide audiences. That is, while the capacity to share information, including fake news, is in one sense unremarkable in a contemporary digital environment, the cultural shift makes sense in the historical development of the digital environment marked as one of participation and democratisation and the dissolution of publishing controls. Or, to put it another way, at the core of the implications of contemporary digital culture is the shift from a one-way sender–message–receiver model of news dissemination to one which is interactive: by which we mean, actively permits the production of amateur content, user-generated content, manipulation of content, and peer-based sharing of content as the culturally demanded tools of both popular and populist media engagement.

Although the concept of interactivity started out as a buzz word to describe online community in general, the term is more popular today as a way of describing contemporary online communication not as the mimicking of face-to-face interaction in real time, but as the ability to generate content, to produce, to create, to share, to remix, to re-utilise and to participate in everyday culture as a creator rather than a reader, spectator or user (Cover, 2006, 2016). It is helpful to foreground some of the ways in which the notion of interactivity points us to the need to think beyond online communication as simply communication that is facilitated through online networks and more towards the implications of digital communication and emergent digital cultures for thinking about authorship, co-creativity or co-participation in the production of texts, which includes the ways in which it may be implicated in the establishment of texts and public sphere debate that varies in factuality and truthfulness. In other words, the concept of interactivity provides, on the one hand, some useful mechanisms for understanding audience co-creativity that moves beyond the traditional twentieth-century frames of gate-keeping and agenda-based public sphere contributions and, on the other hand, a problematic setting in which co-creativity has permitted the broad and somewhat undesirable emergence of a communicative culture in which scurrilous co-creative contributions are produced as a cultural formation that marks and potentially undoes the veracity of public sphere engagement.

What we argue here is that interactive forms of communication must be understood as part of an assemblage of user, culture, norm, technology and practice, all of which are mutually constitutive and built on deep-seated attachments to the desire to participate in creativity, sharing, the construction of personal and social meaning, access to materials and entitlement to share, change, exchange, adjust, re-frame or re-utilise content (Cover, 2016).

Fake news, in this context, is not the attempt to disrupt or screw over this scene of creative engagement, but is itself operationalised by the fact that digital interactivity and participation enable the generation of content of all kinds (real news, fake news) and the capacity of it to be shared and flow for a diverse set of reasons and motivations.

Thus, while interactivity has a 20-year history of being celebrated as the out-pouring of creativity and the democratisation of access to the tools of creativity, the present anti-democratic dangers inherent in fake news, disinformation and misinformation flows are founded in that very democratic project. It is helpful to see the shift from the positive, almost utopian ideal of interactivity to the present, more mundane setting today in which it enables communication and creativity without a unified social goal or ethic. Major contributor to the World Wide Web platform, Sir Tim Berners-Lee, outlined his version of interactivity early on: framed as a site of connection, engagement and the exploration of information (Green, 2008, pp. 2–3), Berners-Lee was in favour of a democratised, engaging communicative setting. As he reflected in a 1999 speech:

> I wanted the Web to be what I call an interactive space where everybody can edit. And I started saying 'interactive', and then I read in the media that the Web was great because it was 'interactive', meaning you could click. This was not what I meant by interactivity, so I started calling it 'intercreativity'. (I don't generally believe in making up words to solve problems, so I'm sorry about this one.) What I mean is being creative with others. A few fundamental rules make this possible. As you can read, so you should be able (given the authority) to write. If you can see pictures on your screen, why can't you take pictures and very easily and intuitively put them up there? (Berners-Lee, 1999)

The web was to be, for everyone, a read–write medium, and Berners-Lee among others heavily pushed for the development of tools and protocols that permitted everyone to 'publish' online regardless of skill. This included tools that simplified HTML protocols resulting in the early explosion of blogging and, then, the capacity for the readers of blogs to reply, respond and write back (Lessig, 2008, pp. 58–59).

Cultural practices of online communication and the site architecture that democratise and make available practices of interactivity, co-creativity, self-publishing and sharing become embedded in the framework of Web 3.0, in which interactivity is practiced even more so through persistent connectivity, mobility, multi-platform movement and the Internet of Things. This means that engagement between human subjects is more and more frequently built around the idea of users as participants, co-creators and generators of content rather than as readers who also communicate back, or writers who publish on websites or blogs. The changes to the practices of being a participant in a communicative culture are also focussed increasingly on the capacity to contribute or what, in early decades, we might have called self-publishing. Techniques and skills in development, content-creation, film production and writing are no longer the sole province of professional/trained web designers and media practitioners; rather the skills are dispersed among 'ordinary' users and become commonplace (e.g., the skills needed to create and/or remix and upload video content to YouTube or to take, filter, photoshop and disseminate an image). Computer-related activities shift from being understood as the domain of the 'nerdy hobbyist' to an everyday pursuit that allows a continued up-take of digital skills and content-creation activities and, indeed, a broad desire to engage in such settings and interactions.

In an always-connected and cloud-driven communication environment, the contemporary digital experience is framed by the trends and practices that developed across social networking's 15-year history. Founded in 2004 and available for use by anyone aged 13 years and above, Facebook had over 1.3 billion active users in 2014 and, a little over five years later, had about 2.8 billion active users. The largest social network by virtue of user numbers, this is approximately one-third of the world's population. Facebook is rivalled by social networks that originate in China such as WeChat and in the west Twitter, which is understood to have an average of 330 million active users per month, 500 million tweets posts daily, and over one-and-a-half billion accounts overall (Ahlgren, 2021). Certainly, Twitter and Facebook have come to stand in for the very idea of online activity in a Web 2.0 era, very significantly outpacing the Web 1.0 idea of users publishing material on discrete websites. In one respect, what this implies is that content is circulated more readily through 'push' mechanisms (deliberately forced into people's feeds, selected by proprietary algorithms that align with a user's tastes) rather than the older 'pull' mechanisms (requiring a person to deliberate seek out and check a website for updates). The relationship with mobile phones as a site through which the push of content alerts appears more closely entwines the practice of content distribution and the human body which, on the whole, remains close to the mobile devices communicating these alerts and updates ubiquitously and instantaneously (Cover, 2016).

Social networking sites have been investigated and discussed by researchers, journalists and public commentators, although a gap emerges in the fact that much of the time the breadth of uses, tools, functions or gratifications of social networking is levelled down to appear as a singular, unified activity or sole 'purpose' of the sites. This includes seeing social networking as a site for the sharing of personal experiences among friends, whether known or strangers (Ellison, Steinfeld, & Lampe, 2007, p. 1143); as a site for the articulation of one's identity-based interests through the construction of taste statements which act as identifications with objects and with others (Liu, 2008, p. 253); as a site for relationship maintenance (Hoadley, Xu, Lee, & Rosson, 2010, p. 52) and connecting unfamiliar people with one another (p. 53); as a networked space for the expression or representation of pre-existing and salient aspects of users' identities for others to view, interpret and engage with (boyd, 2008); as a space for youth to engage with other younger persons outside of the physical world's constraints and parental surveillance (boyd, 2008, p. 18); as a site for the expression and/or self-regulation of narcissistic personalities (Buffardi & Campbell, 2008); being friended and linking to friends whether close friends, acquaintances or strangers as 'one of the (if not the) main activities of Facebook' (Tong, Van Der Heide, Langwell, & Walther, 2008, p. 531). These are all ostensible reasons for the use of social networking – conscious, self-aware purposes articulated by different users in varied contexts.

In that sense, to account for the flow of fake news in interactive and social media settings, we need to pay attention to the multiplicity of reasons why people are present in these sites in the first place – there are no model social media users. In late 2020, for example, it became increasingly clear that the new video-sharing social network service, TikTok, which is owned by Chinese company ByteDance, was the setting for the circulation of false content, some of which claimed it was based on news stories, about the US presidential election. Much of it was sharing disinformation that claimed fraudulent ballots were being counted for Joe Biden. While the company took early action to remove problematic and false content videos, early indications of the cultural framework through which fake news circulated allows us to account for the complex mix of motivations for use of TikTok in the first place. Key distributors of fake news on TikTok included young Republican party influencers (Paul, 2020). Arguably, some influencers sharing disinformational content were motivated by the need to maintain followings, including in cross-platform contexts, by engaging their followers were spectacular content. Other users are present and exposed to fake news because their purpose in engaging with the site involves seeking entertaining videos but were alerted to what they saw as a problem of 'politics' to which they would otherwise not be exposed (Colwell, 2021). Other users would like some of the problematic and disinformational videos not because they necessarily held a strong view, but because their friendship networks – central to a sense of being and participation – liked, flagged or otherwise engaged with a video (BBC News, 2021a). Participation involves acting along with others in a group, and this makes possible the cultural conditions for the flow of fake news without necessarily a consideration for the content. That is, in none of these cases is there a deliberate sense of using interactive protocols of communication to disrupt, resist or undo establishment frameworks, but acts of social participation that serve a cultural, relational and identitarian need that surreptitiously and unwittingly generate and share fake news.

The Dissolution of Gate-keeping and Agenda Setting

In light of the short history of interactivity, we have provided above, it is useful to consider not just that participatory communication means everyday people have overcome the traditional barriers to sharing their creativity with wide audiences, but that we are thereby witnessing the dissolution of the gate-keeping practices which, on the one hand, restricted a whole host of radical and alternative voices, discourses and ways of thinking and, on the other, maintained a certain level of culturally-expected quality, factuality, objectivity, and utility across news and entertainment content. The reduction in the 'power' of gate-keeper institutions to control the production and dissemination of media content has, for these reasons, been both celebrated and bemoaned (Jenkins, 2008, pp. 17–18). Indeed, when one investigates more deeply interactivity's capacity to overcome gate-keeping per se, it is difficult to see this as either positive or negative. It must be remembered in an era of populist politics that minorities, for example, have on the one hand been excluded from opportunities to participate in mainstream publishing, broadcast representation, news-making and other engagement, but at the same time have also been actively protected from some of the hate speech that marks aspects of digital media's environment of hostility and fake news' common anti-immigrant narratives (Wilson & Gutierrez, 1985, pp. 134–135). Whatever our political standpoint on gate-keeping, and cultural studies scholars and sociologists have traditionally held a critical view of the institutional arrangements that empower some individuals, groups and socio-economic interests to serve as gate-keepers, in an era in which we see the impact of fake news, the utility of gate-keeping becomes more prominent and the arguments that bemoan its loss become more than just nostalgia.

Prior to the advent of digital interactivity and participatory internet culture, institutional media played an active role in structuring 'thresholds of thought, knowledge, and communication' (McCoy, 1993, p. 141), and major institutional news outlets were well-positioned to take advantage of gate-keeping to maintain their scale, pervasiveness and forms of ownership (Philo, 1995, p. 176; Turner, 1993, pp. 232–233). At the same time, however, gate-keeping by institutional news organisations was seen as part of quality control marked by the factual basis of news and its grounding in investigation, evidence, interviews and analysis (Borden & Tew, 2007, pp. 303–304; Singer, 2003, p. 152). Journalistic codes of ethics permitted gate-keeping to operate in the West under practices of self-regulation rather than government control and censorship regimes (Henningham, 1993, p. 69), thereby sustaining a liberal-humanist framework that was both pastoral in nature and limited the capacity of radical and transformative discourses to be made available or circulate (Boyd-Barrett, 1995, p. 233). And, of course, the practices of gate-keeping in the pre-digital setting tended to spiral out from those organisations charged with the activity to meet the agenda-setting demands of other institutions, agencies, governments and interests (Dahlgren & Sparks, 1992).

The development of digital interactivity and participatory online cultures, as we have described them above, meant that there was no longer a gate-keeping barrier to subjugated voices, anti-establishment interests, disempowered but critically engaged voices, minorities and others excluded or marginalised from public sphere discourse by normative cultures and the status quo. For Dery (1993), this resistance took the form of media hacking, informational warfare, terror-art and the guerrilla semiotics of work which sought to point out the significatory foundations of existing mass-media texts. This conception of an emerging, diametric war between media creators/industries and audience participation and interpretation can be considered one of the drivers that prompts the cultural demand for a more participatory digital culture at the particular historical instance in which the read–write capacity of interactivity began to emerge. The lowering costs of participation and publication that come with the advent of digital computing and networking also lower the gates in ways which have positively permitted the everyday user to comment, to engage, to 'publish', to express thoughts in a written or recorded audio-visual form, to develop followings, to become nodes in sharing of information, and to taking out of the hands of institutions the capacity to decide which discourses, thoughts, ideas, ideologies and ways of thinking 'will be offered and what will be excluded' (Milner, 1996, p. 96). From a more negative perspective, however, the dissolution of gate-keeping has meant that the capacity to exclude or 'make unavailable' harmful, problematic, unethical, hurtful, damaging or dangerous speech and content is no longer at play. While we deal with arguments about free speech, injurious speech and censorship regimes in other chapters, we note here that the circulation of conspiracy theories, dangerous health information, distrust in, say, official COVID-19 pandemic information and so on sit alongside the capacity of fake news to 'flow'.

Believability of Fake News: Online Echo Chambers in an Era of Tribalism

So far, we have described the digital-cultural conditions that enable the contemporary phenomenon of fake news in four aspects. First, the culture of digitisation and the convergence of digital communication in the everyday. Second, the culture of interactivity and the capacity of everyday users (regardless of motivation, intent or interest) to produce and share material including news. Third, the dissolution of gate-keeping that previously served to limited the circulation of problematic or false content. The fourth, and final aspect of digital cultures that enables the rise of fake news, disinformation and the flow of misinformation through networks is that of the production of what is increasingly referred to as online 'echo chambers', 'online tribes' or 'filter bubbles'.

As with other aspects of digital media and communication platforms, these are often described as alien events that have encroached on an otherwise healthy public sphere. For example, in an otherwise insightful analysis of the relationship between social media and behaviour, Netflix 2020 documentary *The Social Dilemma*, uses the metaphor of human beings manipulating a news feed in order to produce an echo chamber in which a user is cut off from a wider array of media content and potentially subject to disinformation. Here, the construction of an algorithm is seen as the principal cause of echo chambers, as if they would not exist without the introduction of social media platform technology. As Roger McNamee, an early Facebook investor, reinforced in *The Social Dilemma*, resulting from social media's manipulative technologies:

> Each person has their own reality with their own facts … you have the false sense that everyone agrees with you because everyone in your news feed sounds just like you. And once you're in that state, it turns out you're easily manipulated. The same way you're manipulated by a magician. Magician shows you a card trick – pick a card, any card. What you don't realise is that they've done a setup, so you pick the card they want you to pick. That's how Facebook works. Facebook sits there and says 'hey, you pick your friends, you pick the links that you follow. But that's all nonsense, just like a magician. Facebook is in charge of your newsfeed.'

Although alarmist, this perspective is important to communicate, primarily because it alerts us to the ways in which over-participation in social media, and falling into the substantially growing group of users who primarily gain access to news from their Twitter and Facebook feeds (Avnur, 2020), reduces the possibility of exposure to discourses, sites, information and content which may provide us with the necessary range for critical engagement with information.

Critique, of course, is the capacity to call into question the legitimating grounds of a thought, belief, practice or norm, and it relies absolutely on the capacity to undertake an inquiry through the posing of questions (Butler, 2009a, pp. 775–776). An inability to ask questions by not having access to alternative discursive frameworks forecloses critique by prohibiting or rendering certain kinds of questions invisible – primarily the questions that make possible the potential of an oppositional reading of the content one encounters (Hall, 1993). This is not, of course, to say that resistance to content is always desirable; rather, it is to claim that the capacity to pose questions, undertake a reading, formulate the veracity and legitimacy of the text, make sense of the underlying legitimating political, normative and administrative frameworks that make the content and its motivations for communication possible, and thereby make an informed decision is undone for those who are not able to engage with alternative discourses, or who see all alternative discourses and ways of thinking in wholly oppositional, adversarial ways as 'outsider frameworks' to their echo chambers.

Although this problem has been posited as one from 'outside' culture that has come to infect the good operation of literacy, communication and critique (Mara, 2019), the tendency towards such tribalisation is in fact much older than social media, the internet and digital communication. If understood from a cultural studies perspective, we can place echo chambers and frameworks of filtering, tribalisation and affiliation around types of content, ideologies and discourses in their broader historical context of audiencehood (McNair, 2017). From a cultural perspective, we might differently approach the problem of echo chambers as the emergence of long-seeded tendencies towards affiliation and communities, in which different audience groups have traditionally identified with each other and formed affiliation networks depending on pre-dispositions to responsiveness to content and events.

The sociology of community frequently posits two forms: 'communities of place' and 'communities of interest', both of which are recognised as long-standing cultural tendencies. Communities of interest are built on loose affiliations among people, often polarised along partisan political lines (Dans, 2021). This affiliation around communication and content is more readily seen when we consider communication not from its transmissional context but the ritualistic practices of consuming it, engaging with it, and – today – often sharing it and responding to it. Media scholar James Carey (1988) identifies two views of communication practices from a culturalist perspective taking into account the role of the audience – the transmission view and the ritual view. The transmission view is the standard, pedestrian account of communication as it occurs in line with a simplified sender–message–receiver understanding of all communicative processes whereby authorship, communication and audiencehood are understood through key definitional terms of 'imparting,' 'sending,' 'transmitting' and 'giving information to others'. Messages are transmitted and distributed across space for the control of distance and of people (p. 14). In a learning environment, this is the standard formation for understanding the responsive production of student work – authored by a student as if without intertextuality, sent via a hardcopy submission or a private upload for imparting to the examiner.

Carey's ritual view, on the other hand, likens communication to acts of 'sharing,' 'association,' 'fellowship,' 'possession of a common faith'. He suggests it is more ancient than the concept of transmission, and is not directed towards the extension of messages in space, but towards the maintenance of society, community or groups across time (p. 18). In this context, a ritual production of communal small-group grouping is part of the miniaturisation of affiliations around communication. We recognise that in the nineteenth and twentieth centuries, the daily consumption of newspapers helped produce large national communities (Anderson, 1983), often at the symbolic level rather than in terms of the specificity of content (Cohen, 1985). However, resulting from an ongoing historical tendency away from mass media, mass broadcast television and the wide community audience and more towards the narrowcast forms of cable television, multiple broadcast channels and early Internet experiences governed by searches for specific pages as 'pull' information rather than traditional media's widespread 'push' communication (Smith-Shomade, 2004, p. 73), a fragmentation of national communities comes to be not only the preferred social function of communication, but the preferred economic model of neoliberal target marketing (Berlant, 2007, p. 764). This results in both the proliferation of spheres of communication and the shrinking of that which was once figured as a more singular, if not necessarily equitably accessible, public sphere (Duggan, 2003). In one sense, the dispersal of adherents to the national community and the everyday nationalism that underpins it is important, useful and necessarily. On the other hand, the formation of adversarial communities of affiliation closed off to each other's practices, norms and ways of thinking is a tribalisation unlikely to be productive of critical engagement.

In communication terms, the rituals that produce communities of interest around particular types, forms and ideologies of media content include those self-same rituals of other kinds of friendship networking and affiliation in online, social settings (Cover, 2012), particularly emphasising the driving role of similitude and taste (Liu, 2008). Here, we see media information increasingly consumed within echo chambers, which occur when certain information is amplified and reinforced while dissenting ideas are underrepresented (or absent altogether) (Sunstein, 2001). This, in theory, leads to audiences becoming shielded from exposure to information that runs contrary to their pre-existing beliefs (Pariser, 2011). Much as media publications assume a consensus among readers and audiences and thereby invest audience members with an impression of consensus (Philo, 1993, p. 255), membership of an echo chamber or filter bubble actively encourages identification both as and with the cohort as a community.

Discussing the praxis of community, Etienne Wenger (1998) notes that two readers of the same text share a 'mutual link to a common readership [that] creates a kind of community to which they see themselves as belonging' (p. 182). This sort of community, for Wenger, does not necessarily involve mutual relations between the readers, but an imagined conception of a viewing or reading membership (p. 181). Likewise, those whose access to online forums, subscription to specific social media communities and whose feeds are built on the persistent domination of similar rather than conflicting content, form an unwitting community with those who also appear in the echo chamber. And that affiliation of community involves an increased hostility towards those who are outside the community, those who subscribe to different discursive, ideological or interpretative viewpoints. As is common among most of us, a hostile cousin who berates a political perspective shared by us on a social media post is deliberately blocked to avoid further hostility. But that can also block us from the potential growth of critical capabilities and skills that are produced in the ongoing experience of weighing up content, discourses, ideologies, competing understandings and forming views based on engagement rather than merely confirmation of narrow perspectives. In this sense, we must regard echo chambers, filter bubbles and tribalised online communities and clusters not as something new to bemoan, but as the contemporary fruition of much older cultural dispositions of audiencehood.

This is not to suggest, of course, that those who participate in an echo chamber are necessarily no longer exposed to alternative viewpoints or more credible sources of information and factuality, as research is beginning to show that the case is otherwise (e.g., Haw, 2020) and that there are deeper concerns around what makes the information circulating in an echo chamber. While some studies support the idea that many people consume news within echo chambers (Del Vicario et al., 2016; Lazarsfeld, Berelson, & Gaudet, 1944), it is not yet as clear the extent to which an echo chamber framework has a sustained effect on audiences, with some studies suggesting that consuming news within echo chambers does not limit audiences' exposure to dissenting ideas. For instance, Garrett (2009) found that while audiences often seek out content that reinforces their views, they seldom disengage upon encountering contrasting ideas. Similarly, Johnson and Kaye (2013) found that web users regularly search for information that both supports and challenges their own stance on political topics.

Nevertheless, in the context of fake news, what this cultural environment of echo chambers does is provide fertile ground not for its production but for its positive reception. Although a large undertaking to increase media literacy capabilities is sometimes seen as the necessary remedy to fake news, it is not that media literacy is not taught but that critical literacy is not, by some, practiced within those echo chambers and filter bubbles. Fake news arrives and, if it adheres to a set of beliefs (e.g., that Hillary Clinton is corrupt and in the pay of a 'deep state'), and if expands the evidence of those beliefs (e.g., that Hillary Clinton is running a paedophile ring from a pizza shop), the cultural setting for that fake news to be received, on-shared and further embedded in the belief systems of readers is at play.

Chapter Four

The Cultural Emergence of Fake News II: Postmodernism, Sensationalism and the Hyperreal

Introduction

A number of texts, opinion-writers and political figures have insinuated that the relationship between fake news (disinformation dressed up as news stories and circulated as misinformation by trusting audiences and users) and Donald Trump's election is akin to the relationship between propaganda and the Nazi takeover of Germany in the 1930s (e.g., Carey, 2017, p. 5). While narratives that figure the return of Nazism can sometimes be informative as a warning, and also generate a great deal of pleasure for the imaginative amateur historian, the problem with framing fake news and disinformation *as if* it is a new form of Nazi propaganda is that it mis-reads the cultural conditions that make disinformation palatable and believable among certain sets of the public. German nationalism, the politics of Weimar resentment, and the persistence of Prussian imperialism in German cultural forms as it had had been built since the mid-1800s made the claims communicated by the propaganda machinery of the Nazi party believable to an otherwise sceptical German population (Fischer, 1986). The conditions that made the fake news stories about Donald Trump (among many other false narratives, conspiracy theories and problematic communication) are so markedly different from those of 1930s Europe that we may be talking about different planets.

Some of the conditions that emerged in the second half of the twentieth century and have enabled fake news in its present form have been dealt with over the past three chapters – questions of news' authenticity as a social and political issue, the critique of truth and fact, and its development in both older and newer digital cultures of interactivity. One further cultural element takes us into a deeper level of thinking about how truth is perceived within what is sometimes thought of as the 'postmodernisation' of everyday culture, and the role of postmodern sensibilities in changing how meaning, truth and perception operate in everyday culture. 'Postmodern' is a term with multiple meanings, depending on whether we are discussing a set of scholarly theories of critique (often mistakenly including poststructuralism and deconstruction which, on the whole, differ in style and method from other postmodern

Fake News in Digital Cultures: Technology, Populism and Digital Misinformation, 45–61
Copyright © 2022 by Rob Cover, Ashleigh Haw and Jay Daniel Thompson
Published under exclusive licence by Emerald Publishing Limited
doi:10.1108/978-1-80117-876-120221004

approaches), twentieth-century movements in art and architecture, a philosophic rejection of grand narratives and ideologies belonging to the post-1750s Enlightenment era (identity, liberty, rationality, universalism, objective truth, morality, human nature) in favour of the contingency, plurality and relativistic diversity of meaning.

While all of these fields are part of contemporary culture, there is a further aspect in which postmodernism is used to describe aspects of contemporary everyday culture somewhat removed from scholarly, artistic, critical and philosophic practices. Indeed, what perhaps distinguishes postmodern culture from postmodern scholarship is the way in which it has overwhelmed of public sphere discourse with thinking that lacks the critical integrity and motivation of scholarship – an oversimplification, but useful as a starting point to think about the origins of fake news in postmodernity. While scholarly theories might mark the inaccessibility of any 'real' or 'referent' behind symbols, images and textual content, the postmodernised everyday culture also disputes the existence of a real or referent, but without a critical eye for the implications of not even suspending our disbelief.

Fredric Jameson (1985) used the term postmodernism to describe a particular cultural logic of the late twentieth-century marked by the disseminatory practices of mass media, the implications of the shift in the 1970s from Fordist to post-Fordist production of commodities (including information), the promotion of consumption as a way of being, and the cultural responsiveness of scepticism within communication. For Jameson, postmodernism is not just a philosophic tool or a way of describing a zeitgeist of a particular historical era, but a cultural trajectory – one which arguably fashions today's cultural framework that has facilitated the conditions that enable fake news, disinformation and misinformation to flourish, and created the setting in which some of the more ludicrous, out-of-touch, unrealities communicated as misinformation come to be *meaningful* and *believable* to large numbers of people. Jameson (1991) describes this cultural trajectory as involving an 'historical deafness' (p. xi) as a mode of engaging with meaning, a loss of context, and the embedding of communication, thinking and framing within a market exchange system of neoliberal capital. It is worth thinking a little about the latter, since fake news is sometimes seen as being 'at odds' with or working against contemporary neoliberal, Western capitalist regimes, such as the pre-Trump administration of the United States. An alternative is to see fake news as being a logical outcome of that very system, which Jameson described in the 1990s in a way which we continue to see as the core international framework of today:

> [I]ts features include the new international division of labor, a vertiginous new dynamic in international banking and the stock exchanges ..., new forms of media interrelationship ..., computers and automation, the flight of production to advanced Third World areas, along with all the more familiar social consequences, including the crisis of traditional labor, ... and gentrification on a now-global scale. (p. xix)

This framework, for Jameson, did not simply develop through a great rupture in the 1970s and 1980s. Rather, as with all cultural change, its conditions are found in older emergences, including what he identifies as the social and psychological transformations of the 1960s, and the economic and nationalist frameworks that emerged in the post-war 1950s (p. xx). In this context, if we are looking for a cultural formation to hold accountable for the rise of fake news in the 2010s, we have to consider how the 2010s has been built upon the continuities of much of the twentieth century rather than identify a great rupture or crisis that radically transformed social and communicative engagement in the twenty-first century.

It is important to recognise here that no cultural shift is a radical breach or disjuncture from the past. Rather, new cultural formations build upon and extend past arrangements, practices and norms. This is the case whether we're talking about the advent of a postmodern late capitalist culture, the emergence of Web 2.0 digital culture in the mid-2000s with the advent of social media and the reconfiguration of communication from mass media to narrowcast dissemination, the even more recent development of artificial intelligence tools and machine learning's capacity to make fake content convincing, or other generational changes and the development of new approaches to work, entertainment and news consumption. Among those are the reconfigurations of truth, meaning, and reading and interpretation practices which developed across the twentieth century. Rather than these aspects being overturned by contemporary digital culture, they are retained, reproduced and often even *excited* by new technologies and digital communication frameworks.

Thus, while we are suggesting that a postmodernisation of culture that began in the twentieth century and has come to fruition in the 2020s is a key element in setting the conditions for fake news' emergence, this very postmodernism sits alongside, rather than replaces, an even older cultural form: liberal-humanist Enlightenment. The Enlightenment is typically described as a period roughly described as beginning in the 1750s and through which emerged many of the key contemporary western tenets we associate with truth, meaning, rationality, humanism, identity and reason. Fake news emerges as a practice and an issue at the very tension point between the continuity of some elements of Enlightenment culture, and the insistence of some of its dissolution through postmodern practices of meaning. That is, Enlightenment attitudes that understand the human subject as a free, rational subject with agency and capacity to utilise tools of understanding to determine a truth or meaning (Benn, 1982, pp. 4–5) and able to consent to be governed within discourses of meaning (Locke, 1988) who will act with honesty and interest (Mill, 1972) is not at all a thing of the past, but co-exists tactically as a contextual *ideal* alongside postmodern scepticism and dissolution of the fixity of meaning (Jameson, 1985, p. 115). The struggle over fake news as a phenomenon and social issue can, then, be characterised as representing a deeper cultural struggle between Enlightenment truth and postmodern impossibilities of truth, between early modernist elitism and postmodern populism, and between institutionally-governed reason and its postmodern abandonment in favour of pleasure, consumption, entertainment and de-contextualised communication.

In this chapter, we explore some of the ways in which everyday postmodern culture and its relationship with meaning and communication are, alongside digital frameworks, a further pre-condition that encourages the inevitable rise of fake news, disinformation and misinformation as phenomenon and social problem. We will first build on the previous chapter by deepening our discussion of a post-truth era in encouraging the unethical and cynical production of false and misleading content before considering two key elements of postmodern culture's reconfiguration of communication and meaning: the longer-term shift in media consumption from one of information-seeking to the invocation of corporeal and psychic pleasures (including outrage) that are encouraged in tabloid and media sensationalism; followed by the role of postmodern satire, parody and pastiche as setting the model by which fake news circulates and is both recognised and goes unrecognised.

Content Production and Motivation in a Postmodern, Post-truth and Late Capitalist Era

In Chapter Two, we addressed some of the philosophic and theoretical approaches that open the possibilities for thinking about truth and post-truth, and some of the ways in which concepts of post-truth have been associated with the presidency in the United States of Donald Trump. In this chapter, we expand on that discussion to ask how the 1980s and subsequent postmodernisation of truth operates as a cultural formation that sets the conditions for the 2010s rise of fake news as concept, problem and issue. What drives the textuality that marks fake news as unethical, as untruthful and fake – are those who produce fake news merely evil people driven to make a financial or political gain for themselves? Or are they more broadly a group of people who themselves are produced within a contemporary culture that has difficulty 'handling' the complex issues related to ethical communication?

According to an article in the *Washington Post,* a known producer of fake news, Paul Horner, likens it to the production of hoaxes which, in turn, he equates to the contemporary forms of satire and parody (Dewey, 2016). He notes, however, that while there is a 'fakeness' to such hoaxes through which one can earn a living through the production of fake stories which go viral, the market is available because its audience is a group who no longer recognise satire:

> It's great for anybody who does anything with satire – there's nothing you can't write about now that people won't believe. I can write the craziest thing about Trump, and people will believe it. I wrote a lot of crazy anti-Muslim stuff – like about Trump wanting to put badges on Muslims, or not allowing them in the airport, or making them stand in their own line – and people went along with it! (Dewey, 2016)

From a production perspective, we know that Horner monetised the creation of false and misleading stories for profit rather than acting for a particular political, national or foreign interest. The creation of dissent and the creation of social anxiety over race relations vis-à-vis Muslim-Americans is a terrible outcome, of course, but was not the intention. Horner's story here leads to two key questions: what permits a content producer to feel that it is okay to produce misleading content regardless of consequences, and, on the other side of the communication concern, what leads a public to believe stories such as that the former President Trump wanted to put badges on Muslim-Americans?

One aspect of the culture through which textual production of fake news becomes feasible is that of the postmodernisation of meaning – the polysemy of textual production. For over 50 years now, most cultural, literary and media scholarship has recognised the diverse meanings generated by a text. And it has recognised the need, then, to develop theoretical frameworks for understanding how communication happens (at all) and how shared meanings emerge through shared access to available discourses and reading positions, intertextual referentiality and contextual meaning-making, and culturally embedded knowledge frameworks. In other words, we have needed an understanding as to how we can have both polysemy, on the one hand, and reading practices that prevent the total slippage of meaning into infinite diversity and untranslatability in the actual practice of communication. We argue, however, that since the early 2000s, some aspects of postmodern cultural theory have become firmly embedded in contemporary everyday cultural practices in relation to the ethics of content production. In saying this, we are arguing that the recognition of the multiplicity of meaning leads – not entirely logically – to a next step: the infusion of polysemy into communication ethics.

This is a somewhat deeper aspect of the question of truth or, more pertinently, what has been described as the contemporary populist culture that actively disavows the need for a concept of truth (Anselmi, 2018, p. 82). We recognise, of course, that the idea of a universal, accessible truth is mythical at best (Foucault, 1970), and that any production of an idea of truth is firmly embedded in the relationship between power, knowledge and subjectivity (Foucault, 1980). However, acknowledging the inaccessibility of truth is different from considering the issue from the perspective of creative production practices that cynically create and circulate misleading or untrue content. In journalism training, we make use of the notions such as 'facts' and 'fact-checking' as key lynchpins in ethical practice. In a postmodern culture, we see the advent of the hyperreal, what French Situationist thinker Guy Debord (1994) described as the 'society of the spectacle' which he saw, at the early stages of consumer capitalism, as the replacement of the perceptible, referential world with images not only seen as superior to that 'real world' but as losing their function in representing it. Just as the contemporary cultural practice of the selfie involves not just an enhancement of the self but a refiguration that bears less-and-less resemblance to the self (Kwon & Kwon, 2015, p. 305), the circulation of fake news content involves not just a sneaky motivation to trick readers, but an *artistic* practice of creating content that mimics news but bears no reference to real or actual events. This contrasts, then, with communication – especially journalism – which has been built on a tradition that emerged *prior* to the postmodernisation of communication. The primacy of the verifiable fact as truth's referent was a key to its stylisation as informational communication. Fake news, on the other hand, works in the postmodern 2020s because creators are unashamed to produce content that no longer represents reality but replaces it. It is the difference, identified by Manuel Anselmi (2018) between the manipulation of communication and a cultural form that artfully ignores an ideal of truth as a strategy and a cultural operation of production.

There are two levels at which we see a postmodern late capitalist culture provide the conditions that make (for some people) fake news and disinformation 'allowable', despite the continuing force of Enlightenment-era struggles to retain concepts of universality, rationality and factual truth. The first concerns the *primacy of monetising content over quality of truth or fact*. This is to consider the marketised ethos that, within neoliberal postmodernism and late capitalism, infuses all aspects of everyday life, including ethics. The concept of the *laissez-faire* market acts increasingly not as a setting of exchange but as a regime of truth, coordinating practices, ideologies, ways of being and establishing a particular mode of reality (Terranova, 2009, p. 243).

As a framework for being – including, in our case, being a producer of content – this perception of reality serves as one of encouraging, fostering and promoting neoliberalism's regime of truth such that it subsumes ways of thinking in all other fields aside from the economic. It 'involves generalizing it throughout the social body and including the whole of the social system not usually conducted through or sanctioned by monetary exchanges' (Foucault, 2008, p. 243). Every social and identity activity falls under the framework of an economic rationality, including the ethical governance of the self (p. 286). Within this perspective, we argue, content producers of fake news can best be understood not through moral frameworks that ask us to label these figures as liars or people with illicit intent. Rather, they can be understood as an inevitable figure produced through postmodern late capitalism as a subject whose ethical disposition is to produce and marketise content, and to maximise value of that content, without regard for the Enlightenment and liberal-humanist values that previously governed the ethics of communication and institutional practices such as journalism, the regulation of defamation, judicial frameworks, and other professional and everyday social and cultural formations.

The content producer as *homo oeconomicus* is, then, a cultural, ethical and productive disposition not limited to the purveyor of disinformation and fake news, but one which actively saturates contemporary and emergent cultural production. For example, aspects of amateur online production were, in the first years of the twenty-first century, marked by a desire for authenticity in contrast to and distancing from the 'manufactured' glossiness of professional print, magazine and television production (Senft, 2008). Yet the value – financial or otherwise – of the inauthentic and professionalised returns in more recent content production online by influencers, bloggers, Instagrammers, and vloggers who monetise their everyday lives is marked by a knowingly false representation of authenticity, self-branding and activities to maximise the return on self-commodification (Abidin, 2018, pp. 78, 95–96). While this obviously does not represent every individual influencer or online celebrity, it has become the marked ethos in which everyday life is represented cynically *as content* that is manufactured, curated, honed, marketed and distributed for profit. Just as *homo oeconomicus* is a production or construct or outcome of a symbolic system and set of axioms, rules and reasonings related to the self which conforms to economic principles of exchange in all forms of self-behaviour (Lazzarato, 2009, p. 111), the contemporary framework for the creation of content is likewise undertaken not through the practices of art and creativity but through the postmodernised late capitalist approach to profit maximisation through targeted marketing – *at all cost*. Fake news content production thus fits in easily within the emerging ethos of contemporary neoliberal practices, whereby the cost is authenticity, objectivity or, indeed, reality. This is not suggest that fake news content creators are unreflective (Horner above certainly indicates his capacity to reflect critically on his own practice) but that Enlightenment-era honesty, truth, authenticity, integrity and so on are no longer the governing factors for an ethical relationship with communication. The post-truth era is sponsored by a cultural metanarrative and imperative of profit maximisation.

At a second level, what emerges in a postmodern approach is the idea of information bytes available as a smorgasbord of textuality, available to be selected and packaged for an outcome, whether monetary or not. This is perhaps best summed up by the idea of 'alternative facts', a term coined by then White House aide Kellyanne Conway. In January 2017, White House press secretary Sean Spicer had made a number of verifiably false statements about the attendance numbers at President Trump's inauguration ceremony. The then president had stated that he expected his inauguration to have 'an unbelievable, perhaps record-setting turnout' (Nuckols, 2017). Many news services, however, reported that the crowd size was unexpectedly low, with several outlets drawing on crowd scientist Keith Still's verification that numbers were approximately one-third those who turned out for President Barack Obama's inauguration in 2009 (Frostensen, 2017). Contrasting images of the crowd at the two inaugurations circulated widely on social media, demonstrating a substantial difference in attendance. During his first briefing as press secretary on 21 January, Spicer accused the media of deliberately falsifying the reported numbers at the inauguration, stating that it was the 'largest audience to ever witness an inauguration – period – both in person and around the globe' (Cillizza, 2017). During a subsequent interview with Kellyanne Conway, NBC journalist Chuck Todd raised the widespread disbelief at Spicer's statement, asking 'It's a small thing, but the first time he confronts the public, it's a falsehood?' Conway responded with the following: 'Don't be so overly dramatic about it, Chuck. You're saying it's a falsehood, and they're giving – our press secretary, Sean Spicer, gave alternative facts to that'. Todd responded: 'Wait a minute. Alternative facts? Alternative facts? Four of the five facts he uttered . . . were just not true. Alternative facts are not facts; they're falsehoods' (Blake, 2017).

The discussion opened a series of critique and speculation as to the veracity of truth and factuality in contemporary US politics, and associated the idea of 'alternative facts' with the increasing concerns around fake news (Morrissey, 2017). Arguably, the difference in perspectives presented by Todd and Conway is the difference we have been describing above between an Enlightenment-era approach to truth, fact and verifiability, and a postmodern approach in which facts (verifiable or not) become a matter of consumption choice (like choosing between a quality motor vehicle and a lemon – both available to be purchased and both cars). The idea of competition which is a key to postmodern late capitalism and neoliberal commodification is, in this context, extended to an area formerly protected by Enlightenment, liberal-humanist approaches to truth. Competition of facts, no matter how bad or false those facts are, is the outcome of an application of *laissez-faire* neoliberalism to the framework of speech itself. The cultural narrative and imperative of competition, which in late capitalism shifted from one of being seen as zero-sum game to an ethos of significant enrichment (Foucault, 2008, p. 56), infuses the approach to truth, fact and communication, such that a competition of facts to be consumed variously and diversely is perceived through the ethos and ideology of economic growth. Within the postmodern framework that brings the commodification of content and the polysemic competition of facts together, fake news can be seen as constitutive of contemporary communication, not because it is untrue, but because the circulation of content that is 'fake', meaning 'manufactured', is the ideal of postmodern communication within a neoliberal setting. This understanding contrasts, of course, with those views which consider fake news to be a populist, anti-establishment resistance to institutionalised neoliberalism.

Postmodern Culture, Sensationalism and Emotional Responses: Tabloidism as Fake News' Model Form

In considering the cultural setting of postmodernism as establishing the conditions that allow and encourage fake news, we might think too about the relationship between news and fake news. Often, in the criticism of fake news, a dichotomy between news/fake is implied and circulates as the means by which to verify, judge and condemn fake news, as if there is a secure, timeless and ahistorical 'real news' benchmark. As we discuss in the next chapter in relation to the deepfake, any real/fake binary is not only false, but constrains us from apprehending and addressing the circulation of misleading content, since so much of it is not 'fully fake', as it were. Rather, items of fake news are deceptive precisely because they amalgamate fact and fiction, the perceived real and the perceived false (van der Nagel, 2020). This gives fake news a certain kind of believability among some readers, not because they are ignorant but because the mingling of truth and falsity, fact and fiction, creates doubt that, in itself, is immaterial in the context of what we describe here as the emotional audience position that has been coached through postmodern tabloidism. That is, to understanding fake news' believability warrants looking at the emergence in the twentieth century of similar kinds of amalgamations of fact and fiction that effectively 'justify' the rise of fake news: the tabloid press, sensationalist journalism and the form of emotive response it attempts to invoke in its readership through the distortion of facts.

Tabloid media can be described as news content which is considerably exaggerated and comparatively less 'reliable' than more recognised news sources, presenting content that little indication of a referent, fact, objective reporting practices or credible informants. As a postmodern form of consumption that is partly coded more as entertainment than information, it provides a working model for the circulation of disinformation and other fake news dressed up as credible stories. Tabloid media has been described as content which 'exaggerates wildly' and gains value from representing or re-making the recognisable as grotesque, scandalous, in a way that seeks to 'defamiliarize the normal order of things' and thus mock socially legitimated news forms (Glynn, 2000, p. 145). Critiqued primarily from the 1970s, what John Fiske (1992) referred to as alternative news and popular news was already in wide circulation. Fiske differentiated popular news from 'official' news by virtue of what it selects as events and topics on which to report, on its role in suppressing particular topics and thereby politicising its content, and the discursive tools that are deployed to give particular kinds of meaning to events and reports (p. 47).

Although *all* news has an informational function, no news is simply an iteration of 'facts', but a political process that curates knowledge, and gives form to reality and to identity – in this context, popular news does so in a very particular way, often providing knowledge not for the public life (as does official and the more recognised news publications) but for private, domestic life (p. 49). The focus on the domestic and its explicit differentiation from official, formal, recognised and establishment-class media created the space for various slants that were disengaged from certain recognised facts, which thereby allowed much tabloid press to be colonised in the by right-wing views. Cary Nelson and Lawrence Grossberg (1988) point to the way in which British tabloids such as *The Sun, The Daily Mail* and *The Express* utilised domestic focal points in a way that promoted and then glorified Thatcherism in the 1980s (p. 47). We might argue that the relative distinctiveness of, say *Fox News* in the United States in contrast to the now well-establishment outlets such as *CNN* and *The New York Times* permitted a political identification with Trump populism through the similitude of the anti-establishment language of both populists and the *Fox News* viewership.

Tabloid media operate by attempting to invoke a sharp emotional response from readers – it is the fact that a story can be made to appear *sensational* that is for them the conditions of newsworthiness. Sometimes, this is in order to invoke an emotional response based on satiating curiosity about a private or domestic event, drawing from information from the private sphere into the public in order to create content that appeals to their readership. This includes particularly the private lives of celebrities, British royalty, government ministers, politicians and everyday people – in many cases content that is not verifiable because not all of these public and private figures have access to the resources (financial; time; knowledge) to undertake a defamation suit over false material. Tabloid editors are, for Ken Plummer (1995), 'the people who coax, coach and coerce people to tell their stories' (p. 21), but the stories are not always packaged with strict adherence to interviews, releases or press conferences. Rather, they are available for distortion, deliberate mis-reading and re-framing, such that the narrative written differs substantially from the lived reality, context or events experienced in private by the subject of this media. This is especially true if they are stories of scandal, of hurt, of emotional turmoil, of celebratory success – as long as the story is likely to result in an emotional response from the reader. And as long as the stories can be given headlines that will encourage a reader to seek out content that can help gratify that desire for an emotional response, perhaps in place of more meaningful emotional connections and relationalities.

At other times, the key emotional responses sought and invoked are anxiety or outrage. Outrage as a response to tabloid media stories – and, concomitantly, a form of public debate that, although failing to be rational and dispassionate but emotive, angry and sometimes vicious – is part of a wider shift in communication towards outraged responsiveness and a perceived 'right' to be angry on opinions held individually (Povinelli, 2012, p. 84). This is sometimes juxtaposed to the condemnation of any right to anger, rage of grievance among the disenfranchised, marginalised or dispossessed (Cravey, 2021). That is, tabloid media very often invoke outrage as a reader response through sensationalist headlines that claim a status quo is being threatened. For example, in the Australian context, while the more recognised political and social newspapers ran stories in October 2001 – about a month after the World Trade Centre attacks in the United States – about the Australian Security Intelligence Organisation (ASIO) and other agencies finding fake charities operating in Australia that had links to terrorist organisations, the sensationalist tabloid *The Daily Telegraph* ran a headline designed to evoke anxiety, fear, discomfort and perhaps especially anger: 'Terror Australis: Bin Laden groups in our suburbs' claiming falsely that 100 members of international terrorist groups linked to Al Qaeda were living in Sydney (Miranda, 2001). The story was not corrected (Phillips & Rankin, 2003). This and other Australian right-identified tabloids maintained over the next few years a particularly alarmist approach to headlines for stories that similarly located terrorists in Australian 'backyards' or on Australia's 'doorstep', exacerbating, as Poynting, Noble, Tabar, and Collins (2004) have argued, underlying tendencies among the readership to link Arabs and Muslims with terrorism, incompatibility with Australian values, as objects of suspicion and fear (pp. 1–2). It is possible – and, indeed, common – to argue a political motivation from a right-wing corporate outlet, given the ways in which anxieties over racialised others can sway an electorate towards supporting a hard-line government policy.

Significant here, however, is that while sensationalist reporting can invoke anxiety, fear or outrage, there is a *pleasure* in seeking out these emotional responses, thereby tying that readership even more closely to tabloid publications. One aspect of tabloid journalism is the invocation of adversity, often generating emotional responses of affiliation by making a sensational claim to adversity between two groups – citizens and immigrants being perhaps the most common (Edwards, Occhipinti, & Ryan, 2000, p. 300) although between heteronormative families and LGBTQ youth educators is also common (Hegarty, Marshall, Rasmussen, Aggleton, & Cover, 2018). Protracted adversity between two women is also a popular tabloid story that sells (Singer, 2018). For example, some sensationalist reporting in UK tabloids about Meghan Markle, the Duchess of Sussex being 'at odds' with her husband's sister-in-law Catherine Middleton, the Duchess of Cambridge has demonstrated the continuing tabloid intent on pitting two women against each other, comparing their activities, and judging one favourable and the other unfairly. This practice is, of course, widely recognised and criticised by other journalists (Brookes, 2020). Likewise, adversity between the audience and a depiction of individuals represented as the unusual, the scandalous, the marginal, the non-normative, the weird and the outrageous has become a regular staple of tabloid news and media in a way which is designed to differentiate and confirm an audience's normativity (Creed, 2003, p. 30; Gamson, 1998). Finally, the invocation of the socio-economically deprived as 'other' within the tabloid sensationalism of 'poverty porn' is, as Angela McRobbie (2020) has argued, a deliberate mechanism to generate 'hatred, cruelty and aggression' (p. 3).

What is at stake is the prioritisation of sensationalism as a postmodern disposition of audiencehood over journalistic ethical approaches to factuality, objectivity and newsworthiness; that is, the Enlightenment-era frameworks of judging and valuing communication. In the sensationalist invocation of outrage, anger, disgust or hatred, there is not only a pleasure in being positioned in a false adversarial relationship with the object of anger or hate and watching that object fail (Foucault, 2008, p. 301), but a pleasure in experiencing those emotions in themselves, without regard for the object – a postmodernisation of emotion itself. This is not to suggest that such emotions are always negative, politically regressive or relate to attacks on individuals who fall outside of a supposedly desired norm. Outrage, indignation, desire and hope are also bound up with progressive politics, relations of care, and frameworks of inclusive belonging (Butler & Athanasiou, 2013, pp. 66–67), and outrage has historically been a powerful tool to 'support and impel calls for justice and an end to violence' (Butler, 2009b, p. 11). However, this is not the framework in which outrage operates in postmodern tabloidisation of media. Rather, we are speaking of the kind of 'moral outrage' that invokes an abstract and wholly constructed sense of 'violated propriety' against some imaginary rule that shifts regularly depending on the need to maximise that outrage (Warner, 1999, pp. 26–27). For example, the tabloidised morning television *Good Morning Britain* (ITV) has been the site of regular rants from former host Piers Morgan (also a former tabloid editor) about the Duchess of Sussex (Meghan Markle), presenting content designed to set her up publicly through stereotyping her as an adversary such that it would cause public outrage. This began with claims that she was a shallow and ambitious social climber (Hatterstone, 2020) to hostile articulations that she has lied about her mental health difficulties (Chilton, 2021). While it is well-recognised that British royals are subject to substantial false reporting in the UK tabloid press, the particular extent of hostility towards the Duchess of Sussex is an important case study – one to which we return below in the discussion of deepfakes.

Such tabloid vitriol frames public figures through discourses of adversity. A number of writers and public commentators have identified what is beginning to be referred to as 'rage culture', much of which operates separately from tabloid journalism but the content and dissemination of which is able to tap into it as a market mechanism. One insightful online comment suggested that the emotive response of outrage serves to build community and affiliation by an articulation that shows 'the rest of the world that they are of value because of their emotional reactions and vitriol at individuals and corporations they most likely know nothing about' (Holmes, 2019). Rage culture in the 2020s has been associated, albeit not exclusively or quite correctly, with cancel culture and call-out culture, with anti-sexual assault movements like #MeToo, with anti-racist movements like Black Lives Matter and other progressive articulations of anger at the problematic institutional persistence of injustice and inequalities. However, rage also plays a role in the conservative and populist engagement with anti-immigrant, sexist, chauvinistic, homophobic, white supremacist and conspiracy theory expressions, in which outrage is the form of utterance in response to recognition of minorities and marginalised subjects, and/or the response to any assertion of a need for justice or social change, often represented as having been 'provoked' (Cover, 2020; Fozdar, Spittles, & Hartley, 2014). The more palpable, dangerous and problematic form is the kind of rage from those who rally against social change (Anderson, 2016). Such rage, in combination with several years of both fake news (circulating online), false facts (distributed by Donald Trump's Twitter and rallies) and tabloid sensationalism (primarily *Fox News* in the United States), was arguably a key factor in fostering the conditions for the January 2021 Capitol Riots (Shephard, 2021).

Rage and aggression are not only psychic, felt emotions but experienced in a corporeal sense, often related to frustrated expectations and aspirations, and providing a reward in the absence of anticipated achievement (Appadurai, 2003; Kent, 2012, p. 116). For some of the tabloid audience, this 'need' is problematic but marked by being positioned within a consumer culture in which fulfilment and happiness are regularly promised but never satiated (Lazzarato, 2011, pp. 93, 154). Outrage, in the context of our discussion of postmodern tabloid culture is, then, formative of a particular mode of reading and spectatorship that calls upon the reader to again and again seek out and consume media that has the effect of generating outrage as a response.

A reader, then, can be given over to these regular manufactured affective trans-formations and bodily sensations produced in the encounter with content that causes outrage and anger at a para-social figure such as a target celebrity or politician, and often a woman or minority. At one level, this is because the emotions of anger, hatred, outrage and disgust are utilised to establish a confirmation of the normativity of the self – the reader hates Meghan Markle because she is abnormal in her supposed breaches of etiquette, her alleged rampant ambitions or her perceived disruption of the British royal family's mundanity. Confirming normativity, for the reader, is comfortable because the norm is always comfort-able for those who find a way to inhabit it (Ahmed, 2004, p. 147), and the intensifi-cation of the adversarial relationship with the object of tabloid stories is one tool for those who might otherwise not already be the norm to manufacture, generate and sustain a self-positioning as norm.

At an even deeper level, we might even suggest that the corporeal and psy-chic pleasures of being given over to these sudden intensities can be addictive for the right reader in the right circumstances, producing and sustaining a particular kind of tabloid market for sensational content. These emotions tie a subject to the act of reading and the available forms of spectatorship not because that reader is tricked into reading tabloid sensationalism and mistaking it for factual, knowl-edgeable, critical engagement with a topic. Rather, the reader is subjected to the material in such a way as to confirm one's own being that is constructed in that relationship as a subject of outrage. People persist in such subjection not because the emotions themselves are pleasurable but because in becoming that subject – outraged person, disgusted person – they desire the persistent disciplining and confirmation that allows one to persist in one's own being (Butler, 1997a, p. 28) and thereby to achieve the pleasure of emplacement and confirmation within a constructed audience-community of like-minded readers. This is why it is often difficult for an angry individual who vows to become more 'zen' but cannot make the change – not because of over-exposure to a particular emotion, but because the experience of that anger at the level of the body and the psyche is necessary to continue to confirm a coherent, intelligible subjectivity.

Given the power of postmodern tabloid media's sensationalism to evoke emotions of outrage and disgust, and the need for readers to continue to experience these again and again in order to remain coherent subjects, there is a cultural framework in which fake news not only finds a natural home, but actively extends and sustains the 'work' of the tabloid press. While we recognise that much tabloid media exaggerates, misconstrues, represents with bias and uses other tools to evoke sensation, by disregarding even a reference to factual information, fake news is able to shift communication into a realm of even greater emotive responsiveness and sensationalism by the circulation of stories that not only *might* outrage, but that are *designed expressly* to outrage, disgust or reinforce adversarial opinions and hostility. It is, in this sense, like a more pure form of a drug its constructed audience needs – an audience that has been constructed in advance by the tabloidisation of contemporary communication.

Thus, when a fake news story tells us that the COVID-19 virus is a weapon designed by Islamists to wipe out western civilisation (Miller, 2020), it draws on the one hand on tabloid sensationalist headlines designed to alarm, upset, create anxiety or fear and, on the other hand, appeals to an existing tabloid audience who have already been positioned to see people, states and cultures adhering to Islam faith as a dangerous enemy. It has an audience who have been pre-prepared to feel outrage (towards Muslims) when they read the fake news story (Forrest, Blair, & Dunn, 2020; Wisker, 2020), rather than to be critically engaged enough to query the story's veracity. It is an audience that, through tabloid media, has become used to the lack of a clear, authoritative and verifiable source and thereby rarely questions its absence in fake news content. And, finally, it is an audience that seeks out these tales – and shares and circulates them further – not because they confirm a particular set of beliefs but because, through those beliefs, a pleasurable, corporeal and psychic outrage, disgust, anger or hostility is immediately invoked (Dobson-Lohman & Potcovaru, 2020), representing the latest 'hit' in the need to engage with the world through the sensations of provocative content.

The Unrecognisability of Satire, Parody and Pastiche

We discussed above the assertion by fake news content creator Paul Horner that a media culture based on satire and parody makes the distribution of his fake news hoaxes not only justifiable, but a palatable experience for a wide readership. We turn now from the postmodern tabloidisation of contemporary communication culture (as a setting that constructs a ready-made audience for sensationalist fake news) to think about, instead, another aspect of postmodern sensibility in contemporary culture. That is, the cultural setting that produces fake news through the disavowal of truth and the invocation of outrage and adversity is also a culture that has shifted from the fakery of parody to the factuality of pastiche. Parody and satire have been a very recognisable part of cultural production, and the satirisation of ordinary news media is an important part of engagement – actively training up a public in critical literacy while providing entertainment through both the similitude and recognisability of the standard form that is being satirised, and the exaggeration of that form. Undoubtedly, it relies on a more sophisticated taste regime than tabloid media and some other forms of entertainment.

Publications such as *The Onion* have traded since the late 1980s – first in print, then online from the late 1990s – on the production of satire through parodying and sometimes caricaturing news practices, newswriting norms, recognisable routines of communication. Much as fake news takes the banner of 'real' news outlets in order to purport to originate from reputable, mainstream outlets, *The Onion News Network* (ONN) parodied CNN in style, masthead, online banner, and so on in a way that would sometimes fool the reader by positioning the audience deliberately to experience 'outrage' that a public figure, a scandal, a politician or a corporation had finally 'gone too far'. The pleasure factor in parody, of course, is that once one realises that there has been fakery at play, one is expected to turn back to review the communication and its meanings from the perspective of satire in order better to read the political point that is being made satirically.

Satirical parody, however, no longer dominates the framework of public communication. Just as parody and satire rely on imitation and mimicry as both cultural form and critique (Jameson, 1985, pp. 113–114), in a postmodern setting, for Jameson, pastiche is likewise imitation and mimicry but replaces it by presenting that imitation without its critical intent. That is, pastiche differs from parody in its production of a 'neutral practice of such mimicry, without parody's ulterior motive, without the satirical impulse, without laughter … Pastiche is blank parody, parody that has lost its sense of humor' (p. 114). Given that the audience – and particularly what we are referring to as the postmodernised contemporary audience of neoliberal or late capitalism – is culturally positioned to select, read and engage with texts in a particular way that does not dissolve being active and engaged but directs the form of that engagement, the operative reading formation for that audience is to consume pastiche as a normative model of information-sharing de-politicised and removed of both validity as an informational source, and mockery as an entertainment form. As the fruition of postmodern communication in Jameson's terms, then, pastiche is the direct utilisation of the original in order to do something quite different from satire, whether than be simply to adopt a communicative style to be heard or some other end – indeed, any end that is not to draw attention to the original but to obscure the fact that it mimics the original. *Fake news is pastiche, in that sense* – it mimics recognisable form and style, yet also turns away from the critique of the original and turns its attention to achieving a political end through explicitly shrouding its mimicry.

As a form of pastiche, fake news opens the field of play of truth to a range of perspectives, insights, value-laden statements, and what has come to be described as an era of post-factuality. To put this another way: while it is undoubtedly the case that much fake news is the deliberate and self-conscious production of a falsehood designed either to gain hits and therefore financial reward or to produce outrage or hatred towards minorities and therefore a political reward, it is difficult to disavow as simply a breach in ethics. This is because the ethics of journalism as making a claim to truth and responsibility do not have bearing on the contemporary world of digital, internet utterances. Thus, when fake news content circulates, for example, it is recognisable. One example of a monetised click-bait site that uses recognisable material that is not necessarily truthful is *Heightzone*, a site that purports to provide news-style facts about celebrities but monetises that information with an overwhelming number of advertisements (at least 15 per 500 words of content). One notable example occurred in the days after an Australian teenager was beaten to death by gate-crashers at a party in early 2021 – a difficult narrative related to ongoing public concerns about young people's safety at parties that become overcrowded. *Heightzone* provided content and information about Jason Langhans that had clearly been drawn from extant news coverage, but embellished it with material that is misleading and untrue. For example, among naming his parents, his age, the circumstances of his death, and links to his online social media presence, the article contained phrases such as 'Jason Langhan [*sic.*] was a fun-loving teenager. With his charming personality, he became the heart of every party. That's why he was invited to a house party in Tooradin as well' (Kandel, 2021). These are not necessarily the circumstances of how Langhans came to be at the party, nor necessarily an accurate depiction of his personality. The piece also states: 'On April 6, Jason had serious complications and suffered from stroke as well. His family was forced to turn off his life support since he suffered never-ending pain'. Later in the piece, the writer reiterated: 'After the stroke on April 6, the family turned his lifeline off on Saturday and put him to death to save him from the pain' (Kandel, 2021). While the more credible media sites reported the circumstances including his coma and stroke, there is (obviously) no evidence that his family chose to cease artificial life support to save him from pain as opposed to the verifiable fact that he was medically determined to be unrecoverable (Rizmal, 2021). At a time when a police investigation into his murder was progressing and when coronial investigations are likely to be undertaken, the misinformation about the reasons of his death have an impact on recognised institutional and legal practices, as well as substantially misrepresenting the role of his family.

While a difficult piece to read, the *Heightzone* story is a good textual example of the relationship between fake news and pastiche. As a news story, it is in a recognisable format, albeit poorly written. As content, it draws from existing news stories, images, photographs of the victim, and details circulated in elsewhere. As misinformation, it contains recognisable but not necessarily truthful information (a fun-loving teenager, a charming personality, the heart of every party, invited to the party due to his popularity), much of which relies on stereotypes of young Australian men, but is not linked to a source or informant. By drawing together small pieces of information alongside made-up facts, the content fits within a post-modernised form of cultural production. It 'works' because the components and the story as a whole are recognisable and not incredible. Here, we see fake news at work in a way which is not the exaggerated sensationalism of the tabloid press form taken to a dishonest extreme, but the factual compilation of information, albeit untrue. In this respect, we can see the association of pastiche and fake news that produce the deepfake – usually defined as a the production through computer-assisted algorithms of audio and video material that brings together real images and fake images of a person to create an untrue but believable representation, but which in its most general definition is considered deceptive on the basis that it can 'amalgamate fact and fiction' in a way that is 'threatening to our narratives of truth' (van der Nagel, 2020, p. 424). As a form of bricolage, the piece disseminates false and misleading content, some of which may be considered unwittingly dangerous or damaging to the parties involved, and it does so for the purpose of monetisation of this pastiche by drawing readers seeking information to a site that earns from very heavy on-screen and pop-up advertising.

Conclusion

In many respects, what a postmodern, neoliberal culture does involve two intersecting frameworks that not only critique the certainty of Enlightenment approaches to truth, meaning and motivation, but actively undo them in ways perhaps unforeseen in from a scholarly viewpoint that embraced the value of those critiques. On the one hand, the postmodern dissolution of the universality and fixity of meaning opened the path for the production of content that is no longer tethered to a referent, even as a contingency to allow for communication as a form of ethical relationality. Rather, the growth of tabloid and sensationalist news production set a framework for content production that had only a tenuous link with journalistic truth and factuality, and thereby allowing for the emergence of fake news as a form of news as an *extension* of tabloid journalism rather than it's *opposite*. At the same time, the dissolution of satire and parody as critical forms of cultural production were overlaid by the popularity of pastiche and bricolage, not as self-knowing intertextual construction of a text, but as the cynical putting together of fact and fiction, 'real' and 'fake', in ways that can be seen as creative on the one hand but, on the other hand, as dangerous if read *as if* 'truth'. Drawing on new creative tools and computer processing power, the deepfake emerges as a normative form of creative production masquerading as 'truth' through the power of the visual and the recognisable, and we deal with this problematic phenomenon in the next chapter.

At a second level, however, we have the role of the interrelated economic system identified by Jameson (1991) as postmodern late capital, but which other scholars refer to as *neoliberalism*, that is, the cultural mode of polemic that places consumption, commodification and profit maximisation at the core of all relationships and subjectivity, displacing older value systems based on ethics and democracy (Duggan, 2003). The infusion of all forms of communication and exchange with a neoliberal logic sets the scene for the cynical production of fake news, deepfakes, and disinformation which, while sometimes masquerading as anti-neoliberal populism, permits the purveyor of fake news to justify their activities on the basis that it enables profit – whether through clickbait that leads to sites that generate advertising revenue, or through the sale of false or misleading content as monetised good in itself.

As we have described them, neither of these cultural elements is hegemonic in the sense that while fake news, disinformation and misinformation become more normative in our everyday lives, they are not so dominant that they circulate without criticism, investigation, introspection and combat. In later chapters, we deal with some of the specific ways in which fake news is actively resisted, and with some of the emerging ethical positions that restore truth regimes without disregarding the need to critique the power/knowledge gains of certain kinds of truth or the contingency of institutional knowledge. What we can say here, however, is that the postmodern culture that provides the conditions for the rise of contemporary fake news is always one which operates within a push-and-pull struggle between older Enlightenment values which have a continuing cultural role in information concepts of truth, liberty, identity, subjectivity and meaning, and the emergence of postmodern alternatives and their unfortunate cynical use in justifying falsity and criticising valuable knowledge frameworks in favour of conspiracy and profit.

Chapter Five

The Visual in an Era of Hyperreality and Disinformation: The Deepfake Video

Introduction

In our discussion of postmodernism in the previous chapter, we began to explore how several emergent cultural arrangements of contemporary media, literary and entertainment practices, readership and spectatorship together make possible the aspect of fake news known as 'deepfakes'. We build here on our key point that a creative culture that has embraced bricolage and pastiche in such a way as to bring together facts, truthful accounts and false or misleading material into a text that no longer warrants a referent or a grounding in verifiable sources. Although often critiqued separately from the wider issues of fake news and disinformation, the term 'deepfake' has emerged in the past half-decade to describe a significant new tool that draws on advancements in computer processing power to create and make available false and misleading visual material for both powerful creative or artistic purposes and for surreptitious use in creating and 'proving' disinformation.

Most commonly, deepfakes draw on algorithmic powers, machine learning and modern capabilities for processing information to allow users to insert the face, body, and visual information about a real-world person into a false setting. This enables them to replicate voice and mimic movements in a way that looks 'real', for example, representing former US Secretary of State giving a speech she never gave, looking credible and saying things that may persuade people she holds views she does not. What is at stake is the fact the fakery is so well done – this is not fake news in the textual form in which one has to suspend disbelief in order to trust the quotations, paraphrases or narratives presented are real, as this requires a prior belief in its *likelihood* and, as we have been arguing, a giving over of critical readership to sensationalism, or having believable elements because it is a pastiche of fact of fiction. Rather, this is the visual, spoken, computer-generated image that takes us beyond the need for belief or reading practices: by looking believable the deepfake video is presented as the evidence itself.

Rather than condemning the deepfake as a horrific problem, or recommending state regulation – such as the State of California's new laws that make deepfakes about politicians illegal in the lead up to elections – we argue in this chapter that deepfake as a form of disinformation can only be apprehended by putting

Fake News in Digital Cultures: Technology, Populism and Digital Misinformation, 63–76
Copyright © 2022 by Rob Cover, Ashleigh Haw and Jay Daniel Thompson
Published under exclusive licence by Emerald Publishing Limited
doi:10.1108/978-1-80117-876-120221005

the concept in its historical, technological and conceptual contexts. That allows the global community to think through remedies that avoid seeing it as an invasive force and, instead, as an anticipated emergence. That does not mean we can develop genuine, workable remedies in the space of one chapter or one book. Rather, what it means is that we can begin to give pointers to help engage with deepfakes as an issue that is both relative to fake news and supports and expands the dangers of fake news.

To that end, we address three things in this chapter: firstly we discuss how the deepfake is understood and how it operates as an issue for comprehending fake news, disinformation and misinformation. Making sense of it as both a wonderful creative tool and a problematic mechanism for injurious content is, we argue, a significant part of the solution. We then turn to its emergence, demonstrating how it rises as a culturally demanded and foreseen form of creativity at the convergence point between new technologies that were developed precisely to enable digital video manipulation, and the culture of postmodernism's hyperreality, bricolage and pastiche that frame the very idea of content that is cobbled together from faces that were not recorded, voices that never spoke those words, settings and backdrops that were films, and original bodies that are no longer in the picture. Finally, we address what we identify as the four key socio-political issues that result from the deepfake.

The Deepfake as New Issue for Fake News

Deepfakes 'are the product of artificial intelligence (AI) applications that merge, combine, replace, and superimpose images and video clips to create fake videos that appear authentic' (Westerlund, 2019, p. 39). The earliest deepfakes included videos in which an individual's face and body was sutured into scenes from a separate recording in which they did not appear, act in, or were otherwise recorded. At times, it has involved highly believable, correct-sounding computer-generated speech in the person's voice they never recorded. This is often an act of showcasing the creative value of deepfake and computer-generated imaging technologies – often for the sake of humour, satire or critique. A well-recognised example from 2018 involves the actor Nicolas Cage, using deepfakes to build on a much longer-running internet trend or meme that involved circulating images of a wide-eyed, maniacally grinning, over-the-top acting Cage, often with layover text to make a political or social point or as a creative way to express an emotion or viewpoint. Compilations of these images came to be known online as 'Cage Rage', and the re-utilisation of still images from films has come under criticism – perhaps unfairly – for undermining the integrity of the original work (Pulver, 2018). The re-utilisation of recognisable content is, of course, part of the interactive engagement with textuality we described in Chapter Three: a cultural form that binds communities in a shared practice of re-utilisation and manipulation.

Similarly, in 2019, a video circulated online depicting the face of Tom Cruise merged onto that of comedian Bill Hader (Wang, 2019). Others make use of a combination of existing images and new, such as of former President Barack Obama or Facebook co-founder and CEO Mark Zuckerberg giving a speech, but using software that mimics the voice such that they are speaking words they never actually spoke (Gilbey, 2019). Such videos demonstrate and show off the power of emergent technologies, including freely available apps such as FakeApp which was developed using open-source deep-learning software from Google. These technologies are part of the outpouring of the creative potential of interactivity envisaged by the creator of early World Wide Web platform technology, Tim Berners-Lee. Berners-Lee (1999) imagined a future in which texts were edited, changed and further developed freely by other users, combined with the postmodern taste for pastiche, bricolage and creative assembly of disjunct components. While the technology is new, and is beginning to be discussed with alarm in public discourse (Robertson, 2018; Robinson, 2018), as a creative and artistic form they are not in themselves new. Rather, they are an expansion on existing creative practices of 'remix', including particularly those fan activities which – from the early 2000s – took video footage from television shows and films and combined it with audio from songs in order to create a new work built from old that had new meanings (Cover, 2010). Remixed texts have been positioned as a new and transformative form of art that, despite industry copyright concerns, do not compete with existing texts but makes use of them as 'found material' that can be manipulated, mashed-up, converged, packaged into each other and juxtaposed in order to produce an ostensibly intertextual experience (Lessig, 2008). It is part of the ongoing practice of consumer co-creation of audio and video texts (Burgess & Green, 2009).

As an interactive and deliberately intertextual text, the remix, mash-up and now the deepfake is best understood as *layered intermedia*, that is, as a narrative comprised of – or fused between – moving image and sound, audio which includes dialogue, effects, incidental and narrative-related music. In that context, no individual component of the text can be understood or analysed away from the elements into which it has been remixed. New meanings emerge in intermedia remixes not simply because original or new intertextualities are produced by user-creators relying on existing sources, but because those sources themselves no longer operate with the same set of meanings and significations, allowing the productive activation of new meanings. This outpouring of creativity adopts new technological developments at different points in time, whether that was the widening access to video-editing software and the requisite skills to use it in the 2000s or the access to simple apps that use machine learning for the more advanced forms of insertion of faces as a new kind of layering we see in the 2020s.

There is much to celebrate about the technological capacities of digital advancements for creative industries. Film and television have long taken advantage of ongoing advancements in computer processing to produce digital effects that enhance storytelling (Alexander, 2017; Hashim, Mohamad Salleh, & Mohamad, 2015). Arguably, such advancements not only represent the artistic practices of hyperreality, bricolage and pastiche in positive and productive ways; they enable creative producers to overcome obstacles such as the death of an actor who can later be sutured using deepfake technologies into unfilmed scenes, or replacing an actor, producing more effective doubles without the use of green screen and body doubles, and placing actors into scenes which would otherwise be dangerous or threatening (Debussman Jr, 2021).

That is one angle. Another, however, returns us to the point made in Chapter Three that while technological advancements emerge from culture and are actively sought and foreseen, they are not always utilised in those foreseeable ways but adopted for other uses that meet a cultural need. Again, a postmodern practice of hyperreality that has not an artistic but an insidious quality is at play. Deepfake videos that utilise the likeness of known people take the artistic practice to a deeper, more problematic level – using machine learning software that, for example, places reproductions of Nicolas Cage not only into films in which he did not act, but representing his character or person believably punching women – something which is neither representative of himself or the characters he has *actually* played, and has the potential to damage his reputation or, perhaps more importantly to a Hollywood, his marketability for future roles (Gerstner, 2020, p. 1). The capacity to use deepfake technology to produce falsehoods as *evidence*, not just *accusation*, is substantial. In March 2021, for example, the mother of a schoolgirl cheerleader in Pennsylvania, United States, used deepfake technology to produce videos of three rival cheerleaders nude and using drugs and alcohol in an effort to have them removed from the team (Bellware, 2021). While a police investigation was able to find the material created to embarrass the three young women was false, a successful deepfake is more than an accusatory statement made for scurrilous purposes but serves as a piece of evidence, not necessarily requiring efforts to create wider context.

Deepfakes also include videos that are sexually explicit and pornographic in nature. A 2019 study found that 96% of the internet deepfake videos are pornographic (Wang, 2019). These videos have included the faces of actresses such as Gal Gadot and Emma Watson (Ohman, 2020, p. 133), and of Hillary Clinton (Collins, 2018). In 2018, journalist Rana Ayyub reported that she had been made the subject of a deepfake porn video after publishing an article about the rape of a young Kashmiri girl (Maddocks, 2020, p. 415). Pornographic deepfakes are often designed to objectify women sexually, and to humiliate their targets. There is a long tradition, of course, of 'celebrity porn' in which look-alikes are used in poorly lit and poorly shot scenes to allow viewers to fantasise they are seeing a particular celebrity engaged in a sexual act. Deepfakes further enable the capability to produce such work without the need for a look-alike or, indeed, to shoot a new scene, but can rely on the computer-processed insertion of the celebrity into a scene from an older pornographic work. Finally, pornographic videos are sometimes posted in retaliation for perceived wrongdoings or missteps on behalf of the target, and as such fit the genre of revenge porn (Wang, 2019).

Perhaps the most substantial difference between the celebrity Cage and Cruise deepfakes (and the thousands doing something similar for entertainment purposes) and the deepfakes used to humiliate, whether through creating pornography or other embarrassing scenes (equally for entertainment and/or insidious or reputation-damaging purposes) is not in the fact that the latter are sexual or may involve subjects in compromising. Rather, it is again in the push-and-pull between different modalities of cultural production: a creative pursuit designed to showcase technological film-making skill and to demonstrate that skill by announcing publicly how such a work was made – part of the wider genre of behind-the-scenes and how-to that has accompanied major visual creative endeavours for several decades. Yet, the utilisation for purposes that are other than entertainment, fascination, enjoyment of the 'trick', is the deepfake that is produced in order to masquerade as 'real'. Here a real/fake is, interestingly, restored in contemporary cultural production, such that the hyperreal fakery of film-making acknowledges its postmodern, technological and pastiche framework of production, while the insidious deepfake is distributed in a pre-critical framework in which the viewer is expected to believe 'the camera never lies'.

Deepfake's Rise: An Interactive Postmodern Cultural Technology

In discussing the technological development of the television, Raymond Williams (1990) provided a useful cultural framework for making sense of how technologies emerge and why they are not alien to culture. Williams was critical of technological determinist theories that viewed the invention of a technology as an accident or an invention unrelated to any need that then goes on have an impact on society, change institutions and practices, and produce other unforeseen consequences (pp. 10–11). A cultural approach is to understand technologies, platforms, communication tools and recording devices and practices as developed from *within* culture over time, rather than the more pedestrian binary approach of identifying a technology's moment of invention and then attempting to understand culture in terms of 'before' and 'after', often either celebrating or denouncing that 'after' (Flew, 2005, p. 25). This view, which despite being used uncritically in popular discourse has been the 'orthodox' public view of technological development since the twentieth century (Williams, 1990, p. 12), is the one which governs much of the discourse of both celebration and alarmism over deepfake applications. For example, one report from investigative cluster *Deeptrace* which researches cybersecurity detection technologies, described the advent of the deepfake as an unsettling phenomenon, quickly changing the landscape of pornography, security and institutional authority (Ajder, Patrini, Cavalli, & Cullen, 2019). Others have described deepfake technology as bringing about an 'infocalypse' (Lenters, 2021), implying an instance of crisis or rupture that bears witness to something extraordinary or from out of this world to destroy the civilisation and cultural practices that are recognisable to us today.

In criticising technological determinist assumptions for their narrow understanding of the cause and effect of new technological developments, Williams (1990) offered an approach we have come to know as 'cultural technologies'. He sought to restore *intention* to the understanding of technological development, such that new technologies are not seen as an accident or the work of an individual 'inventor' who discovers a technology that unleashes change on the world, but as actively 'actively looked for and developed with certain purposes in mind' which includes primarily 'known social needs, purposes and practices to which the technology is not marginal but central' (p. 13). In the example of the television, he points out that there is no single event or moment of television's creation – despite the popular myth of 'invention' by John Logie Baird that is taught to all children.

Rather, it developed over more than a century of deliberate research, investment, trial, and related technical artefact construction. The purpose for which television was invented was to respond to several intersecting cultural needs, including the need for mass communication (p. 17), the expansionist desires of industrial capital (p. 19), and cultural demand for entertainment that crossed over and inhabited domestic spaces subsequent to the move towards nuclear family homes and the concept of a public/private threshold (pp. 20–21). In other words, without a set of cultural demands to make the development worthwhile, there would have been no serious investment in the cost and effort of research and development, the labour involved and the wider infrastructure framework, since such technologies are never developed without that intentional investment and research.

In the case of the deepfake, the same approach to investment, research and development has applied, indicating that they emerge from within culture as the everyday way of life and system of meanings and understandings experienced socially. That is, deepfake applications were not an accidental discovery, nor the brainchild of a young app developer working from a bedroom in her parents' home (although these are always part of the emanation of the cultural desire or demand for the technology). Rather, deepfake technology develops over time in response to a perceived cultural need, desire or demand for the capability to generate images that are as good as or better than recorded footage. Early work on visual facial reanimation in combination with sound from elsewhere dates back at least as far as the late 1990s (Bregler, Covell, & Slaney, 1997). Building on other developments in artificial decision-making and deep-learning – themselves the subject of long-standing cultural desires and demands for forms of automated thinking and creativity – alongside massive increases in computer processing power resulted in the substantial capability for applications that can operate on personal computers using accessible software interfaces by the 2010s. The practice of video-editing and digital image manipulation had already transitioned from professional to personal settings with software such as Adobe's Photoshop and Premiere Pro. Commercial development of deepfake applications such as FakeApp and the open-source FaceSwap and the mobile application Impressions were developed and made available in 2018, 2019 and 2020, respectively. The research that went into the underlying platform technologies, such as neural auto-encoding, and generative adaptation algorithms are part that wider developmental picture, as has been the entire digital video effects (DiVX) industry supporting major film and television production for over 15 years. In other words, a very large number of people, institutions and practices over a protracted period were involved in the development of software that would enable the computer-generation of believable audio–video content that depicted a person who was not recorded, but placed into a recording or other setting, doing or saying things they had not said.

To what, then, does the deepfake respond? What is the cultural need, demand or desire that made such investment possible? At its simplest, we can say that deepfakes are deliberately developed to support a film industry that has invested in and pursued constant improvement in DiVX (Naruniec, Helminger, Schroers, & Weber, 2020, p. 2). However, they respond to a much deeper cultural need, which is most easily expressed as the desire for real-looking, non-authentic visual content, as part of the wider cultural practice of interactivity with texts that manipulate and play with meanings, timing, framing and other aspects as part of a deep-seated human desire to co-create (Cover, 2006). Deepfakes respond to this desire, which is one that becomes expressible in a cultural framework that deliberately disregards or disavows authenticity, as we discussed in the previous chapter, in favour of hyperreality.

This hyperreality is culturally demanded within the late capitalist postmodern framework that, as Slavoj Zizek (2002) described it, warrants content that is *'unreal,* substanceless, deprived of material inertia' (p. 13). That is, it is a loss of the myth of authenticity that constrained creativity as representative rather than as liberated. In obliterating the boundary between the authentic and simulation, contemporary postmodern culture not only produces the idea of the fake as a creative form, but embraces the potential to explore alternative ways of being, communicating and engaging (Filiciak, 2003, p. 98). The postmodern cultural setting described in the previous chapter as that of production and pastiche without referent, and which enables at one level the acceptability of the fake in fake news, is the cultural formation which demands the tools not only for more spectacle and simulacra that trumps any concept of real, but also the tools that allow the everyday subject to participate in building the hyperreal. Aside from what we might personally feel about authenticity, and in a contrastive struggle with Enlightenment-era demands for the authentic, the normal, the real and truthful, the participation in the production of the hyperreal underlies the contemporary condition of human communication and engagement.

According to Henry Ajder et al. (2019) report, 96% of the deepfake videos they identified online were pornographic in nature, the majority representing actors and singers (p. 2). That figure *may* have re-balanced more towards non-pornographic deepfakes, particularly given conspiratorial controversies over COVID-19, vaccinations and the US election subsequent to that report. However, what it indicates is that a very sizeable majority of deepfakes have been produced not for the purposes of demonstrating creativity, producing humour, or use for the creation of art. Rather, they have been produced for surreptitious purposes of a kind that was not intended (van der Nagel, 2020). Pornography, of course, has been the product of every medium of record known to global human cultures, from drawings to tiled mosaics, from painting to magazines, from video to cassettes to amateur online videos, from sexting to deepfakes. As Emily van der Nagel (2020) notes, it has very substantial implications for how we perceive violation and sexual harassment, particularly in cases where a woman's image has been taken in a public setting and then converted into a false pornographic piece (p. 426). This is clearly at some remove from the cultural intentions that compelled the development of deepfake software, skills and capabilities. Likewise, the use of deepfake for other non-entertainment purposes as Ajder et al. (2019) identified: accelerating political unrest and scandal in Gabon and Malaysia (p. 10), the use of deception to defraud businesses and everyday users (p. 13), including through synthetic voice simulation (p. 14). These more recognisable forms of illegal, criminal or illicit activity are, of course, in addition to other kinds of everyday use such as the smear campaign by the cheerleader Mum discussed above (Bellware, 2021).

In other words, while the cultural desire for the development of deepfake technology may well be grounded in a deep attachment to creativity that has become creativity within hyperreal formations over the past few decades, the technology has been put to uses other than those intended.

To make sense of this aspect of the deepfake, then, requires us not to turn back to a technological determinism (and thereby assume that the availability of deepfake technologies has fostered an environment in which people do things differently), nor to disavow Williams' (1990) highly important contribution that allows us to comprehend deepfakes as a cultural technology, actively sought and intentionally developed with explicit purposes in mind. Rather, to understand what is often at an overly simplistic level called 'mis-use' requires us to think from a 'uses and gratifications' approach. This is a set of theories that asks not what causes a technology, but how technologies are utilised for gratifications that may not be part of the foreseen need that drove the intentional development. Rather, deepfakes, are put to other purposes to satiate other kinds of desires and needs that are not necessarily incompatible with the underlying cultural demand for hyperreality. Uses and gratification is a set of theories that examine what people do with media content, technologies and practices (Perry, 1996, p. 47).

Developed initially in the late 1950s, the uses and gratification approach turns away not only from technological determinism but also from 'effects' models, these being the idea that the content access through communication technologies have a direct behavioural impact on the user, reader or viewer who is seen in such approaches to lack agency. Uses and gratification, rather, looks not to the impact but to what people do with media, technologies, platforms, content and other artefacts of the communication process (Kaye & Johnson, 2002, p. 55). One of the key pioneers of the uses and gratification approach, Elihu Katz (1959), argued that in contrast to understanding a media process as doing something to a recipient, '[t]he 'uses' approach assumes that people's values, their interests, their associations, their social roles, are pre-potent and that people selectively "fashion" what they see and hear to these interests' (p. 3). Such selection and fashioning of use according to a particular cultural positioning applies to technologies as well. This is not to suggest that the subject who uses deepfakes to defraud a friend was somehow always a person with criminal intentions. Nor is it to say that a certain kind of criminality came about once deepfake apps began to be available. Rather, it is to say that in the interaction between a certain technology and a certain cultural formation driven by a need separate from the one that fostered the development of that technology, an unforeseen cultural activity emerged. And in the case of the surreptitious use of the deepfake for the purposes of disinformation and misleading content, this unforeseen effect of the relationship between the technology and the people using it becomes an 'issue' for what would otherwise undoubtedly have been a relatively benign but useful creative platform.

Deepfake as a Social Problem: Four Key Issues

While we celebrate the technological advances that enable a truly amazing capability to produce real-looking audio-visual material, we also need to observe the ways in which they both re-shape and embed the issues around disinformation, misinformation and false or misleading news and other problematic content. This is not to suggest that the very idea of the deepfake is such a problem that the activity should be banned or regulated, nor is it to say that the creative benefits outweigh the problems of their misuse. Rather, it is to argue that – as with any cultural or creative reconfiguration – they emerge in ways whereby a struggle for the control of content, meaning, utility, value occurs, with consequences that may be undesirable, problematic, damaging and available for acts of violence to public figures who are otherwise acting good faith. To that end, we argue, there are four key issues that emerge with the deepfake in terms of the wider problems of fake news and disinformation.

Firstly, deepfakes extend the boundaries of fake news and support it. Although fake news and deepfakes have commonly been criticised simultaneously, their relationship is somewhat more complex, with some writers suggesting a symbiosis (e.g., Blitz, 2018; Westerlund, 2019). Such arguments often suggest that both fake news and deepfakes are examples of communication in a post-truth era, which Westerlund (2019) describes as being 'characterized by digital disinformation and information warfare led by malevolent actors running false information campaigns to manipulate public opinion' (p. 309). However, we argue that this is more than simply being two examples of post-truth communication, and suggest that the relationship is one in which the deepfake serves to strengthen fake news in other forms, while both are the emanation of postmodern cultures of pastiche and hyperreality. There are an increasing number of cases in which a fake news story circulating in print form includes a link to a deepfake video as the 'evidence' of the fake news, in much the same way a story in *The Guardian* about a political policy might include an embedded video of a government minister announcing that policy. The journalism products that emerge from the cross-media news-room and multi-modal news-sharing arrangements have become so familiar to us since the 2010s that embedded and linked video material operates as part of the expected package for those who are reading news online or through social media. The utilisation of the deepfake, then, operates not only as a form of disinformation and misleading content alongside fake news, but serves as the 'proof' of the fake news by presenting a real-looking bricolage of an actual person's recognisable face speaking or doing something they did not do.

Secondly, we have the wider issue of the potential a proliferation of deepfakes does for the capability to balance postmodern critical engagement with texts and the reliance on Enlightenment-era practices – if not universally accessible or 'truthful' – of fact, evidence and shared meaning. What a proliferation of deepfake does is undermine confidence not only because misleading but 'believable' manufactured footage is in circulation, but because it leads to doubting any other kind of footage as the 'fake' and the 'real' become increasingly indistinguishable. In that sense, they both serve and can become 'news' in themselves, particularly when they involve public figures, or be 'taken' as news by those who have been misled or are otherwise positioned to believe these texts. This is because they primarily purport to present 'evidence' of events that 'actually happened'. As one study noted:

> Digital images and videos are a powerful form of persuasion on a fact of a matter being asserted ... Visual representations of an alleged fact can be more convincing than words. (Maras & Alexandrou, 2019, p. 257)

This use of visual media sets deepfake videos apart from other forms of fake news, which can be visual *or* text-based. Fake news can sometimes be quickly debunked via fact-checking, whether by a professional post-hoc fact-checking organisation, a journalist or an 'everyday' internet user. Conversely, establishing the veracity (or otherwise) of deepfake videos can be profoundly challenging.

Some of the ramifications of the widespread availability of technologies and applications that allow everyday users to develop deepfake video content were spelled out in a letter by US lawmakers to the US Director of National Intelligence:

> Hyper-realistic digital forgeries use sophisticated machine learning techniques to produce convincing depictions of individuals doing or saying things they never did, without their consent or knowledge. By blurring the line between fact and fiction, deep fake technology could undermine public trust in recorded images and videos as objective depictions of reality. (cited in Chakhoyan, 2018)

Andrew Chakhoyan (2018) suggests that deepfake videos can increase the political polarisation that has been prevalent in contemporary democracies, and that was particularly evident during the 2016 US presidential election. He cites as an example a Buzzfeed video from 2018 in which footage of Barack Obama was manipulated to make it appear as though he was making ludicrous statements. This video was designed to illustrate how deepfaking works, but it's not unimaginable that it could be used to demonise politicians and polarise the public even further (Chakhoyan, 2018).

Research is being undertaken on technology to authenticate deepfake videos; this appears to be in its early stages. However, it has also been suggested that the exponential advances in AI mean that 'it is only a matter of time before fake videos are so convincing that they are difficult to identify as fakes' (Maras & Alexandrou, 2019, p. 260). Whether technological intervention can provide a permanent solution to identifying manufactured content from recorded footage is unknown, but as with all problematic or unintended uses of digital a media, an ongoing set of push-and-pull developments between the problem and the remedy is anticipated (Cover, 2006). At the same time, then, there is a risk that the real press conference, the real speech, the real activities that have really been undertaken by a public figure, are likewise more difficult to identify as real. The US state of California has enacted legislated to make it illegal to post or distribute any video content that deliberately manipulates the face or speech of a political candidate 60 days prior to an election – while important symbolic legislation to indicate concerns over electoral implications, doubts have been expressed as to the real capacity to police such videos given the likelihood of the anonymity or invisibility of the creative source (Karr, 2019). The wider capability among everyday readers and viewers to distinguish between manufactured content and actual footage packaged as a news story becomes less accessible to the broader future public. Or, at the very least, creates substantially more labour for those who are attempting to determine the 'truth' behind a news story and assess whether it is representative of facts or a form of disinformation.

Thirdly, is the fact that the existence of deepfakes in general sabotages confidence in all forms of visual evidence, and the impact that has on the workability of institutions. This is because deepfakes create a glut of information online that cannot easily be picked through to find the facts, truth and value of information. In earlier examples of fake news and disinformation, a claim about a particular event can be doubted due to the lack of any visual evidence (e.g., fake news claiming hordes of immigrants are breaching borders and recognised institutions are taking no action). In the era of the deepfake, not only can the visual material provide so-called 'evidence', and the fact of deepfakes make us doubt any actual evidence, the ability to determine whether or not an event is really taking place, whether or not key institutions, governments and agencies are trustworthy and reliable, and whether or not a person actually said something or not is difficult to determine. Not only does this increase the labour of genuine journalists and critical readers, but it broadly undermines confidence in public institutions and figures. For example, a low-quality deepfake of US House of Representatives Speaker Nancy Pelosi that circulated in 2019 had used basic video-editing tools to slow down 'real' footage of her speaking in an interview in order to show her as either drunk or impaired, such as by a stroke (CBS News, 2019). Widely distributed and remarked upon, it made it into political news outlets not as an object of critique but as evidence for political statements.

For example, a *Fox and Friends* broadcast contribute stated on 24 May that 'She always looks like she's a non-functioning alcoholic' (Towers-Clark, 2019). A related video was then notified by then US President Trump who tweeted 'PELOSI STAMMERS THROUGH NEWS CONFERENCE' (CBS News, 2019). While the effect of these lower-level deepfakes was not necessarily that serious, it had the potential to undermine confidence in the US legislature, its leadership and the Democratic Party in the year prior to an election. While confidence in governance institutions may already be eroding due to a range of factors, the immediacy of the inability to unpack the glut of information that may or may not be real has genuine impact. As one computer scientist, Hany Farid, noted in an interview with CBS News, the ability to trust may not just be a matter of the erosion of confidence in institutions or leadership over time, but have a problematic immediacy. As he put it:

> What if somebody creates a video of President Trump saying, 'I've launched nuclear weapons against Iran, or North Korea, or Russia?' We don't have hours or days to figure out if it's real or not. The implications of getting that wrong are phenomenally high. (Karr, 2019)

This is not to account for the fact that a well-developed deepfake could use computer-generated footage to provide further 'evidence' of a nuclear strike by providing images of actual nuclear missiles being launched. The Cold War frameworks in place to prevent an international misunderstanding and accidentally trick an opposing foreign actor into thinking a launch has taken place may no longer be up to the task in an era of convincing deepfakes. In that sense, the deepfake as the 'evidence' of deliberate fake news sabotages confidence (Robertson, 2018) such that what even content that was created as a joke, an entertainment or showcasing of skill may influence decisions, opinions, ways of reacting that are not limited to ballot box voting but may have significant and unforeseen consequences on a wider population as a matter of public interest (Muller, 2014, p. 80).

Finally, there is the ethical angle. Deepfake videos can seriously transgress ethical boundaries in such a way that it is not matter of bolstering fake news and disinformation, creating additional labour for journalists and viewers, or having an effect on decisions, confidence or trust, but may be an act of violence in themselves. At one level, the more innocuous videos have the problem of consent over the use of images: certainly, in the case of the Cruise and Cage videos, there is no evidence that either actor consented to have their images used and publicly distributed in those ways. More significantly, however, is the ethical violation of the pornographic deepfake as a form of disinformation that has a negative impact on the public image and the credibility of the individual being deepfaked. On the one hand, these videos fit into the gossip or entertainment news category of the leaked celebrity sex-tape that is usually never widely seen but presents a celebrity as being a certain type of celebrity. On the other hand, by circulating as a text that humiliates, shames or embarrasses a public figure – which is not to suggest that sex or the recording of a sexual act is in itself shameful – is not just something which may have a material impact on a decision about a subject, but is something which does violence to a subject. That is, when the Hillary Clinton video deepfake pornography was distributed on several platforms during the 2016 electoral year – including on a pro-Trump subreddit (Collins, 2018) – there was a likely damage to Clinton's standing in a way that may have had an impact on that election.

However, while the deepfake pornographic video of Meghan Markle, the Duchess of Sussex, circulates in a way which does reputational damage, as a public figure neither standing for office nor reliant on acting jobs, there is an act of violence that is simply about reputational damage, per se – the desire to shame. The Meghan Markle deepfake circulated in 2019 on pornography platforms, which built on widespread tabloid criticism of her 'raunchy' scenes in previous films and television (Mail Online, 2017). Fake news claims circulated across a number of blogs, including the personal blog of the B95 iHeartRadio online station, that a 'real' video had been sent to a Canadian woman who had contacted former pornography producer Kevin Blatt who had previously negotiated the release of various celebrity sex tapes (Carmen, 2019).

The story is undoubtedly false, as it cannot be corroborated. However, as the Question and Answer forum site, Quora, indicates, the idea of the existence of a Meghan sex tape is widely believed, and a sizeable number claim to have viewed on various porn sites where it is easily available and believed it to be real, rather than a deepfake. From the perspective of the fact that deepfakes are produced without the consent of their subjects and can be classified as 'image-based sexual abuse' (Maddocks, 2020), we might consider the act of violence that the deepfake of the Duchess does – not merely to shame or humiliate her, but as an act of sexual violence by visualising her *as if* in a sexual scene, regardless of its believability. In this context, we see fake news stretch its impact from one that affects decisions, trust and knowledge to one that is used as a tool of harm and hostility. This is an issue we take up again in later chapters on trust, attitude and ethics.

Conclusion

We discuss ethics in the final chapter in this book where we make the case that fake news entails a particular kind of violence that obliges all members of the global community to participate in suspending our disbelief in concepts of a universal truth, accessible facts and shared realities through an engaged and renewed critical practice that prompts both interrogation of meaning while permitting communication, information and collective knowledge-sharing to flow for the sake of a peaceful, ethical, inclusive and sustainable future. In this brief conclusion, it is worth making a few preliminary remarks about the ethical framework in which deepfakes are perceived. Marc Andrejevic (2002) noted nearly two decades ago that conditions of power in the context of entry to what he referred to as 'the digital enclosure' are at the heart of our legal, ethical and political issues of the future of communication. These conditions include not only the denied access to skills, technologies and networks that comprised a digital divide, but also the compulsion to participate in both watching and being watched (p. 246). Since then, the question of skill has changed in relation to the technologies of creative production – while skill is not eradicated, machine learning, automated processes, simple apps and accessible practices have made entry to the creative processes easier, which has in part resulted in the increased ability of those with ill-intent to produce and circulate deepfake videos.

Where the ethical question of access remains, then, is in the context of spectatorship. On the one hand, there is now the possibility that any presentation of the self online, whether in a blog, being recorded at a party, a photograph on Facebook, might be used without consent to generate a deepfake that serves as evidence for an act of disinformation. On the other hand is the question of a different kind of exposure: the fact that the existence of the deepfake calls upon viewers to question whether what they are seeing is actually a framed recording of an actual event or personage, or not. In raising these as ethical questions rather than ones of political communication, we are not suggesting this warrants a regulatory framework to prevent the creative use of deepfakes, only that there is an ethical undecidability in which preventing the use of a technology would be an act of violence but permitting the problematic mis-representation of people – whether public or private figures – is also an act of violence. It is an impasse that requires a third position before we can begin to remedy fake news.

In light of the deepfake's role both *in* and *as* fake news – that is, as evidence supporting disinformation and as the content of disinformation itself – the ethical questions are now no longer just about what impact fake news might have on democratic decisions and the integrity of institutional processes. Rather, they become a matter in which all subjects, users and anyone who has had images circulate in digital form is available to be the object (and target) of fake news and misleading content. Just as the cheerleader mother we described above utilised deepfake technologies to embarrass her daughter's rivals, any everyday person may unwittingly find themselves investigated for participating in activities they had not participated in – whether that is being represented in convincing (fake) footage being drunk at a work party, or taking part in an insurrection that never happened. We might predict that one of the results of this goes back, then, to Andrejevic's ethical concern over being watched, albeit in a different way: the need for increased surveillance and self-surveillance in order to always have 24 hour, 7-day-a-week ready-to-go alibis, lest we – everyday people, rather than politicians – be the unwitting subject of damaging fake news.

Chapter Six

Fake News and Conspiracy Theories

Introduction

In June 2020, the era we are now living in was described as 'the golden age of conspiracies' (Stanton, 2020). *Politico* journalist Jack Stanton was referring to the proliferation of conspiracy narratives in the digital media ecology. Other than perhaps the adherents of conspiracy theories, most people would agree with that assessment, since reporting about conspiracy theories has become commonplace in mainstream media over the past half-decade, particularly in relation to COVID-19, vaccinations, climate science and political extremism. There has also been increased conspiracy theory activity across social networks and online forums in relation to a wide array of ideas, from claims that the Moon Landing was a hoax to claims of a conspiracy among airline pilots to hide what they believe is the 'fact' that the Earth is flat.

While these are the kinds of statements one found on flyers in the 1990s or occasionally in speeches given by well-meaning but misguided members of the public addressing crowds on a street corner, the principal vehicle by which conspiracy theories circulate today is online fake news stories. In many ways, the proliferation and hardening belief in conspiracy theories is disappointing to those of us who were present in the early years of the internet: while online communication once represented the capacity for fact-checking, knowledge accessibility and collective intelligence (such as through the cooperative building of wikis), more recent formations of digital culture have seen the circulation of suspicions and beliefs that were once marginal at best, and the hardening of adherence to conspiracies in ways that work against the values of the early internet.

This chapter situates the proliferation of conspiracy theories within the context of fake news. We begin by tracing the mass distribution of conspiracy theories not only to the rise of global digital networks, but also to what we have described in Chapter Four as the postmodernisation of communication content. In the twenty-first century, the potency of conspiracy theories lies not merely in the pleasure of consuming the fantastic, the spectacular or the stories of clever twists and hidden agendas (Berkowitz, 2020), but in the fact that they traverse the real and the hyperreal. Even the most outrageous and improbable of these theories is able to draw together facts and recognised knowledge in ways which distort the factual elements into what, for many, is the truly ludicrous, but for others,

Fake News in Digital Cultures: Technology, Populism and Digital Misinformation, 77–91
Copyright © 2022 by Rob Cover, Ashleigh Haw and Jay Daniel Thompson
Published under exclusive licence by Emerald Publishing Limited
doi:10.1108/978-1-80117-876-120221006

represents a deeply held belief. We present these points, then, through a case study of the QAnon conspiracy theory. This is one of the best-known contemporary conspiracy narratives, and an unmistakeable product of the current moment of postmodern hyperreality. QAnon conspiracists have exploited the affordances of modern web technologies to advance their cause. Given the dangers of the re-circulation of conspiracy in credible news media, we conclude this chapter by exploring some of the ways in which journalists can report on conspiracies in as ethical a manner as possible. The challenge, we suggest, lies in reporting on these movements and their purported aims without giving them credence, but also without demonising their proponents, since doing so sets up an adversarial relationship with purveyors fake news stories in ways that strengthen their following and harden the mistrust of credible journalism.

Conspiracy Theories and Their Cultural Role

The term 'conspiracy theory' encompasses factually unverified (or unverifiable) attempts to explain certain phenomena. This kind of text, content, belief or discourse typically takes the form of narratives that allege secret plans by powerful entities (the government, the super-rich, the old European aristocracies, and so on) to harm or destroy a section of the population (Singh Grewal, 2016). Those plans are usually framed as being both elaborate and actively concealed from the general public, though the conspiracy theorist is (somehow) alert to them and able to provide content that claims to be evidence, albeit usually only a small part of a picture that remains otherwise hidden. The conspiracy theorist is thus usually self-positioned as a subject whose role is to 'educate' others about those carefully concealed plans, and heroically to uncover fraud or corruption, prevent a global catastrophe or deaths, or stop a radical curtailment of liberties or substantial change to civilisation.

Information that is apparently unrelated to a conspiracy can, for the conspiracist and their adherents, be utilised as evidence of that conspiracy. For example, one Facebook user actively interpreted President Trump's clothing choice of a yellow tie as evidence the COVID-19 virus was a fraud, claiming:

> He is telling us there is no virus threat because it is the exact same color as the maritime flag that represents the vessel has no infected people on board. (LaFrance, 2020)

In other words, Trump's clothing colour choice is drawn – using a very long bow – to be seen as proof that the COVID denialist conspiracies are correct. Rather than a rationalist or critical analysis, or indeed even an Occam's Razor approach (removing assumptions about the then president's yellow tie to leave only the most obvious and logical reason such as that it was an ordinary, unrelated choice), the conspiracy itself obliges a particular kind of logic by which unrelated matters are interpreted not only as *causative* but as *evidence*. The yellow tie incident is a good example of what Australian communication strategist Parnell McGuiness (2021) described as the misguided views of a group of people 'who pick up an idea and knit it into a system of beliefs that becomes their whole world, to the exclusion of reality'.

Conspiracy theories precede the contemporary use of the term 'fake news' by about a century, but as we will show in this chapter, fake news extends, exacerbates and affirms the reach of conspiracy theory beliefs. The word 'conspiracy' is drawn from the Latin terms *con-* (meaning with) and *spirare-* (meaning to breathe). It means literally *breathing together*, invoking the image of a small group discussing, planning or plotting. The term 'conspiracy theory' has its origins in the nineteenth century although one of its more prominent early uses in writing was in a 1909 article noting the false origins of, and reasons for, a legislative appeal in the state of Missouri (Johnson, 1909). Across the twentieth century, conspiracy theories emerged and waned, often in relation to a controversial event that had broad social impact. The conspiracy theory claims over who killed US President John Kennedy nearly 60 years ago re-emerge from time-to-time, not as a point of interest but as one which results in broad public concern about a hidden agenda of faceless conspirators. For the conspiracist, the broader public are being denied the 'fact', regardless of how unimportant those facts might be to everyday life.

Importantly, since at least the 1990s, conspiracy theories have been formed in a social setting in which the dividing line between reality and popular culture is increasingly blurred. Resulting from the increased saturation of popular culture in every aspect of our everyday lives, the pleasure of the conspiratorial twist that has become a staple of contemporary film and television narratives (especially science fiction, action and thriller genres), moves increasingly into a pleasure to consume the conspiratorial twist and hidden agenda in relation to the real-world everyday narratives of social and political life. We have seen this shift of the pleasure and mechanism of conspiratorial narrative in relation to popular entertainment stories about UFOs and aliens. In *Aliens in America*, Jodi Dean (1998) noted that stories of 'abduction and conspiracy are uniquely influential in the current technological context, a context where information travels at the speed of light and everything is entertainment' (p. 7). Such narratives played out in particular in relation to the highly popular 1990s and early 2000s texts such as *The X-Files*, which drew public interest in the otherworldliness of extra-terrestrial life, its presence on Earth and narratives of alien abduction into stories of government cover-ups, conspiracies, collaboration in invasion and other frameworks that provide a 'logic' to explain the complexity of everyday contemporary life. Notably, even as recently as 2021, the entertainment-spawned idea of government involvement in UFOs and extra-terrestrial presence has received both media coverage and genuine investigation in the United States (Gabbatt, 2021), indicating the potency of the conspiracy narrative to encourage fixations and beliefs outside of the entertainment text.

The cultural role and circulation of conspiracy narratives have sometimes been treated with disdain in scholarly writing. For example, Fredric Jameson (1988) famously described conspiracy as 'the poor person's cognitive mapping in the postmodern age ... a degraded figure of the total logic of late capital' (p. 356). At other times, conspiracy theories and their proponents have been perceived as bizarre and irrational, figures of pathos and humour who are not to be taken seriously. The popular 'tin foil hat' stereotype, for example, has its origins in Julian Huxley's (1927) short story 'The Tissue-Culture King', in which characters wore tin foil on their heads to prevent their private thoughts being read by others. The use of the phrase 'tin foil hat' brigade is now regularly used to describe both the avid adherents of conspiracy theories and those who suggest a framework of hidden meaning that is at odds with prevailing community views. The term has certainly extended into the 2020s in relation to claims that COVID-19 is a hoax and that vaccination programmes have a hidden agenda (Harvey, 2021); it has also been deployed as a term of abuse for those who have advocated a stronger investigation into the origin of the virus, arguably reducing the efficacy of any public communication on investigation and examination that assesses the full range of possible causes (Knott, 2021). In contemporary scholarship and among the more rational settings of public discourse, then, there is a tendency to eschew anything that might risk one being labelled part of the tin-foil hat brigade, despite the need to understand the normative, cultural role of conspiracy theories as a mode of communication and how they are interrelated with contemporary frameworks of disinformation and misinformation.

Nevertheless, there is some scholarship that demonstrates how conspiracy theories have, in some cases, been historically and sociologically useful, particularly in providing insights into the cultural frameworks that encourage their proponents to solidify beliefs that are otherwise difficult to apprehend in rational terms. For example, while the shortcomings of conspiracy theories are recognised when they compete with more rigorous and nuanced critiques of neoliberal capitalism, systemic inequalities or the disciplinary roles of institutions, there is a gap in understanding the *role* of the conspiracy theory in the context of interpersonal relationalities, the framing of personal subjectivity as an outsider, the *social need* for a belief in hidden agenda beyond the mundane everydayness of bureaucracy and slow change. David Singh Grewal (2016) gets a little closer to the significance of conspiracy theories when he writes that 'the charge of conspiracy may tell us something about the relative opacity of the operation of power in any social setting' (p. 40). To put it another way, in an increasingly complexified biopolitical framework of national and global governance, it is not always evident who wields power, and to what ends (if any).

The complexity and density of governance experienced today is the historical outcome of the development governmentalities since the late nineteenth century resulting not in efficiency but in power mechanisms and complex formulations for securitising the population (Foucault, 2008, p. 61). This opaqueness may encourage scholarly and political investigation into the structures of power and exclusion among those who are equipped to engage in those critiques and, among others, encourages a belief in agendas that 'impute causal agency behind otherwise oppressive social structures where there may be none (at least, none presently operative)' (Singh Grewal, 2016, p. 40). Either way, the conspiracy theory serves then as a powerful marker not of a hidden truth but of a widespread, global problem in who is and who is not empowered to engage in knowledge frameworks. In this vein, the tin-foil hat wearer is, then, not an irrational subject acting individually, but actively formed through the frameworks of complexity in governance that have developed over the course of the twentieth and twenty-first centuries.

To put this at the level of the individual subject drawn into a conspiratorial belief, conspiracy theories serve as a compensatory explanation when, among some people, an existential need is threatened (Douglas et al., 2019, p. 8). This has, of course, been witnessed substantially during the COVID-19 pandemic. On the one hand, attempts to 'explain' the outbreak have resulted in a massive and unprecedented increase in public knowledge of virology, epidemiology and genomics as they circulate in everyday communication. For those, however, without equitable access to such information (or the capacity to engage with the complex reasons for a viral pandemic), the conspiratorial belief compensates and replaces anxieties that are otherwise caused by attempts to engage with discourses of the complicated, the accidental, the inevitable and of population risk. The conspiracy beliefs here, of course, range from the view that the virus is an insidious and deliberate invention of a Wuhan laboratory for the purposes of Chinese world domination, a by-product of 5G wireless communication technology, or that the virus is a tool used by governments to vaccinate and control their citizens.

While such explanations are not only unverified and remain outlandish in the context of rational scientific discourse, in addition to highlighting how some individuals have tried to make sense of the apparently insensible, they point to the inaccessibility of the knowledge frameworks that allow a nuanced understanding of a very complex and worrying situation. They also suggest how individuals can attempt to gain a sense of agency in circumstances of diminished agency by uncovering the hidden 'truth' behind that situation (Singh Grewal, 2016, p. 26). In a period of increased precarity over labour, housing and health, the conspiracy theory adherent remains steadfast and intellectually frozen in the knowledge that (unlike their peers) their eyes are open to what they believe is 'really' going on.

As we have begun to unpack in this chapter, conspiracy theories are not concocted in a vacuum and their believers and adherents are not individual actors behaving in a deluded fashion. Rather, conspiracy theories reflect and perpetuate the anxieties and prejudices of their day, working both as a logic and a remedy for those anxieties. By suggesting they have a cultural role is not, of course, to suggest that they are healthy for a society, since most conspiracy theories produce social fragmentation and adversarial behaviours. For example, the 'Chinese lab leak' and 'Chinese world domination' conspiracy theories about the origin and purpose of COVID-19 reflects and perpetuates anti-Chinese prejudice in many Western countries, which we discuss in more detail in Chapter Seven. Alongside the anti-China rhetoric of current and former world leaders such as Donald Trump in the United States and Prime Minister Scott Morrison in Australia, conspiratorial beliefs have contributed to an environment in which discrimination and violence against people of Asian descent has flourished (Wu, Qian, & Wilkes, 2020). The key, then, is to unpack the power of the conspiracy theory, and turn it into a harmless event by returning to the pleasure of other complex but more rigorously sound knowledge frameworks for making sense of the world. To do so is to remove the underlying belief system that fuels a large amount of the content generation of disinformation and misinformation. In the form of the look-alike news article, the deepfake video or the spread of piecemeal claims across social media commentary, fake news drives the outward push of conspiracy theories into the feeds of those who may 'need' them or find pleasure in them. Given the potency of conspiracy theories, fake news content that circulates, extends or sustains conspiracy beliefs encompasses perhaps the most secure forms of disinformation, and the most difficult to disprove among its adherents given the conspiracy theorist's rejection of the veracity of fact.

The Networking of Conspiracy Theories

A 2019 article revealed that 50% of American residents believed that at least one conspiracy theory, ranging from the idea that the 9/11 attacks were fake to the birther theory which holds that Barack Obama was born in Kenya and not the United States as required under the US constitution (Vittert, 2019). In a June 2020 interview, conspiracy researcher Zack Enders reported that his polling had revealed that '30 percent of the American mass public believe in some coronavirus conspiracy theory' (cited in Stanton, 2020, see also Uscinski et al., 2020). Why have conspiracy theories gained such traction in the twenty-first century? We have described above the cultural role of conspiracy theories across the twentieth century as the antidote to the complexification of governance and everyday life, and the ways in which that antidote has drawn increasingly on popular entertainment narrative mechanisms and applied them in real-world settings. What we need to examine now is, however, the increase in the distribution of the conspiracy theory such that it has moved from obscure books, pamphlets and local meetings of like-minded adherents, to playing a widespread role in everyday communication.

One approach is to consider the nature of the contemporary networked media ecology in which conspiratorial narratives are disseminated. We addressed some of the role played of our contemporary interactive, user-generated digital communication framework in the circulation of fake news in Chapter Three. Here, we focus on the network morphology that underlies digital communication and provides the means by which fake news, disinformation and misinformation drawing on otherwise irrational beliefs is circulated, repeated and sustained across a broad social setting. Sociologist Manuel Castells has provided a powerful framework for making sense of the network logic that permeates all aspects of economic, material, cultural and social life since the era of the early internet (Castells, 2010). For Castells, the network morphology encourages a persistent expansion and reconfiguration of communication into a setting of increased complexity. In more recent work, Castells (2012) has explored how social movements such as Occupy Wall Street gained traction in this networked society. These 'movements spread by contagion in a world networked by the wireless Internet and marked by fast, viral diffusion of images and ideas' (p. 2). In thinking about conspiracy beliefs as they are disseminated and consumed across contemporary digital networks, we might consider some of the ways in which networks play a role not merely in communicating the belief but in forming the social movement of their adherents.

Certainly, digital media has been responsible for forging communities of disaffected persons, allowing the production of new knowledges, languages and sensibilities and in many cases, empowering those communities in the act of creatively discussing alternatives that make lives more liveable for those who find themselves un-represented. At the same time, the networked environment also provides those individuals and communities with voices that can actively challenge dominant ideas, expert-derived discourses, and the taxonomies that routinely leave large numbers of people feeling that the available categories are narrow, regimentary, constraining and unliveable.

This has certainly been the case over the past decade in the formation of sub-cultural communities who, dispersed in small numbers around the world, develop practices of everyday living, interpretation and meaning-making through engagement in networked communication. These practices enable individuals to form communities and social movements, often coming together to fulfil an underlying need for increased engagement and to take pleasure in the interactive discussion of an otherwise minoritarian belief (Dobre, 2012). Bearing in mind that all communities, whether formed online or in geographical or affiliational settings, precede the identities they claim to gather and are thereby 'imagined' into existence (Anderson, 1983, pp. 6–7) and sustained through shared practices of belonging, affiliation and behaviour. In these spaces, a shared language is constructed and in doing so, the discourse for a new identity is articulated. The conspiracy theory networked community is, in that context, formulated, produced, repeated and sustained through digital networking and the establishment of 'virtual' communities that unwittingly encourage practices of interpretation, intelligibility and iterability.

Online conspiracies take a number of shareable forms. These include media articles that report uncritically and/or affirmatively on conspiracies. They also include user-generated content, that is, content produced using web affordances. This includes memes, GIFs, and videos featuring interviews with, and monologues by, conspiracy proponents. On some occasions, these items of communication are overt in their intentions, such as the QAnon 'Q drops' whereby the alleged agent or group known as Q engages their followers. On other occasions, these texts are more coded, usually to avoid platform censorship. For example, the Australian celebrity chef and reality television star Pete Evans drew on and extended conspiracy theory material about the COVID-19 virus, vaccines, mask-wearing and 5G networks in 2020 and 2021. He used his vast social network following across Instagram and Facebook and his website to circulate these ideas, while simultaneously attempting to sell his own cure (a plasma lamp that has no therapeutic value or capability to treat or prevent a viral infection). At the same time, Evans actively networked his minority conspiratorial beliefs by cynically attempting to woo an extant white supremacist community by adopting their symbols (BBC News, 2021b). As with other purveyors of conspiracy theories, these examples show how the spread of disinformation takes advantage of online networks of followers and expand those with crossover tactics using the tools not of the twentieth-century conspiracy theorists but of twenty-first century influencers. That facilitates the capacity to push, promote and grow followings, and to do so in ways which often include financial gain rather than genuine belief in the conspiracy theory.

While the network morphology is a boon to the contemporary form of conspiratorial fake news and disinformation, it is also its greatest risk. The key emergence measure to attempt to curtail the spread of conspiratorial disinformation being used since early 2021 is the act of isolating the influencer in question from their own network by cutting them out as a content generation hub. In Evans' case, this occurred through his ban from Facebook and Instagram in 2021, much as Trump was banned from several social media platforms to reduce the violence his disinformation and conspiracy claims was causing. While those who generate conspiracy disinformation often migrate to other platforms, and the deliberate disruption to their network creates greater suspicion of a conspiracy among their adherents, such bans are an indication of the centrality of the network morphology to disinformation.

The Postmodern Hermeneutic of Suspicion

A second reason for the current popularity of conspiracy theories concerns what we label 'the postmodern hermeneutics of suspicion'. The term 'hermeneutic of suspicion' has been used it to describe approaches to power relations that, while diverse, are united in their suspicion towards institutions and authority figures, asking the key question as to whether or not governance institutions and actors are intent on oppressing subjects. The term is commonly associated with Paul Ricoeur (1970) who wrote of a 'school of suspicion' comprised of thinkers such as Karl Marx, Friedrich Nietzsche and Sigmund Freud, all of whom sought to critique their contemporary regimes of truth in favour of new modes of interpretation and social configuration (p. 33).

A hermeneutic of suspicion is not, of course, problematic in itself, since it is a powerful tool of democratic critique of the genuinely hidden agendas of governance systems, practices, frameworks and knowledge regimes. Questioning 'truth' (whether this is a truth purported in news content, a politician's press statement, a policy or an opinion by an empowered agent) is a crucial step in sorting the meaningful and verifiable facts from fake news, and differentiating between the outlandish conspiracy and genuine corruption. This can mean asking whether a version of truth reinforces a particular ideological outlook on the world, and asking who benefits from that outlook. In that sense, suspicion is not always irrational and paranoid. Indeed, the ability to ask such questions and to hold leaders and empowered actors to account remains a hallmark of functional liberal democracy. However, the mode through which suspicion is deployed in an era of fake news and disinformation is one which emerges in part from the reduced efficacy of the force of verifiable, factual information to serve as an answer to suspicion as a mode of disbelief or uncertainty. In other words, the nineteenth century practice of suspicion and the critique of truth was one grounded in rationalist methods of criticism and interpretation, relying on facts organised through systems of belief that did not ignore but sought to engage with incompatible or marginal facts, and arranged a hierarchy of knowability and knowledge.

As Didier Fassin (2021) notes, 'there is a leveling on the internet of all available data instead of a differentiation according to their scientific or journalistic credibility' (p. 134). A scan through everyday social media platforms reveals regular posts about COVID-19 that cite everything from peer-reviewed scientific research on the virus to the 2020 documentary *Plandemic*, which proposes an unproven theory about the novel coronavirus, and was available on YouTube and Facebook before being removed from both platforms (Cook, van der Linden, Lewandowsky, & Ecker, 2020). The rapid and widespread dissemination of conspiracy theories does not necessarily translate to more conspiracy proponents; as Fassin (2021) points out, these theories tend to circulate in groups who already believe those theories.

The conspiratorial hermeneutic of suspicion, then, is one which does not utilise the tools of critique and interpretation, but merely gathers content – most of which is unverifiable and delivered through fake news – to sustain, extend and expand a conspiracy theory. The catch-cry response directed to non-believers of the conspiracy theory is the slogan 'do your own research'. This phrase is commonly deployed by proponents of the anti-vaccination and COVID-19 denialist movements, and relies on the fact that digital networks have made available content in a manner with which authority, verifiability, credibility and scholarship are no longer part of what makes content authoritative – whether that involves news or fake news, scientific validity of vaccination practices or a claim that the injection will insert a trackable chip. The framing, then, of conspiracy theories and the claim that they are based on 'research' (meaning: looking things up online) indicates the need to understand conspiracy theories – as a core element of fake news – as emerging from the increasing unwillingness or inability to distinguish some content from more credible sources. This is further complicated by the complicated claims to authority made by conspiracists. For example, *Plandemic* takes the form of an interview with Judy Mikovits, who was a virologist before her research was discredited, and who is eloquent and speaks with the form, tone and style of an ordinary medical professional or health scholar. Here, we see the distorted and fuzzy arrangement of fake news and disinformation become misinformation – her work and her words are easily circulated to a wider audience beyond conspiracy adherents, since she does not fit the stereotype of the tinfoil hat-wearing paranoic.

We argue that the hermeneutic of suspicion animates the circulation of disinformation that draws on and sustains conspiracy theories for several reasons. Firstly, conspiracy theories usually involve interpreting all phenomena, social action, political speech and everyday events through the lens of corruption, hidden agendas and illicit scheming. The term 'apophenia' has been used to describe 'the tendency to perceive a connection or meaningful pattern between unrelated or random things (such as objects and ideas)' (Berkowitz, 2020). Apophenia fosters paranoia and distrust. Secondly, conspiracy theories and the disinformation discourse are framed in heroic terms: not only interpreting events, but taking on the supposedly democratic task of publicly exposing wrongdoing. We thus recognise that conspiracy theory discourses do not produce liberation, emancipation and consciousness (Fassin, 2021, p. 136), but their opposite by disempowering a population from the capacity for genuine critique of the power relations that govern social participation.

Fake News and the QAnon Conspiracy

In this section, we will now expand on the cultural role of conspiracy theories, the generation of conspiracy in digital networks, and the postmodernised practice of suspicion by addressing the QAnon conspiracy, which has been the source, content and interpretation of very substantial fake news pieces. Indeed, in many ways, QAnon operates at the intersection between the historical emergence and exacerbation of conspiracy narratives, the hyperreality of postmodern knowledge frameworks, and the contemporary formation of fake news. We focus here on three key aspects of the QAnon conspiracy: firstly, its pastiche of tropes and characters from older conspiracies (from the shadowy cabal to the devil); secondly, QAnon's resemblance to Baudrillard's understanding of simulation and simulacra; and, thirdly, the way in which QAnon proponents have fashioned themselves as user-generators of content in a form that simultaneously self-promotes their cause and builds a community.

Although the QAnon conspiracy has its roots in much older conspiratorial beliefs, both repeating and elaborating on an established narrative of a secret society, one key incident of the past decade is a foundational moment indicating the centrality of conspiracy disinformation to contemporary North American and global politics. On 4 December 2016, Edgar Maddison Welch was arrested at a Washington D.C. pizzeria after entering the premises wielding a rifle. He claimed he was in search of what he firmly believed was the paedophile ring headed by Hillary Clinton and headquartered in the pizzeria's basement. This paedophile ring was believed across some social media platforms to be actively abducting children and conducting satanic rituals (Fassin, 2021, p. 132). Rumours about the ring and the ludicrous claims of Secretary Clinton's involvement had begun on 4Chan (a platform notoriously popular amongst the Far Right) shortly before the 2016 US election, and so-called 'evidence' of those rumours had been posted to Reddit (Sebastian & Bruney, 2020). Conspiracy theory adherents persisted in their claims, initially on social media platforms, that they had deciphered key terms in leaked government documents that were cryptic code words for child abuse, human trafficking and satanism, and these exchanges were then posted on fake news websites such as *Your News Wire* (Silverman, 2016). Edgar Welch had read of the claims that the pizza shop was the headquarters of this organisation, and the 28 year-old took it upon himself to help the children he believed were imprisoned there having read about the story online. As it turned out, there was no basement, no paedophile ring and no involvement of the then Democrat presidential candidate. Welch was sentenced to four years imprisonment for his crime. The conspiracy to which he subscribed earned the internet moniker 'Pizzagate'.

The trope of a secretive cabal attempting to control political governance is an old one, popularised many times throughout history. These include some of the more instances of popularisation such as the claims made in the pseudohistorical 1982 book *The Holy Blood and the Holy Grail* of a secret society extending from Mary Magdalene and controlling royalty, governments and politicians all the way through European history (Baigent, Leigh, & Lincoln, 1982), conspiracies around the real-world Club of Rome, the marginal but potent fascination with claims of a conspiratorial cabal of contemporary Illuminati, and the popularisation of many of these together in the best-selling novels of Dan Brown. Significantly, these fanciful stories are based on piecemeal speculation about the intersection of religion, satanism, royalty and contemporary governance, political power and corporate finance.

While such conspiracies took the form of low-brow books in the 1980s, followed by popular fiction in the 1990s, and newsgroups and online forums in the Web 1.0 era, they have increasingly found a communicative home in fake news and disinformation that is dressed up not as fiction or low-quality scholarship but as the reportage of fact. At the same time, moral panics about devil-worshipping paedophile cults, broadly disconnected from powerful institutions and operating away from the major centres of power, circulated as genuine media stories. Here the moral panic format of media reports in spectacle-based tabloids, with their long history of putting forward an unpalatable 'other' to shock a fascinated readership (Hebdige, 1979, p. 94; Zylinska, 2004), drew together the everyday construct of the folk devil (paedophiles and child-abusers) and the construct of the 'real' devil (depicted as devil-worshippers) to establish the conspiracy of satanic ritual abuse, which has remained a staple of conspiracy theory lore, likewise since the 1980s.

QAnon, in that sense, is not new but builds upon the much older conspiracy theories for a new generation and a new framework of disinformation, that being the digital dissemination of fake news. The 'Q' is a mystery figure who first surfaced on 4Chan on 28 October 2017, claiming he had seen evidence that Hillary Clinton would soon be arrested and tied at a military tribunal for the supposed transgressions described in Pizzagate. Thereafter, 'Q' posted regular short missives ('Qdrops'), alleging that President Trump was on a secret mission to expose the conspiracy and bring down the conspirators who were depicted as comprised of literal blood-drinking elites. In the following years, 'Q' continued to post, albeit on a range of different platforms (LaFrance, 2020; Rothschild, 2021). The QAnon conspiracy sustained significant traction across the internet, proliferating as social media users spread Q's messages in cycles of misinformation. QAnon supporters have been implicated in acts of public violence, including the January 2021 insurrection. From a rational perspective, the QAnon conspiracy theory is widely debunked and discredited, albeit with concern that it not only has circulated far-right rhetoric but has solidified networks of extant far-right extremist groups around a cause, with expectations of continued risks of public violence.

Perhaps the most striking aspect of QAnon is its pastiche of tropes and characters. Pastiche, which we described in Chapter Four, is a key aspect of the cultural framework of postmodernism that contributes to the circulation of fake news and the means by which it is both recognised and goes unrecognised. Pastiche can be understood as a neutral imitation or mimicry, similar to parody but without the satirical or critical motives of parody (Jameson, 1991). Pastiche assembles cultural references within a single text, not to generate humour or subvert the texts. In the case of QAnon conspiracy, taken as an interwoven set of texts, the conspiracy brings together older conspiratorial material not as reiteration or citation, but as pastiche. The shadowy cabal of elites, for example, are depicted anew in this conspiracy with neither the depth of claims from older versions, but as a mundane core *expectation* of the contemporary conspiracy genre. The trope of children abducted for their blood or for ritual satanic abuse draws on the older conspiracies, going back to twelfth-century anti-Semitic discourse (Greenspan, 2020), but again as a banal inclusion in the patchwork of conspiracy figurations that are then on-communicated in fake news. Such satanism claims, which draw on historical European and North American moral panics in which satanic cults and witchcraft were blamed for issues such as crop failures, irreligiosity, teen suicides and violent crime (Hughes, 2017), are reproduced as part of the *mise-en-scène* of the conspiracy narrative. Finally, paedophilia and child abuse as ongoing sources of cultural anxiety (Angelides, 2005), are incorporated into the QAnon conspiracy in a way that produces the conspiracy not as a worked out alternative logic, like older forms, but as a catch-all of recognisable conspiracy stories (with perhaps the exception of moon landing hoax claims or UFOs). In turn, this patchwork becomes a fertile field on which to pick components to be circulated as fake news as each new 'Qdrop' piece of false evidence is released. At the same time, fake news circulation of this narrative strengthens the reach and efficacy of the conspiracy story, and for all the reasons we described above about why conspiracies are successful.

We suggest that the feverish, pop culture-inflected world of QAnon can be best understood not as an alternative cultural narrative or way in which to perceive the world built on frail and non-credible stories, but as simulacra, a product of the culture of hyperreal spectacle we described in Chapter Four. Jean Baudrillard (1988) described the late twentieth century as 'the age of simulations', in which references to the real were liquidated in favour of their 'artificial resurrection' as non-meaningful systems of signs (p. 167). The patchwork narrative of QAnon is, in this sense, a world of familiar signs and popular cultural intertexts. In this context, verifiable truth matters less than the generation of spectacle and an effect of outrage, anxiety or fear. Here, any evidence of the conspiracy's baselessness or any content that discredits the QAnon narrative is reincorporated and harnessed by proponents of the conspiracy theory as evidence that 'Q' is right (and the majority of the population has been fooled into believing a false narrative of everyday life). Central to the QAnon simulation is the fact that the mysterious and unknown 'Q' is simulation itself. The 2021 documentary *Q: Into the Storm* explored the fakery, disinformation and unlikelihood of 'Q' as a genuine figure or personage (LaFrance, 2020). We argue that even if there is a singular individual behind the 'Qdrops' this figure is pure hyperreality – the 'deep throat' in an *X-Files* episode, the shadowy informant from any political thriller – or what Baudrillard (1988) described as 'a real without origin or reality' (p. 166).

What is distinctive about the circulation of the QAnon conspiracy content through fake news is the fact that, regardless of any real or mythical 'Q' source, the proponents and purveyors of this conspiracy are interactive users, simultaneously generating and consuming content. This is the form of internet use described as 'produsage' whereby everyday communication today conflates the roles 'producer' and 'user' (Bruns, 2008). Rather than QAnon being sourced, as with older conspiracies, in a core storyteller with the conspiracy passed on by paranoid spectators, the adherents and proponents of QAnon are *active co-creators*, either using social platforms to embellish and sustain the conspiracy or dressing it up in the mimicry of news content and circulating its myths and falsehoods as fake news (Gillespie, 2020). They also participate in the control of the narrative by limitation and deletion as much as proliferation and circulation

(Nieva, 2021). While this culture of hyperreal disinformation may barely register with non-believers, it has proven to resonate with its proponents and those who are otherwise adherents of other marginal extremisms, operating as a call to arms which has rightly 'spooked' administrations all over the globe.

Conclusion: The Ethics of Reporting Conspiracy

We end this chapter by considering some of the difficulties in reporting, investigating and discussing conspiracy theories, given two significant problems that emerge in a setting in which verifiability and fact alone are no longer significant in debunking disinformation and falsehood: firstly, that in addressing conspiracy theory lore, particularly those that encourage violence, one puts the conspiracy into further circulation and, secondly, that in framing conspiracy theory adherents as ignorant dupes, one further alienates the group and thereby solidifies a marginal population and exacerbates the strength of their beliefs. We outline in this conclusive section a few of ways in which our discussion of conspiracy theories as a core component of contemporary fake news, disinformation and misinformation highlights the importance of considering how journalists can ethically report on conspiracy theories and their proponents. Journalists are significant here because, even in an era of social media and the everyday non-institutional generation of content, they remain agenda setters who establish the terms and topics of public debate, and do so in ways which continue to have an impact on politics, policy and governance. Although we address some of the wider philosophic ethics of fake news within a culture of digital disinformation in Chapter Ten, we use the term ethics here to describe those principles that guide our understandings of what is 'right' and 'wrong'; of how best to treat others; and of how to minimise harm towards others and oneself (Thompson & Muller, 2021).

Conspiracy theories rely on the generation of attention and spectacle, and conspiracy proponents are often motivated as much by public interest as by any desire to circulate their beliefs. Indeed, one of QAnon's best-known slogans is 'You are the news now' (LaFrance, 2020). Yet, ignoring conspiracies is not an ethical option for news media. In today's networked media ecology, conspiracies such as QAnon are more publicly visible than ever. Refusing to report on these narratives lends tacit support to the conspiracists' cause, primarily because it establishes the impression that news media are not up to the task of unpacking corruption, hidden agendas, problematic interpersonal networks and underlying motivations in politics (despite a very long history of having done so). It also risks reinforcing the conspiracy among its believers by suggesting that news media is following a deliberate agenda to obscure from their readership and the public what the conspiracists believe they have otherwise 'found out'. There are four key principles at stake in which, we argue, the motivation for quality reporting undertaken carefully and ethically can be found.

Firstly, there is an imperative for journalists to provide fact-based reportage on conspiracies. Given news outlet's greater capacity to provide verifiable information in the form of statistics, real-world examples, and expert opinion, this puts into circulation the necessary material for others to continue to debunk conspiracy theories, rather than rely on adversity or hostility as the counter-measure to conspiracists. This is particularly important when reporting on health-related conspiracies such as anti-vaccination claims for example, whereby reportage on the anti-vaccination movement provides the opportunity to circulate factual information about the benefits of vaccines and to critique myths expounded by the anti-vaxxer movement. Debunking such myths through, for instance, 'explainer' pieces can be a crucial step in preventing conspiracy movements from growing further.

The second principle relates to the problems of giving credence to conspiracy theories by reporting them and re-circulating them without taking the necessary action to debunk them using factual information. Although the credibility and authority of journalism and institutional news outlets has been on the wane among some sectors of the public over the past two decades, it is unhelpful to foreclose altogether on the potential appeal of credibility into the future. Lastly, journalists should avoid demonising conspiracy proponents, for example, by drawing on problematic stereotypes such as labelling them 'tinfoil hat-wearers'. While such stereotypes are both amusing and help to focus dissent on conspiracy theory adherents, they serve to shame and insult conspiracists in an often dehumanising manner, exacerbating the adversity between the proponents of reason and the proponents of these fantasies. Indeed, conspiracy proponents are as diverse as any other social group (Douglas et al., 2019), and the denial of that diversity through a reductive ad hominem approach furthers the 'us-versus-them' adversarial framework which, as we have been arguing in this book, is a key component in the generation of the cultural conditions for a fake news ecology. The key risk here, is that conspiracy-based fake news will circulate through flows and networks that are wholly separate from the wider media ecology if the conspiracists are further alienated from engagement with more credible media sources.

Indeed, a useful step in preventing the problematic 'othering' of conspiracists and those who believe in fake and misleading news content involves journalists actively listening to conspiracists. As an ethical approach to engagement, listening rather than stereotyping is a key mechanism for building the kinds of pedagogies that rely on connection and a shared sense of belonging rather than conflict, adversity and silencing (Dreher, 2010, p. 100). While conspiracy theories have provided a substantial amount of the content for fake news and disinformation – and while the culture that encourages conspiratorial fake news is one which has emerged historically in ways which are difficult to undo – solving the problems of fake news will not happen through alienating conspiracists or expressing outrage at what are otherwise ludicrous ideas. Rather, it is in listening to the case and engaging with the conspiracists as subjects and members of the community that inroads into undoing the belief in disinformation can begin.

This chapter began by describing conspiracy theories as being a prime example of the 'hermeneutic of suspicion' in action. We examined some of the factors behind the appeal and the uptake of conspiracy theories. These include online networks, as well as the feelings of powerlessness that many people have felt due to various instances of social unrest and upheaval (including the COVID-19 pandemic), and the 'postmodernisation' of contemporary society. We also examined how the points raised above played out in one very specific case study, the QAnon conspiracy, and concluded by exploring some of the ways in which journalists can report on conspiracies in a manner that is as ethical as possible and avoids further perpetuating fake news. Conspiracy theories represent a particularly insidious and particularly pervasive form of fake news. As such, we have argued that their proliferation can be attributed to the affordances of a digital media ecology on the one hand, and a desire to engage in the hyperreal spectacle of otherwise unverifiable fantasy. Conspiracists are not just dedicated believers; they are also generators of content, constructing and disseminating the videos, memes and GIFs that promote the conspiracy and create the fertile field for fake news. The January 2021 Capitol Riots in the United States is just one example of the risks of violence and chaos the public belief in falsehood and hidden agendas creates. While, as we have argued, a healthy democracy warrants a sceptical public capable of using critical tools to understand and make sense of the genuine interconnections between institutions, governance, power and agenda, the belief in the patchwork quilt of contemporary conspiracies that underlie fake news and disinformation today is not only not the same thing as critique, but poses a genuine ongoing threat to public safety.

Chapter Seven

Marginalising the Marginalised: Fake News as a Tool of Populist Power

Introduction

A key dimension of fake news is its dependence on trouble, crisis and social unrest and, simultaneously, its capacity to nourish, reinforce and sustain these. As crises become fertile ground for the spreading of fear, uncertainty and misinformation, fake news finds its audience. Our collective understanding of important global issues such as climate change, migration, displacement, and pandemics undergoes a substantial impact when disinformation and misinformation circulate in competition with verified, factual content and recognised news (Ireton & Posetti, 2018). One part of the reason for this relates to the informational function of communication, in contrast to its entertainment, affective, spectatorial or communitarian roles. When crises occur, publics both desire and demand information quickly, placing substantial pressure on journalists and other content providers to communicate timely updates (van der Meer, Verhoeven, Beentjes, & Vliegenthart, 2017).

Consequently, the proliferation of fake news, propaganda and conspiracy theories presents a complex challenge for news organisations and emerging rival content providers such as social media channels, bloggers and influencers, as the viral spread of disinformation and misinformation persistently undermines societal understandings of important issues (Tandoc & Takahashi, 2017). For instance, as Kwanda and Lin (2020) observed in their study of news coverage of disasters in Indonesia, viral fake news stories on social media led to widespread panic and substantial social unrest. The challenge, therefore, is to find ways which not only immunise against fake news stories, but re-balance in favour of factual information and simultaneously provide readers, viewers and users better opportunities to assess the factuality of the content they encounter about key social issues, particularly during times of unrest, crisis, chaos, disaster or emergency.

In the previous chapter, we explored the proliferation of false claims and conspiracy theories related to the novel coronavirus outbreak (COVID-19) and the anti-vaccination movement. We established that fake news can have significantly problematic social, political, economic and cultural outcomes, especially when it comes to issues where understanding observable facts about other human beings

Fake News in Digital Cultures: Technology, Populism and Digital Misinformation, 93–107
Copyright © 2022 by Rob Cover, Ashleigh Haw and Jay Daniel Thompson
Published under exclusive licence by Emerald Publishing Limited
doi:10.1108/978-1-80117-876-120221007

is essential. In turn, the dissemination of fake news contributes to the insidious undermining of democracy, whereby, as we argue, the only beneficiaries are those with the power to shape public perception to fit a narrative that aligns with their own interests. One aspect of the anti-democratic potential of fake news is its significant role in creating racial discord, social disharmony, anti-minority sentiment and hostile perceptions of migrants. In this vein, fake news both feeds into underlying social segmentation, inequality, hatred and stereotypes, but also circulates new material posing as evidence of that both affirms such hostilities and exacerbates violence against those positioned as more vulnerable than others. It is within these conditions that right-wing populists promote a climate of fear, which makes scapegoats out of already marginalised people.

We have seen an abundance of false reports, racial scapegoating, and manipulated videos flood the digital sphere in response to several major events occupying the global social conscience over the past few years. Two notable examples are COVID-19 and the Black Lives Matter (BLM) protests. Over the past few years, BLM has been a key target of disinformation, largely attributed to the populist strategy of discrediting protesters to undermine the veracity of the movement. COVID-19, in addition to its significant impact on global health and the economy, has been the focus of campaigns of misinformation, conspiracy theories and racist propaganda, especially in pluralist, western nations such as the United States, Europe, Australia and the UK. Here, we are seeing strong anti-immigration sentiment justified and legitimised through problematic discourses and false or misleading content that vilify the groups whose health, economic stability, and social cohesion outcomes are most adversely impacted by the pandemic. Social and economic consequences of crises have a persistent tendency to create or reinforce environments in which minorities – particularly racial and ethnic minorities – are scapegoated (Carland, 2020). We argue that the circulation of disinformation, misinformation and false content the fortifies stereotypes of minorities and their marginalisation or 'othering' has a normativisation effect, that promotes disharmony and reduces the capacity of all citizens to participate equitably in social, political and democratic life.

Against the backdrop of present global events and their impact on minorities, this chapter explores the role of fake news in the reinforcement of inequitable power divisions, analysing how prejudiced discourses and the sustaining of negative stereotypes are strategically introduced into the public domain. Through the circulation of 'believable' misinformation that relies on existing prejudices, marginalisation is further legitimatised and bolstered. We explore this form of normalisation as part of a deeply entrenched discursive process of enacting extreme positions to rationalise and reframe harmful ideologies as acceptable elements of public discourse. The result is a pronounced social division that further disenfranchises society's most marginalised people, with dangerous implications for public attitudes, policy, democracy, and human rights. We address this first by providing a framework on how fake news reinforces inequitable power relations, followed by a discussion of its role in presenting problematic content about race, immigrants, refugees and people of colour. We end by discussing the role of fake news in promoting a xenophobic response to the COVID-19 pandemic.

Fake News and Populism's Reinforcement of Inequitable Power Divisions

Speaking truth to power requires us to have some truth to speak, but what about those without power? Within western liberal democracies, the most marginalised members of society face significant barriers to accessing accurate information about the world around them. In the realm of disinformation, the consequences can be dire. Lower-income people, for instance, primarily access the Internet for entertainment and/or to forge and maintain social connections (Ognyanova, 2016). The most common setting for this is online social networking environments, where disinformation and misinformation prosper. While online media was, in earlier iterations, considered a revolutionary mechanism for promoting cosmopolitan understanding, cross-cultural belonging, and globalised responsiveness in the reduction of violence against difference, it is frequently mediated today both through powerful organisations whose decisions and motivations are aligned more closely with self-interest than an objective to inform publics (Flew, 2019) and through cultural practices of adversity, hostility and hate speech (Thompson & Cover, 2021).

As we have been arguing throughout this book, the content we find online exists within a cacophonous environment where accuracy and reason must constantly compete with hyperbole, hostility, and disinformation. It is within this landscape that, in recent years, we have collectively witnessed a sharp rise in populist rhetoric in many pluralist liberal democracies. Events such as Brexit and the 2016 election of Donald Trump in the United States represent two notable examples of an insidious backlash against established political elites and the institutions that enable them. As discussed in Chapter Four, this new right-wing populism is underscored by a highly pervasive discourse of post-truth politics, where social media acts as a vehicle for amplifying 'alternative facts'. These alternative facts are often strategically deployed to rationalise and exploit collective fears and hatred of the 'other' (particularly the racialised other), legitimising discriminatory treatment of the most marginalised groups within a given society (Speed & Mannion, 2017). It also relies on the politics of alt-right theatrics, spectacle and the production of outrage which, themselves, demand the circulation not of mundane, everyday news but of content deliberately designed and shared to evoke an emotional response which, in the case of racial and ethnic minorities, involves positioning the adherents of populism for a negative emotional response – often anger – about minorities through false claims about affirmative action or unfair preferential treatment under the law.

It is important to interrogate the flows of anti-minority disinformation and misinformation and the circulation of false content that is designed to foster adversity towards minorities. Populist elites routinely identify opportunities to enlist their supporters as conduits of their messages by exploiting the human desire for social connection – a desire that, for many, drives our propensity to publicly share content that speaks to us. A particular danger here is that much of that social disconnection is, in populist discursive frameworks, constructed not through the promotion of relationalities and belonging, but around the identification an 'other', an outsider group, a threat to some kind of norm. Consequently, people with limited access to independent, public service media (and/or those who cannot afford subscription fees for quality news) become especially vulnerable to the effects of fake news (Ireton & Posetti, 2018). Additionally, for those with limited opportunities to partake in digital literacy training, disinformation represents yet another barrier to civic engagement.

In this sense, fake news finds a willing target audience among those who are often identified within populist frameworks as the mainstream 'forgotten people'. The twentieth century articulation of the notion of an authentic, middle-class population as a 'forgotten people' is often credited to Australia's longest-serving prime minister, Robert Menzies who served in that role during the pivotal mid-twentieth century and post-war years (1939–1941 and 1949–1966). He is remembered as much for his most famous speech 'the forgotten people' (1942) as for his key role in forming the early ideology of Australia's liberal-conservative political party. Not unlike Franklin Roosevelt's 'fireside chats' radio broadcasts between 1933 and 1944, Menzies gave a number of talks, radio speeches and written texts that appealed to the figure of an 'ordinary', hard-working, middle-class Australian. These speeches actively constituted a particular mode of belonging to a particular segment of Australian national population and constructed a shared sensibility among the target audience of this communication of having been somehow 'neglected' while others were given more attention by the then government. Menzies was attempting to immunise against the formation of a consciousness of class difference framed by the Marxism he feared (Brett, 1992). He thereby invented the figure of an Australian middle class that would see itself as simultaneously *neglected* and *authentic,* arguing that the very rich can look after themselves and the mass of unskilled labourers are looked after by organisations such as workers' unions and by some legal protections, but the middle class had been forgotten because – unlike the rich and the workers – they were unable to command political attention in a democratic climate.

While Menzies' construction of the forgotten people in the mid-twentieth century was relatively benign (Cover, 2020), it is a good example of the way in which earlier modes set the model for more recent, cynical production of such population blocs who, through the populist politics of resentment and the alt-right theatrics of generating outrage will be a willing target for false information that promotes and sustains an authoritarian and extremist leadership figure. Often both neoliberal and conservatively nationalist, political incompatibilities are covered over by utilising or relying on disinformation that embeds the distinction between a multi-class population segment of supporters (positioned as forgotten people) and a mythical 'other' within the population, such as migrants, refugees, welfare recipients, gender-diverse persons or sexual minorities (positioned as dangerous usurpers or undeserving of affirmative legislation, policy protections, aid or agency). In this more insidious form of population segmentation and the production of resentment, the term 'silent majority' has been deployed as a common synonym for forgotten people in political and protest rhetoric in the United States since former US President Richard Nixon's use of the term in the 1960s (Mudde & Kaltwasser, 2017, p. 24). The Nixon approach was further entrenched in North

American political and social culture through the 'wedge politics' of former US President Ronald Reagan. Reagan, again, used alarmism and sensationalism to create both discord and population demarcations that firstly built *resentment* and then actively *mis-directed it* along gender, ethnic and racial lines rather than lines of class (Fiske, 1996, p. 31).

Rather than a middle class 'silent majority', today the populist base is consti-tuted of a wholly different class: typically not those who are the genuine middle class of relative comfort or those genuinely struggling through the decline in wel-fare and support (Simic, 2016), but individuals from a wider range of classes who have been brought together through social media networking, marginal online publications (the alt-right), disinformation, and the sustaining circulating of fake news stories. Through these various mechanisms, they are able to recognise or, more rightly, rethink themselves as a community or class who make a claim to have been silenced or forgotten in favour of *both* the figure of the liberal elite and the figure of the minority – often the welfare recipient and the migrant (Daniels, 2018; Salazar, 2018).

The reinvigoration of a forgotten people concept in the United States through the electoral campaign of Donald Trump thus built on *both* the older frameworks of silent majority and the newer production of a populist right. Trump's ability to assume leadership where other contemporary populist politicians had failed (e.g., Sarah Palin and other members of the Tea Party movement) was not the result of being viewed as a sensible or capable political leader, but in his encour-agement of the support base to – again – perceive themselves as vulnerable to loss (national greatness; resources; national military strength; perceived sovereignty; dominance of other world powers; dignity). Here, such loss was positioned as that which is either not experienced by an enemy within (left-liberal politicians) or that which is not adequately cared about or understood (by foreigners or migrants). This, likewise, is to *project* vulnerability onto a group in a way which simultane-ously bestows violence upon them while also serving to institutionalise violence onto others through a circuitous route that 'plays off' different segments of a population via hiding or forgetting the in-built 'unequal distribution of vulner-ability' (Butler, Gambetti, & Sabsay, 2016, pp. 4–5). This is achieved through a combination of decontextualised facts, disinformation, viral misinformation, fake news and the subsequent reportage of fake news by politically-biased real news services, in order to make one group *feel* they have been treated as dispos-able as a means of marginalising or disposing of another set of groups. In this context, fake news both targets and constructs a minority in order to utilise an 'other', which is demarcated from the forgotten, silent but 'deserving' majority, sustaining this demarcation and the support for a populist leadership through the persistence of resentment.

At the same time, fake news has a secondary impact on minorities. While in the case of the above, its *content* about minorities is the question, it also involves its effect through the targeting of its *practice* at minorities. People of colour, for instance, encounter numerous barriers to accessing information, thus increasing their susceptibility to believe and re-share fake news (Hamilton & Morgan, 2016). In the United States, for instance, a lack of digital literacy is one of the leading factors for Latinx communities' vulnerability to disinformation campaigns – a fact that purveyors of fake news often use to their advantage (Mercado, 2020). Targeting a marginalised individual with fake news ensures that power rests with the deceiver. As MacKenzie and Bhatt (2018) assert, this deepens inequities through 'the spread of prejudice, confusion and distrust in institutions, news sources and figures in whom we normally have grounds to grant epistemic trust' (p. 12). Fake news therefore has significant implications in terms of democracy, politics and belonging in the context of its role in constructing a set of minorities and then relegating them as unworthy, dangerous, problematic or deceptive.

A central goal of fake news, particularly in the context of elections and referendums, is not necessarily to convince publics of the veracity of a given idea, but to aid in agenda setting by signalling what issues people should be paying attention to. In other words, fake news serves to distort forms of belonging that have become normative by creating discord that both draws on and expands the underlying popular concerns, but doing so by both confusing and simplifying key political, social and cultural understandings and thereby weakening the rationality factors that underlie citizens' decision making. We saw this play out during the British EU referendum campaign, where 'Vote Leave' repeatedly disseminated false claims about the high costs of EU membership – a claim that was widely debunked through fact-checks undertaken by *BBC News*, as well as multiple independent experts (Speed & Mannion, 2017). Naturally, the oppositional framework established by an 'authentic' British population and an undeserving (continental) European governance structure and population is exacerbated by false stories that create resentment and hatred.

In addition to being harmed through their exposure to fake news, marginalised groups disproportionately find themselves as the subject of misinformation and disinformation campaigns. Thus, they are marginalised both through their susceptibility to fake news and their own representation within it. A notable example involves transgender communities and gender-diverse persons in the UK. In February 2021, the Maternity Services team of the Brighton and Sussex University Hospital trust in the UK announced via Twitter that they will be incorporating more gender-inclusive language by adding terms such as 'chestfeeding' and 'birthing parents' to their everyday practice in an effort to better support to their transgender and non-binary patients. They stated:

> we want everybody who uses our services to see themselves reflected in the language that we use. This means not only pregnant women, but also pregnant trans, non-binary and agender people. Our chosen approach to inclusive language is additive rather than neutral. (BSUH Maternity, 2021)

Following this announcement, the UK's *Daily Mirror*, known for its anti-minority and sensationalist mode of tabloid reporting that distorts facts in favour of engendering emotive responses that generate sales, suggested that the policy at BSUH requires midwives to stop using terms like 'mothers', 'breastfeeding' and 'maternal' altogether (Taylor, 2021). This claim was disseminated widely via social media, instigating a global deluge of transphobic rhetoric based solely on misinformation. In one notable example, Australian wellness influencer and alternative health practitioner Nat Kringoudis re-shared the *Daily Mirror*'s erroneous claims with her 56.5 thousand Instagram followers, which incited several comments, many of which decried the adoption of inclusionary terms for transgender men and argued that BSUH's policy 'erases women'.

Kringoudis' post attracted considerable push back, with many commenters pointing out the falsehoods contained within the *Daily Mirror* article and attempting to explain how re-sharing these claims is harmful to the transgender community. Australian feminist author Clementine Ford, for instance, took to her own Instagram to publicly urge Kringoudis to engage in trans-inclusive education:

> This is not education that should be sought on your own Instagram page, typically at the expense of trans people who are expected to maintain grace and kindness while their very existence is questioned and discredited. If you are calling yourself a professional in this area, you have a moral responsibility to seek trans inclusivity training.

This critique was largely met with defensiveness by Kringoudis and her followers, many of whom lamented dissenting commentary as 'bullying'. Kringoudis even privately contacted Ford to threaten legal action before doubling down on her stance in a follow up post where, in line with arguments about freedom of speech, she proclaimed 'I too am entitled to my beliefs'. This sparked further debate, including transphobic remarks among Kringoudis' supporters. Indeed, Kringoudis' position as a public figure with a social media following of over 50,000 people places her in a highly privileged and influential position. In this instance, her influence became a mechanism for legitimising and amplifying bigoted ideologies that substantially harm those who occupy a considerably less privileged place in society. Despite eventually admitting to her wrongdoing in sharing the false reports about BSUH, Kringoudis continued to share falsehoods via the 'stories' feature on her Instagram account until platform intervention eventually resulted in the posts being deleted.

The implications are considerable, however, for a minority group targeted through disinformation, misinformation, non-factual and sensational reporting, and the outrage that is generated as this fake news circulates widely. In the case of transgender persons, there remains an alarmingly high rate of mental health and suicide (National LGBTI Health Alliance, 2021), some of which has been linked to online harassment, including digital hostility generated through false or sensational statements (Zwickl et al., 2021). Kringoudis' re-circulation of the *Daily Mirror*'s dubious claims indicates some of the ways in which fake news viral circulation of what would otherwise – in a pre-digital sense – be limited to that publication's readership exacerbates practices of marginalisation and anti-minority violence to sometimes dangerous levels. When publics are encouraged to feel resentment and outrage resulting from false assertions that are presented *as if* factual, not only are exclusionary policies less likely to be questioned or addressed, but more mundane and everyday prejudicial attitudes are reinforced to the point of violent behaviour. We see similar dynamics at play in the context of racism, racial violence and anti-racism efforts, which we begin to unpack in the following discussion.

Racial Stereotypes and Fake News

As we have been arguing in the previous section, fake news deepens social divisions that further disenfranchise vulnerable communities and groups through their use as a wedge, through their being the targets of hate campaigns spread through fake news, and through their greater susceptibility to disinformation and misinformation. We would now like to take this to a deeper level by discussing not only how fake news makes use of minorities, but how it is an effective tool in digital spaces entrenching negative representations of minorities and their perception in wider society (Mercado, 2020). This is particularly pronounced for Black, Indigenous and People of Colour (BIPOC) who face continuous adversity, much of it as a direct result of disinformation and misinformation – a problem exacerbated by online platforms' disproportionate and inconsistent moderation of racist content. As Mercado (2020) points out, such inaction enables the safety and human rights of BIPOC communities to remain precarious, and the knowledge of this precarity is then further utilised by knowledgeable white supremacists.

Although fake news, disinformation and misinformation come in many forms, from the deep fake manipulations used in organised crime as phishing attacks to misguided ideas about vaccines that circulate in online communities, we argue that fake news cannot be understood separately from cultures of hate and manipulation in digital spaces. As racist rhetoric circulates widely in online spaces, real-life manifestations of racially fuelled violence increase in frequency and severity. For instance, following the 11 September 2001 attack on the World Trade Centre in Manhattan, Islamophobic rhetoric reached new heights in media and political discourse, western nations witnessed a sharp rise in verbal and physical attacks against people of Middle Eastern appearance (Abbas, 2004; Morgan, 2016). Both false and true claims about Muslim communities celebrating the collapse of the Twin Towers circulated in the pre-social media, Web 1.0 internet by email, through forums and news groups, and conspiratorial websites. While CNN showed footage of a group of Palestinian men and women celebrating the attack, a false counter-claim circulated online claiming that CNN had deliberately misled the public by using stock footage of Palestinian families celebrating the 1991 Iraqi invasion of Kuwait. The claim has been repeatedly fact-checked over the past two decades (Mikkelson, 2020). The footage, the claim, the counter-claim and the subsequent confusion contributed to a widespread *uncertainty* that fed into existing and new fears, converting these into campaigns of racial hatred (Poynting, Noble, Tabar, & Collins, 2004, p. 241).

One of the effects of fake news that is based on racist ideas is the fact it re-circulates prejudicial stereotypes about minorities. A common way this occurs is through the reporting of inter-group conflicts outside of their fundamental sociological, economic and political contexts. This, in turn, feeds a climate where administrative racism becomes more likely and thus, discriminatory and exclusionary policies that further harm BIPOC groups are legitimised (Pate & Idris, 2017). In these conditions, legacies of racist fake news shape contemporary debate surrounding issues of integration and difference with significant democratic implications (Heckler & Ronquillo, 2019). For instance, it is well documented that fake news is a weapon routinely wielded to procure public support for policies that exclude racial minorities in the United States, especially the growing Latinx community (Mercado, 2020).

Stereotypes are 'taken to express a general agreement about a social group, as if that agreement arose before, and independently of the stereotype' (Dyer, 1993, p. 16). A stereotype, as Mireille Rosello (1998) has pointed out, transmits 'ideas, images, and concepts, but it does so by freezing a certain stage of the production of the text' (p. 23). The widespread understanding of stereotypes in liberal-humanist discourses is that they transmit and fix an *un-truth* about a group of people. Stereotypes are a linguistic tool that 'package up' information, establishing and freezing an often erroneous link between an *identity* (e.g., Arab-Americans) and a presumed set of behaviours, attributes, desires, motivations or aspirations (e.g., to undermine white America, to undertake terrorist acts in the name of religion). They work by making that linkage, freezing it *as if* an historical and observable fact, and circulating to reinforce that fact. And, of course, they serve among the range of cultural identity resources that can then be taken up by that particular group, further reinforcing the stereotype and giving it its own problematic legitimacy (Cover, 2004a). While they are easily refuted by facts – including particularly the fact that not all members of a minority identity group can be found to share the same attributes, behaviours, attitudes or patterns of thinking – they remain a powerful communication force because they serve as a shorthand for a quick, non-critical assessment of a person or group of persons.

Stereotypes have a particularly powerful relationship with fake news because they rely for their strength on circulation. Any citation of a stereotype (including even to denounce it) puts it into further circulation, thereby adding to its presumed legitimacy and the 'certainty' by which an unthinking subject cites it (Rosello, 1998, p. 29). At the same time, fake news depends on stereotypes because they serve as a mechanism of agreement – for example, a fake news story about immigrants cheating on welfare not only riles up a particular target audience, but plays into existing stereotypes about immigrant welfare cheats. The story is believable from the start not because it confirms the stereotype but because the extant belief in the stereotypes confirms the story. And, finally, because stereotypes often use images to circulate a package of information about a minority group (e.g., an image of an effete man conveys a stereotype of non-heterosexuality as an easy-to-read package), they are well suited to the fake news environment of Twitter and other social media in which an image and a short description can be used to invoke a stereotype, circulate stereotypical information and rile up a group of supporters. For example, during his term in office, President Trump regularly used images that played into existing stereotypes to make erroneous and inflammatory remarks and share misinformed rhetoric about immigrants in the United States. On one occasion, he falsely attributed an image of people fighting at Morocco's border to Mexican immigrants attempting to gain entry to the country (Collins, 2016). Unsurprisingly, the image circulated virally, inciting several other politicians and social commentators to replicate and advance this misleading construct of Mexican immigrants in a dehumanising and homogenous way, further distorting perceptions of a Mexican immigrant minority in the public sphere.

Fake news has also relied on the re-circulation of stereotypes about refugees, including particularly refugees from Muslim backgrounds, in ways which engender a strong and negative emotional among audiences (LaChine, 2017). For instance, fake news which has framed refugees as a national security threat (linking the identity 'refugee' with the attribute of 'threat to stability'), adds to the intensification of social division between those who believe this erroneous stereotype and those refugees seeking safety, security and hospitality in a foreign country (LaChine, 2017). Such division prohibits members of the public from recognising refugees' and asylum seekers' shared humanity. Lerbaek and Olsen (2020) analysed a dataset of 14.3 million tweets related to the 2016 refugee crisis in Syria, finding that depictions of refugees were overwhelmingly negative. These tweets also appeared to amplify fearmongering by presenting fabricated and sometimes extremist claims about refugees, which were presented and readable as fact due to the existing stereotypes of refugees, people of Arab descent and people of colour as threat. The Syrian crisis was, at the time, a global discussion and in turn, this fake news content became a central facet of disinformation campaigns driven by conservative political groups seeking to undermine the credibility of their opponents and misinformation circulation by those who had less to gain other than perhaps pleasure in expressing a negative emotional response of outrage at the presence of the 'other' (Lerbaek & Olsen, 2020).

Fake News and Black Lives Matter

It would be remiss to talk about fake news in the context of racism and the ongoing inequities it legitimises without addressing some of the ways in which fake news operated in the context of the BLM movement. On 25 May 2020, 46-year-old George Floyd died after he was arrested in Minneapolis, Minnesota for allegedly using a counterfeit bill. Viral footage of the arrest showed Floyd pinned to the floor while a white police officer, Derek Chauvin, knelt on his neck. Later, transcripts of the police bodycam footage revealed that Floyd repeated over 20 times that he could not breathe. The incident triggered widespread protests around the world and the #BlackLivesMatter hashtag was tweeted a record 8.8 million times during the peak of the protests on 28 May that year (Anderson, Barthel, Perrin, & Vogels, 2020).

Although social media platforms contained during this time many necessary conversations about BLM, racial injustice, police procedures in regard to minorities, and a very powerful engagement with a serious issue of historical and current justice, with so much speech on the topic, digital culture became a setting for the expanded circulation of fake news about racial minorities (Georgacopoulos & Poche, 2020). False claims and conspiracy theories aimed at to discrediting and demoralising the movement ran rampant, including stories suggesting that Floyd is not dead, and that billionaires supplied protesters with weapons (Alba, 2020). Furthermore, President Trump tweeted in 2020 that Martin Gugino, a peaceful protestor who received life-threatening head injuries about viral video footage showed him being pushed to the ground by Buffalo police, could have been a provocateur of far-left anti-fascist group Antifa. Journalists from the Associated Press reported that Trump was referring to a report from the One America News Network (OANN) that claimed Gugino was using Antifa tactics to monitor the location of police, a claim that was debunked by top tech experts (Georgacopoulos & Poche, 2020).

As Humprecht (2019) argues, disinformation – particularly when amplified in digital spaces – is reflective of controversial discourse surrounding race and difference and thus, gains traction by playing into audiences' pre-existing anxieties about the 'other'. Indeed, people are more inclined to believe fake news when it confirms their worldview. Psychologists have long found that confirmation bias leads people to believe false information when it aligns with their existing beliefs (Taber & Lodge, 2006). In this vein, when President Trump suggested that Muslims in New Jersey applauded during 9/11 (Carroll, 2015) and that Mexican immigrants are rapists and murderers (Lee, 2015), these claims were more likely to be taken seriously by people who already associate Muslims with fundamentalism and Mexicans with criminality. As we discussed in the previous section, digital and media users who encounter false and misleading information about racial minorities are more inclined to believe and share fake news when it confirms and amplifies their fears about the world (Hochschild, 2016; Polletta & Callahan, 2017). In the Australian context, for example, news audiences often decried fake news about asylum seekers and refugees to emphasise their own position on the topic (Haw, 2021). Here, media messages that were at odds with participants' pre-determined views were routinely dismissed as misinformation and/or disinformation, aligning with studies showing that people often denounce fake news to discredit ideas they disagree with (e.g., Farhall et al., 2019; McNair, 2018).

Racist fake news is also a powerful way to mobilise far-right movements by uniting people who share xenophobic beliefs, offering them a sense of community. As we noted in Chapter Three, audiences and social media users regularly form both temporary and long-standing communities around issues, even among people they do not know and will never meet, but recognise they share a form of belonging, often in opposition to some framing of an 'other' or 'outsider' group. When the attitudes of these groups are legitimised through false narratives and stereotypes circulating as fake news, the trauma from witnessing institutionalised violence against minority racial communities is trivialised through discursive strategies deployed by those who benefit from reinforcing centuries of racial hatred, discrimination and segregation. We turn in the next section to some of the ways in which fake news surrounding the pandemic has become a vehicle for intense scapegoating, xenophobic hate speech, and violence against racial minorities.

Fake News and Xenophobia in the COVID-19 Pandemic

Much like the BLM protests, a major global event framed as catastrophe – the COVID-19 pandemic – provided a setting that permitted the circulation of fake news stories that drew on racial stereotypes to connect racial and ethnic minorities with disease. The emergence of coronavirus pandemic, apparently from Wuhan, China, in December 2019 was quickly met with research, policy and governance frameworks that understood that effective management of the pandemic response required addressing the spread of misinformation about the virus, its source, the cause of its circulation, treatment and, more recently, vaccination (Depoux et al., 2020). Indeed, communication – whether through government agencies, news media, or digital platforms – is integral to how we are able to respond to a crisis, and as we pointed out in Chapter Five, COVID-19 represents a significant setting for the circulation of problematic information that has been implicated in the intensification of panic and insecurity (Kim & Sue, 2020).

In the UK, an OfCom report (2020) revealed that almost half (46%) of the country had been exposed to fake news about the virus. Similar results were reported in the United States, with 48% of US residents reporting exposure to fake news about COVID-19, of whom, nearly two-thirds (66%) had seen false stories on a daily basis (Mitchell & Oliphant, 2020). This is alarming considering that repeated exposure to fake news has been found to increase peoples' susceptibility to believing it (see, for example, Pennycook, Cannon, & Rand, 2018). The World Health Organization labelled this emergent framework as an 'infodemic', where an overabundance of information, including disinformation, misinformation, conspiratorial beliefs and misleading health advice, infiltrates the public sphere (World Health Organization, 2020; Zarocostas, 2020). The implications of fake news on quality of health communication was recognised, of course, before the pandemic (Burkhardt, 2017; Mason, Krutka, & Stoddard, 2018).

Misinformation and disinformation in relation to COVID-19 has routinely contained a racial element, including stereotypical responses related to the fear of the racialised other and assumptions that link minorities to the spread of illness. Examples include the conspiratorial claim that the virus was bioengineered in a lab in Wuhan as part of a Chinese attempt to damage economies, take over the world or further strategic aims in the South China Seas (Andersen, Rambaut, Lipkin, Holmes, & Garry, 2020), and that it was caused by the use of Chinese-originating technologies in the roll-out of 5G mobile telephony in many parts of the world (Bruns, Harrington, & Hurcombe, 2020). Fake news relating to COVID-19 has also been implicated in racialised violence, including mob attacks, mass poisonings (Depoux et al., 2020), acts of vandalism (Spring, 2020), and other racially charged violence (Noel, 2020; Tan, 2020). Such incidents highlight the disruptive potential of disinformation and misinformation to ignite the kind of panic, division and fear that gives rise to racism and xenophobia (Albright, 2017; Schäfer & Schadauer, 2018; Shimizu, 2020).

The widespread racialisation of the crisis – most notably, the scapegoating of China and Chinese people, including immigrants in the West – has signalled an urgent need for scholarly and public policy focus on the role of disinformation in fostering and sustaining Sinophobia and anti-Asian racism. In Poland, for example, before the first local case of COVID-19 was confirmed many Asian medical students were subjected to xenophobic responses from their peers and members of the general community (Rzymski & Nowicki, 2020). In the United States, former President Trump and his administration's reckless claims that the virus originated in China (Jaiswal, LoSchiavo, & Perlman, 2020), coupled with sensationalised and xenophobic terminology such as 'Wuhan virus' and 'Kung Flu', have been shown to propel panic, prejudice and discrimination towards Asians (Das, 2020; Person, Sy, Holton, Govert, & Liang, 2004). Data collated from the Asian Pacific Policy and Planning Council on Affirmative Action revealed that, within a two-week period in late April 2020, there were 1,135 incident reports of verbal harassment, shunning and physical assault in the United States (Jeung, 2020). In one incident, a man encouraged a bus to run over a Chinese woman and then proceeded to spit on her (Tavernise & Oppel, 2020). The fatal shooting of eight people, including six Asian women, in Atlanta on 16 March 2021, has been attributed by many social commentators and political figures, including US President Biden, to the sharp rise in anti-Asian hate that permeated public sphere discourse through fake and misleading news stories, misinformation and the problematic association of the racialised other with questions and issues of disease (Forgey & Din, 2021; Lenthang, 2021).

Multiple social media posts circulating false claims have relied on the stereotyping practice that links an identity group (in this case, Chinese persons) with a set of attributes (in this case, untrustworthiness, disease, virus-carriers). For example, a false claim that Chinese passengers with a fever evaded quarantine at Kansai International Airport was disseminated in January 2020, becoming viral and evoking fears that linked Chinese travellers – or, indeed, many travellers of East Asian origin – with the risk of the spread of disease (Shimizu, 2020). Despite Kansai International Airport promptly denying this claim, discrimination against Chinese people remained widespread in the immediate days afterwards, with the hashtag #ChineseDontComeToJapan trending on Twitter during this period. Again, the stereotype at play draws on much older, false beliefs in Western cultures that erroneously link the 'foreign body' with concepts of disease, smell and a lack of hygiene (Bhatia, 2012; Cover, 2015). Chinese-Australians experienced substantial racial violence during the first year of the pandemic (Tan, 2020), and pandemic-related racism made up one-third of complaints made to the Australian Human Rights Commission in 2020 (AHRC, 2020). Again, this drew on older Sinophobic fears and attitudes in Australia, the discourses of which have been present since the nineteenth century (Donegan & Evans, 2001; Hollingworth, 2002). The assignation of unhygienic bodies to East Asian identities has the power, as philosopher Alphonso Lingis (1994) suggested, to pain some subjects while gratifying others (p. ix), thereby exacerbating the experience of difference, the border-policing of bodies of difference, and eroding the available frameworks for working in solidarity to prevent the spread of disease and find solutions to the crisis.

Anti-Chinese rhetoric circulated through disinformation that drew on conspiracy theories in ways which furthered the cause of populist political actors seeking to cement adversity. Much like the Trump examples of racism cited above, the pandemic offered the opportunity for far-right populists to play into existing stereotypes and anxieties by circulating deliberate disinformation. For example, Australian far-right politician Pauline Hanson of the *One Nation* political party, circulated through her political Facebook profile several misleading statements that drew on conspiratorial ideas about COVID-19 being developed in a Wuhan laboratory. She claimed that China had 'unleashed' the virus on the rest of the world, and used these claims to urge the public to boycott products made in China and advocate for Australia to cease its trade agreements with China (Dreher, 2020; Sengul, 2020). Here, we see the pandemic used as an excuse to draw again on the 'forgotten people' framework we identified at the start of this chapter as being a key component of the populist use of fake news.

Hanson herself initially gained notoriety (and, among some sectors in Australia, popularity and support) through a populist articulation of a forgotten white Australian population who were at risk of, in her claims, being 'swamped' by immigrants (those from East Asia in the 1990s; later, those from the Middle East from the 11 September 2001 attacks onwards), in claims which always positioned non-white persons as a threat to security, health, wellbeing, financial stability, land, home ownership or cultural specificity (Stratton, 1998). Unlike some of the earlier populist formations of a 'forgotten' middle class normative population, Hanson's populism has been executed through the continued re-invention of a group within the Australian population who are encouraged through disinformational claims to see themselves not only as *distinct* from other parts of the population, but as wholly *at risk, vulnerable* and *threatened* by the mobility of other parts of the population – the ease of movement 'into' the West of the migrant racialised other perceived as threat. This populism based on exclusionary discourses (Moffitt, 2017, p. 11) actively reinforces the idea of an external other who should be feared, hated, excluded or vilified on the basis of a misperceived threat. The early conspiratorial claims about a deliberate construction of COVID-19, long proven false by genomic analysis, were easily taken up and re-circulated by Hanson as fake news because they had a good fit with her longstanding populist racism, and thereby received a substantially wider audience that, alarmingly, exacerbated racial hatred and racial violence in Australia.

What these troubling examples highlight is how fake news circulates a linkage between minorities and disease (in various formations) in such a way as to both draw on existing anxieties and establish new forms of stigma that can result in racial violence, the embedding of racial hatred and the sustaining of adversity and hostility in place of more ethical discourses of belonging and the universality of risk of disease among all citizens. These examples highlight the significant role of fake news, disinformation and the easy circulation of this content among misinformed users as a driver of xenophobic rhetoric. As Hoppe (2018) argues, 'promoting an association between foreigners and a particular epidemic can be a rhetorical strategy for promoting fear or, alternatively, imparting a sense of safety to the public' (p. 1462). Given the readily accessible nature of globally circulating conspiratorial misinformation about the origins of COVID-19, it is not surprising that we have witnessed a proliferation of racially charged attacks on a global scale.

Conclusion

Periods of social, economic and civil unrest provide opportune moments for the manipulation of public perception. The resultant sense of fear, frustration and resentment among publics creates a volatile environment where our collective understanding of important events and issues declines and social divisions thrive (Georgacopoulos & Poche, 2020). Without a clear idea of what constitutes truth, we cannot create spaces to engage in a meaningful and constructive dialogue about the most pressing issues impacting society, let alone hold elite political actors to account. The subsequent harm to marginalised members of society and to democratic processes and practices is the ultimate propagation of inequality.

There is little doubt that the ascendancy of a partisan populist politics, especially within today's highly fragmented, post-truth media ecology, deepens existing inequalities and reinforces power imbalances that perpetuate real harm. This harm manifests in two profound ways: citizens' limited capacity to delineate reliable, factual information and in turn, make informed decisions about important social, economic, and health issues that affect their lives; and the insidious spread and legitimation of discriminatory, exclusionary, and bigoted ideas that jeopardise the safety and wellbeing of society's most marginalised people. As we have posited in this chapter, both scenarios allow inequitable power structures to remain intact and unchecked, often with deadly consequences.

As we argue in this book, addressing the growing, global spread of misinformation and disinformation in the digital sphere presents a substantial challenge for digital media and journalism professionals, researchers, educators, political figures, and the broader society. In the following chapters, we begin to unpack current conversation and debate concerning the impact of fake news on audience trust and how to address the problem of fake news and mitigate its harmful effects. Although journalists and other content creators have long deployed fact-checking practices to verify claims and sources, today's era of misinformation and disinformation occurring alongside one of the most serious global health crises experienced in the lives of many means that we have entered a crucial time for addressing fake news, not as a matter of political expediency or a matter of inconvenience but as a matter of life and death – which is one which, in light of the misinformation related to the BLM Movement and the experience of Chinese citizens during 2020, indicates the differential impact of fake news on the lives of minorities and vulnerable communities.

Chapter Eight

Audiences, Trust and Polarisation in a Post-truth Media Ecology

Introduction

The principles of rationality, electoral accountability, and access to credible and accurate information have long been treated as central tenets of liberal democracy (Jamieson, 2015). Although the reality of an engaged and knowledgeable public sphere remains the subject of much debate and derision, the ideal of an informed electorate is ultimately what sets democracy apart from other political systems (Karpf, 2019). In a truly democratic and fully enfranchised society, each citizen is, in theory, equipped with the capacity to partake in the electoral process by casting a vote as an informed member of society (Lau & Redlawsk, 2001). This, however, requires each individual to demonstrate an equitable level of motivation to seek accurate political information and exercise the right to vote (Austin & Pinkleton, 1999). Without engaging with reliable information about the political, cultural economic and social framings of their country, region or the world, however, it is less unclear if voters can be expected to make a genuinely informed decision at the ballot box.

In what has sometimes been referred to as a global era of post-factual democracy (Allen & Stevens, 2018, p. 11), the task electors face in making an informed vote is becoming increasingly difficult as *trust* in politics (and in political figures) is in rapid decline – a phenomenon Flew (2019) describes as the 'crisis of trust' (p. 4). Closely connected is the issue of how people are making sense of the vast array of publicly available information about important democratic issues, and how trust is connected to the proliferation of a post-truth political discourse where fake news, sensationalism and hyperbole run rampant. As Nielsen and Graves (2017) summarise this relationship,

> the fake news discussion plays out against a backdrop of low trust in news media, politicians, and platforms alike – a generalized scepticism toward most of the actors that dominate the contemporary information environment. (p. 1)

Indeed, public opinion studies indicate that overall trust in the news has reached an historically low point (Newman, Fletcher, Kalogeropoulos, Levy, &

Fake News in Digital Cultures: Technology, Populism and Digital Misinformation, 109–124
Copyright © 2022 by Rob Cover, Ashleigh Haw and Jay Daniel Thompson
Published under exclusive licence by Emerald Publishing Limited
doi:10.1108/978-1-80117-876-120221008

Nielsen, 2018), with the existence of fake news feeding into 'a bankruptcy of the so-called fourth estate' (Fisher, 2018, p. 19).

As we discussed in Chapter Seven, fake news can not only leave its audiences misinformed, but can also substantially increase their vulnerability in the face of crises and social inequalities. An area we are yet to explore in depth, however, is how fake news works to further undermine the public's confidence in the media, as well as how this is connected to cultural shifts in public trust for institutions more generally. In critical studies of media, trust is broadly understood as a prerequisite for public connection and social engagement: it is only when citizens hold the news in high regard that they are in a position to wilfully engage with it as a means of performing citizenship. While there is a long history of questioning the veracity, credibility and reliability of news, contemporary distrust in news services and institutions occurs in the context of a precarious historical moment for media and political credibility that is characterised by the global destabilisation of journalism institutions, shifts in news routines, and changes to the news production business model (Fisher, 2016). This gives rise to a media ecology that is increasingly arduous to navigate and in which dubious content such as fake news, disinformation and misinformation can pass as 'news', sometimes because they are viewed as more trustworthy than institutional journalism and other times because that trust is levelled across the credible and the non-credible (Szostek, 2018).

This chapter explores some aspects of the role of shifts in public trust in providing a cultural and media consumer framework for disinformation and fake news. Understanding trust as a relational attitude and orientation towards a source, idea, concept, speaker or ideology, we consider how contemporary audience relationships are increasingly produced within the tribalisation of attitude, culture and politics, and how they operate within an era in which evidence, reporting methods, news structure, and the intertextual relationship between news stories has dissipated in favour of trust in sources that are *familiar*, regardless of their objective or assessed credibility. The resulting tribalisation reduces the capacity of journalism to participate in framing public sphere debate, since different audiences with varying ideological perspectives are increasingly less likely to participate in the consumption of balanced news in the context of fragmented publics and are, instead, more inclined to engage in dichotomised and adversarial flame wars in online spaces.

We begin this chapter by theorising trust in the context of its role in sponsoring the circulation and acceptance of fake news. We then present two case studies drawn from the United Kingdom: Brexit, the protracted departure of the UK from the European Union in 2016; and 'Megxit', the highly publicised relinquishment of royal duties by the Duke and Duchess of Sussex in 2020. Both cases represent key cultural instances in which questions of institutional trust, veracity of news and sources, and adversarial hostility come together in ways which demonstrate some of the cultural complexities of the contemporary digital and news media ecology. We highlight how a rising lack of trust in traditional elites and expertise nourishes the kind of post-truth politics that enabled the 'leave' vote to flourish in the *Brexit* referendum and facilitated a hostile media environment characterised by highly sensationalised fake news about the Duke and Duchess of Sussex, both prior to and following their move from the UK to California.

While we agree with the notion that blind faith in the news is not a desirable outcome for a democratic society, the case studies we discuss in this chapter highlight an important complexity with this idea: that a more insidious crisis of trust – in both journalistic integrity and broader institutions – is a central mechanism for the production, spread and acceptance of fake news. Thus, fake news is no more a determinant of mistrust than mistrust is a causal factor for fake news. Ultimately, we argue that the crisis of trust at the centre of this chapter is one of the key cultural mechanisms by which fake news finds its audience and by extension, its power.

Conceptualising and Measuring Trust

We would like to start by considering the wider historical emergence of the concept of media trust, and the ways in which it is understood and measured in the context of the news audience. In the words of Tsfati and Cappella (2003), 'trust plays a part in almost every human interaction' (p. 505). As the concept of trust is multifaceted, it is subject to a wealth of definitions – most of which assume a situation where uncertainty renders an individual vulnerable and, in turn, they must rely on the capability and integrity of another person or system to help them vanquish this vulnerability (Ogonowski, Montandon, Botha, & Reyneke, 2014). In sociological terms, trust has come to be understood as 'the chicken soup of social life' (Uslaner, 2002, p. 1) because it enables people to act despite uncertainty and precarity. Distrust, on the other hand, deepens societal divisions (Lewis & Weigert, 1985).

Trust has long been identified as a vital component of community-building that promotes civic and political engagement (Brehm & Rahn, 1997; Davidson & Cotter, 1989). From the perspective of social capital (Bourdieu, 1983) which foregrounds the cultural perception of institutionalised social networks, trust can be regarded as a fundamental aspect of social cohesion and cooperation (Putnam, 1993, p. 171). In highlighting the role trust plays in developing social synergy, we can begin to appreciate how institutional and social trust work together to facilitate social connectivity and collective action. Trust is, at its core, a heuristic through which people can make decisions on the basis of a belief that their actions will give rise to certain outcomes. News trust is one such heuristic, premised on the belief that the news media represents a reliable and competent public service and is thus distinct from other forms of trust. Ultimately, by establishing trust, media outlets can set the public agenda and in turn, bridge the gap – politically, ideologically, and socially – between newsmakers and their audience.

Questions of trust in the news have been a central scholarly concern for many years, especially in the context of journalistic ethics and guidelines (Fisher, 2016, 2018). An abundant body of literature indicates that trust in the media is in continuous decline (e.g., Edelman Trust Barometer, 2019; Newman, Fletcher, Schulz, Andi, & Nielsen, 2020). This is important considering research findings showing that audiences who demonstrate low levels of trust in the media are less inclined than their trusting counterparts to accept accurate, factual information and are instead more prone to believe misinformation and disinformation (Ladd, 2012). What, however, do people mean when they articulate their claim that they do not trust the media? Kohring and Matthes (2007) offer four elements of the assessment of trust in the news media process:

1. trust in media institutions' selection of topics about which to report, that is, trust in the agenda setting mode of news outlets;
2. trust in how content is chosen for inclusion in those reports;
3. trust in how journalists evaluate that information; and
4. trust in the accuracy of those representations.

A study of news media audience members' understanding of trust in the United States found that, broadly, respondents were interested in discussing trust of news content, trust of the individual journalists delivering that content, trust of specific media organisations, and trust in the media industry as a whole (Williams, 2012). News trust is therefore about more than the *accuracy* of the information presented. Rather, it also frames the ways in which media organisations work to meet public expectations, including how news content is (or is not) reflective of audiences' lived experiences and social realities.

Upon assessing the utility of a source, audiences are traditionally recognised for their capacity and active engagement in making choices to find sources they trust over those they distrust (Knobloch, Carpentier, & Zillmann, 2003). Additionally, it has long been recognised that audiences are more likely to believe a news story when it contains ideas consistent with their pre-existing attitudes, whereas stories that challenge these perspectives are often dismissed as inaccurate (Metzger, Hartsell, & Flanagin, 2015). As an example of the kind of 'confirmation bias' (Nickerson, 1998) that occurs when people seek out and favour information supporting their own views while discounting ideas that do not, the audience has an active incentive to gratify that bias by developing a trust relationship with particular kinds of sources. While these theoretical approaches tend to individualise audience members as sole actors, and disavow the possibility of audience members who perceive themselves not as individuals but as members of the kind of audience-as-community we discussed in Chapter Three, they usefully point out the ways in which trust is performed diversely, not as a given in the relationship, but as a mechanism for shopping around for the kind of gratification that satisfies a desire for trust through finding recognisable discourses in media content.

It is also worth noting that evaluating credibility based on shared political interests has also been shown to positively influence whether audiences share a news story with others, especially on social media (Stefanone, Vollmer, & Covert, 2019). Perceptions of trustworthiness are, in that sense, positively linked to the overall reach of news. Conversely, when audiences mistrust news content, they not only refuse to share it with others, but they will often turn to non-mainstream sources in the future. Fletcher and Park (2017) notably observed a strong relationship between low trust in mainstream media content and a preference for alternative news sources. Some scholars argue that this trend diminishes the media's capacity to provide a public service (Cappella & Jamieson, 1997; Tsfati & Cappella, 2003). In other words, journalists cannot serve their important function as watchdogs when citizens no longer trust professional news organisations.

A low level of trust in the news is also conducive to broader trends of dein-stitutionalisation and deregulation, which can, in turn, result in audiences elect-ing to value individual experiences over expert knowledge (Van Zoonen, 2012). There exists a clear relationship between mistrust in the news media and mistrust of other institutions, notably the government (Hanitzsch, Van Dalen, & Steindl, 2018), which feeds into a growing disconnect between having an informed citi-zenry versus one that is increasingly sceptical (Edelman Trust Barometer, 2019). These issues are exacerbated by the difficulty of re-establishing trust once it has been lost. For example, in Australia, people who express a mistrust of news have been found to offer few suggestions for regaining their trust, indicating that once news organisations have lost credibility in the eyes of their audiences, it is consid-erably difficult to gain it back (Flew, Dulleck, Park, Fisher, & Isler, 2020).

A further (and arguably more dire) consequence of audience mistrust is that it can give rise to individuals withdrawing from news content altogether. Some have argued that this leads to audiences becoming less informed and in turn, less able to perform their duty as citizens (Prochazka & Schweiger, 2019). This is a legiti-mate concern, however, it assumes that news consumption is primarily motivated by conscious and rational assessment of the trustworthiness of a given source, outlet or story (Tsfati & Cappella, 2005; Williams, 2012). It also assumes that citi-zens only engage with content they trust (and vice versa). This makes sense from a *uses and gratifications* perspective, and studies have indeed found that positive perceptions of credibility predict higher rates of engagement with a given source of news (e.g., Winter & Krämer, 2012). Some research has, however, shown that people do not always trust the news that they consume (Park, Fisher, Fuller, & Lee, 2018; Swart & Broersma, 2021; Tsfati & Cappella, 2005). According to a 2020 Reuters report, fewer than half (46%) of news consumers trust the sources they regularly engage with (Newman et al., 2020).

Similarly, fewer people have been found to trust social media as a news source than more traditional forms of media such as newspapers, broadcast televi-sion and radio news (Barthel & Mitchell, 2017; Elvestad, Phillips, & Feuerstein, 2018). Paradoxically, however, social media is increasingly used to access news content (Newman et al., 2020). These apparent contradictions raise important questions about how patterns of news engagement impact (and are impacted by) perceptions of trustworthiness. One such consideration is that, within our already media-saturated lives, the way we consume news is often unintentional. For exam-ple, rather than intentionally searching for news content, people regularly stum-ble upon it while using social media for other purposes, such as keeping up with the activities of their friends and family (Boczkowski, Mitchelstein, & Matassi, 2018; Fletcher & Nielsen, 2018; Haw, 2020). Although media trust appears to be an obvious precursor for news engagement, trust can be (and often is) irrelevant to situations where news exposure happens incidentally, which, in today's media and information ecology, is becoming more and more widespread.

In summary, while there is no definitive answer as to the best mechanism to measure audience trust – or, indeed, if it can be measured at all – the common thread in much scholarship suggests that continuing to interrogate the percep-tion of trust and trustworthiness of news remains a critically important aspect of attempting to understand how and why fake news, disinformation and misinformation has an appeal. By thinking about trust, we are able to move beyond any media effects approach that assumes the audience member's attitudes are produced first and only in the repetitive encounter with a particular form of untrustworthy content. Rather, it enables us to suggest that a key part of what makes fake news palatable, desirable and gratifying to some audience members is trust. And that this is a case of trusting what the rest of us find untrustworthy – whether the conspiracy theories discussed in Chapter Six, or the deepfake video of a politician saying something the viewer finds unbelievable, as we discussed in Chapter Five. In other words, making sense of audience trust is the start of the necessary work in attempting to unpack, address and remedy fake news, disinformation and the persistent circulation of misinformation and content that *ought not be trusted*.

The 'Crisis of Trust': Audiences in a Post-truth Media Ecology

In the previous chapter, we noted the term 'infodemic', which was coined by the *World Health Organization* (World Health Organization, 2020) to describe the abundance of content about the COVID-19 pandemic across the wide media ecology. This term has relevance both inside and outside the context of COVID-19 as it encapsulates the kind of 'info-smog' to which we are continuously exposed in the face of any major event or crisis. And within an infodemic, it is increasingly difficult for citizens to locate reliable information they can trust. By understanding what factors lead people to trust news, we can not only provide valuable insight into the role of news in shaping public opinion, but we can also identify potential strategies for reducing both the spread and negative impacts of misinformation and disinformation (Sterrett et al., 2019). As we have discussed at various points in this book, false information – whether deliberate or not – persistently undermines public trust, not just in the media, but in the very institutions whose normative operation is largely dependent on gaining (and maintaining) a certain degree of trust among the broader society. The need to delve into the link between fake news and audience trust is, therefore, a no-brainer.

We demonstrate in this section some of the ways in which the crisis of trust is productive of the post-truth framework in which fake news is generated and consumed. Journalism scholar Katherine Fink (2019) is right to claim that 'the single biggest challenge facing journalism today is the public's lack of trust in it' (p. 40). While legitimate news is primarily constructed by journalists and media organisations, fake news is co-constructed by the audience because fake news, by design, relies heavily upon deceiving audiences into believing it is real (Tandoc, Lim, & Ling, 2018) and on-forwarding that news to others who may have trust in that audience member. This at least partly accounts for why fake news regularly mimics the format of legitimate news content. Without attaining audiences' trust and thus, ensuring they are duped into believing the content is true, fake news outlets cannot continue to generate the views and shares they require to sustain themselves. We noted earlier in this chapter that audiences generally trust media content when it presents ideas that align with their pre-existing views and mistrust content that challenges them. It is therefore no surprise that purveyors of fake news can reel in audiences by appealing to partisan bias and fuelling political division. This is why we routinely see scandal and incivility in news coverage gain considerable traction among audiences while their political trust declines (Bowler & Karp, 2004; Mutz & Reeves, 2005). Indeed, the demand for fake news is born out of the relationship between the media crisis of trust and the simultaneous loss of faith in public institutions (Flew, 2019). In this vein, although fake news itself can severely jeopardise trust, believing and sharing fake news is actually a symptom of the broader crisis of trust that existed long before the concept of fake news entered the public imaginary.

There is much empirical evidence linking exposure to misinformation with institutional distrust – both with respect to mainstream media and the federal government. For example, one survey of 3,000 US residents representing a range of political views found that fake news exposure is associated with an overall decline in trust in mainstream media (Ognyanova, Lazer, Robertson, & Wilson, 2020). Furthermore, for liberals, fake news exposure correlated with low levels of trust in political systems, whereas exposure to fake news was associated with an increase in political trust among moderates and conservatives. These findings highlight how the consequences of fake news cannot be examined without consideration of mitigating factors, especially within the current media and political environment. Indeed, properly comprehending the real-life consequences of fake news narratives in the context of trust requires us to first explore how media users perceive fake news and the subsequent effects on their media engagement. The fact remains that much research into how audiences make sense of fake news has yielded nuanced and oftentimes conflicting results, largely due to the fact that there are substantial trust-based variances in terms of what kinds of content audiences see as constituting fake news. The Reuters Institute's *Digital News Report 2018*, which measured perceptions of fake news across 37 countries, found that despite a significant degree of public consternation in relation to fake news, very few respondents were able to offer concrete examples of fake news they had encountered, and that audiences regularly conflated fake news (disinformation) with biased journalism (low objectivity and institutionally affiliated news outlets) (Newman et al., 2018).

At the same time, digital platform users have been at a disadvantage in distinguishing real news from fake news and other forms of disinformation for the many reasons given in Chapters One, Two and Three. Many users, for example, express a general distrust in all forms of news media (Fletcher & Nielsen, 2017). These blurred definitions illustrate how fake news as a concept is not sufficiently understood among the wider populace, despite it representing a common source of concern among audiences. Hence, our very real concern is that apprehending fake news means starting from the question of audience cultures, and considering how audiences are positioned through various complex trust relationships to distinguish (or not) between credible and non-credible news sources.

This becomes more apparent when we look at how the fake news *label* is conflated with the fake news *concept*. In research by Nielsen and Graves (2017), for instance, audience members often conceptualised fake news as a term that is deployed to meet certain political ends. Likewise, Zaryan (2017) found that some audience members regard fake news as a tactic deployed by political elites to undermine counter positions. This is an example of the *fake news as label* phenomenon (Egelhofer & Lecheler, 2019) outlined in Chapter Two in which we explained some of the ways in which fake news is thrown around by political elites to discredit legitimate information that calls into question their own position, beliefs or actions. We believe that by weaponising the term 'fake news' as a means of crushing dissent, political adversaries undermine one another in the eyes of citizens and thus further erode public trust in wider political systems, actors and liberal-democratic ideals. In clouding the distinction between fake new as insult and fake news as concept (or social issue), actors can actively embed and sustain the wider crisis of trust in media, institutions and democratic practices. We turn in the next two sections to two recent case studies that demonstrate the complex interrelationship between erosion of trust in news journalism, the reduction in trust in the political institutions that uphold public life, and the framework that enables the flourishing of fake news.

Brexit

There is enormous value in the critique of institutions of power, including national and supra-national governance structures. Critique is the first step to ensuring actors act in good faith, that key stakeholders remain within the purpose and legal frameworks, and that institutions in democratic settings operate for the benefit of the people. Critique allows us to make sense of what benefit might mean, the limitations of power and the value of an institution. Critique operates, as Judith Butler (2009a) has noted, every time the question of what constitutes a legitimate government action, command or policy is raised, meaning it takes a multiplicity of forms beyond those more familiar philosophic argumentation frameworks (p. 780).

Critique implies not accepting authority, frameworks, languages, ways of speaking, norms that establish intelligibilities on face value but being in a permanent process of asking questions about the regimes of rationality, including particularly contemporary liberal-humanist institutions of governance (p. 789). The social and democratic imperative of critique is not, however, antithetical to trust or warrants a permanent state of paranoid distrust in all institutions, practices and people. Rather, it calls upon or interpellates the ethical actor to critically evaluate legitimacy, value, meaning and ways of perceiving trust itself, without necessarily dissipating it or falling into the chaos and violence of radical mistrust. We therefore value trust because it is inextricably related to the problematic but necessary institutions that help societies manage practices of care of the people, the avoidance of war and violence, the distribution of food, shelter and comfort, the meaningful deployment of education in all its forms. We can both trust the working of an institution and critique it without necessarily demanding that any institution that is questioned is instantly dismantled because some people have developed distrust in it.

During 'Brexit', the United Kingdom's 2016–2021 process of withdrawal from its 40-year membership of the European Union and its precursor institutions, we saw the consequences of a growing crisis of trust in both a democratic and social cohesion context. The background that led to Brexit is complex, including the persistence of nationalism, the suspicion of global interconnectivity and the strange appeal of populist leaders and speakers, has been dealt with elsewhere with far greater depth and detail than we can address in a few lines on a book about disinformation and fake news. What is important to note, however, is that the campaign that led to the Brexit referendum was, at its core, an ideological exercise that was 'divisive, antagonistic and hyper-partisan' (Moore & Ramsay, 2017, p. 168). It was the product of style of adversarial argument over substance of meaning, and serves as a notable example as to how, during times of crisis and socio-political upheaval, ongoing dispute over a nation's collective identity become not only discursively weaponised to legitimise or delegitimise a particular course of action (Bennett, 2019), but also takes advantage of the crisis of trust, fuelling it with further distrust through practices of disinformation and the circulation of fake news.

Throughout Brexit, immense propaganda, myths, semi-truths, claims, and counter claims created a volatile media environment – both in terms of formal, traditional news and less formal modes of online communication. Opinion rather than fact contributes to a broad decline in trust in established institutions, sources and forms of authority, including information, policy and leadership (Marshall & Drieschova, 2018, p. 96). Indeed, Brexit is a key example of post-truth politics, whereby a growing distrust in formal institutions, political elites, established expert knowledge, the credibility of media organisations and the veracity of news sources led to the establishment of what we call 'alternative trust frameworks', in which questionable sources of information become more trustworthy to some audiences than traditional sources. This is one of the instances in which fake news operates not by mimicking 'real' news sources, styles of journalistic writing or practices of the style of authorised speaking positions. Rather, it is a case where opinion-writing, non-factual accounts, poorly written misinformation and, indeed, the circulation of brief memes on social media platforms come to be felt as more trustworthy than the complex 'elite' debates occurring about a very complex national and international issue in the United Kingdom's more recognised media sources. In that sense, a combination of declining institutional trust, heavy social media reliance and a rejection of the complexities of contemporary political discourse drove members of the British public towards emotionally charged, misinformed and adversarial dialogue that ultimately resulted in a poorly understood referendum to leave the European Union. It is precisely within these conditions that a strong foundation for post-truth politics is laid.

On both 'sides' of the Brexit debate, an insidious battle of political propaganda took hold, the likes of which we have witnessed in many democratic campaigns in the past. What set Brexit apart, however, was the persuasive techniques deployed through the strategic circulation of false information, simultaneously propagated through a populist rhetoric of overdue change and a nationalist political imaginary. Such ideas were succinctly codified in disinformational slogans such as 'Take Back Control', popularised by those in favour of departing the European Union including particularly the 'Leave' campaign group (Corner, 2017).

This claim of national sovereignty being threatened is a myth produced through the misapplication of discourses of risk and vulnerability, and is built on a successful generation of anger, outrage and dissent across recent populist movements in Western liberal democracies from the United States' Trump presidency to Narendra Modi prime ministership in India, from the Bolsanaro movement in Brazil to the authoritarian populism of Hungary's Viktor Orbán (Inglehart & Morris, 2016). All populist movements depend on the establishment of adversity through creating a sceptical position of distrust in political leaders and institutions (typically described as elite or out-of-touch) and the things that are being reported and said about them in mainstream, credible media (typically described as partisan or false). The 'Euroscepticism' through which distrust in the United Kingdom was channelled into adversity (Daddow, 2013) is a good example and reflects a post-imperial nostalgia that sees British citizens longing for the 'mythical golden age of sovereign nation-states defined by cultural and racial homogeneity' (Virdee & McGeever, 2018, p. 1803).

The 'Leave' campaign took advantage of this culture of distrust, creating and spreading numerous, false accounts about British governance and international relations, notably relating to the economy and immigration (Yerlikaya & Aslan, 2020). These claims included that the UK provides the European Union with £350 million per week, and net migration to the UK was rated annually at 333,000 persons. These controversial claims were highly salient in online misinformation, memes, snippets, anecdotes and personal debates that took place in less formal public settings, notably social media, indicating not only distrust of institutions, but of the settings through which political debate has ordinarily taken place in media, parliament and more formal public events. Although these claims were revealed to be false, opinion polls found that they were widely believed among members of the UK population (e.g., Whatukthinks, 2016a, 2016b). In many ways, the increasing trust in alternative communication settings, and the shopping around by media consumers for other settings of trustworthiness created fertile ground for the Leave campaign to gain traction by relying more on Twitter (Hänska & Bauchowitz, 2017). Indeed, the Leave narratives were found to be four times more prominent on social media than those of the Remain campaign (Grčar, Cherepnalkoski, Mozetič, & Novak, 2017). Leave supporters were also more passionate, outspoken and adversarial when engaging in online discussion and debate, posting about the referendum almost five times more frequently than their Remain counterparts (Polonski, 2016), again indicating a greater trust in adversarial mechanisms of dialogue than in the ordinary practices of British institutional debate.

An additional problem emerged when members of the *Remain* campaign sought to refute the *Leave* group's false claims, which instead had the effect of augmenting their reach. This also occurred when journalists sought to challenge these mistruths. For example, the British Broadcasting Corporation was duly criticised for giving equal airtime to the Leave campaign's misleading claims and refutations from credible experts (Gaber, 2017). Jack (2019) describes this as 'unintentional amplification' which occurs when merely repeating false information lends credibility to it. From a strategic political campaigning standpoint, however, there was nothing unintentional about it. Rather, the amplification that occurred was actively exploited, further reflecting the potency of intermedia agenda setting in the digital age (Gaber & Fisher, 2021).

While both 'sides' of the Brexit debate actively accused each other of acting dishonestly as a means of scaremongering their way to victory, these discursive tactics did little to inspire trust from the public. Citizens were instead encouraged to distrust political messaging altogether. Lopez-Smith's (2017) investigation into how news audiences perceived media representations of *Brexit* revealed that, for all sides, the narratives within coverage after the vote led them to doubt the veracity of the campaigns, and many felt they had been misled into voting a certain way (or not voting at all). For example, there was a tendency to assume that a *Remain* outcome was inevitable, which negatively affected the degree to which *Remain* supporters engaged with the debate, leading several to experience regret for not engaging more. It is important to clarify here that the perception of *Remain* as inevitable was a product of a perceived hegemonic authority of *Remain* and the option to leave the EU therefore represented an opportunity of resistance. This assumed hegemony often prevented critical individual and collective engagement with the campaign, leading to a sense of civic regret for many Britons following the outcome.

Lopez-Smith (2017) concluded that the outcome of Brexit is reflective of a tendency for news narratives to mirror a culture of post-truth hostility and hyper-partisanship over the provision of information voters need so they can make electoral decisions that are in their best interests. In turn, elite representations of news fed into citizens' contextualised mistrust of political institutions, further illustrating how a lack of faith in traditional elites and expert knowledge enables the amplification of post-truth politics. We saw a similar dynamic play out in news and social media discourse surrounding another notable event that has gained global attention in recent years: the decision of the Duke and Duchess of Sussex – Prince Harry and Meghan Markle – to leave their royal duties in 2020.

Megxit

As unpacked in the previous discussion, some of the rhetoric surrounding Brexit, particularly for the *Leave* campaign, was underscored by a sense of post-imperial nostalgia (Gilroy, 2004). This nostalgia is, understandably, closely connected with the country's idealisation of the British royal family – the family of Elizabeth II who is sovereign of the UK as well as several other Commonwealth realms, including Canada, Australia and New Zealand. Indeed, in one sense the royal family symbolises the remnant of the UK's colonial and imperial history, invoking strong nationalist notions of a united, proud Britain that was once the centre of the world's largest empire. At another level, the royal family is symbolic of the social power of celebrity, and the capacity to be famous and newsworthy no matter the contribution that is made or the views that are held. Both are ideals that are constructed in news media as well as in misinformation, tabloid spectacle, gossip writing and the circulation of content that many members of the public dismiss as immaterial while others consume, share and comment upon as a matter of serious engagement.

The entry into the junior echelons of the royal family of Meghan Markle, the first mixed-race woman to marry a British prince, was widely hailed as an advancement for the royal family and for British society more generally. It was also condemned by a small minority of white supremacists and 'old-school' nationalists who felt the marriage to the North American television actor and social activist was too large an adjustment to their ideal of a very English royal family. Following the highly publicised decision of the Duke and Duchess of Sussex to relinquish serving as working royals (representing the Queen in her official duties as sovereign) in early 2020, the neologism 'Megxit' – a play on 'Brexit' that names Meghan – was coined by tabloid newspaper *The Sun*. It subsequently became the moniker for the protracted story around the world. In their article headlined '"Megxit" is the new Brexit in a Britain split by age and politics', *The New York Times* argued that, like Brexit, Megxit represents 'a convenient proxy, allowing people to argue about race, class, gender and British identity (New York Times, 2020).

It is well documented that much of the negativity, hostility and outrage in public and media discourse in relation to the Duke and Duchess of Sussex was levelled at Meghan, who had initially been constructed as bringing a modern approach to gender and her mixed-race status to British royalty (Clancy & Yelin, 2020). Like Catherine, the Duchess of Cambridge, who was widely celebrated for 'rescuing the House of Windsor from its unpopular post-Diana years by transforming it from an insular, rigid and outdated establishment to an open and modern institution' (Repo & Yrjölä, 2015, p. 742), Meghan's status as a woman not raised in a family of royalty or nobility, and as a woman of colour, situated her as someone who could align the monarchy more closely with the average citizen and with the UK's position as a multicultural society (Weidhase, 2021). Indeed, her entry into the royal family coincided with a tumultuous time for Britain's racial politics, as it occurred subsequent to the Brexit vote which had raised racial tensions and been pivotal in an increase in reported hate crimes towards people of colour across Britain (Lumsden, Goode, & Black, 2018).

Where the British royal family symbolised not only the unity of British and/or Commonwealth peoples, but also Britain's imperial past (Randell-Moon, 2017), the arrival of the Duchess of Sussex was logically seen as a positive new era, capable of mediating old and new tensions (Weidhase, 2021). However, what was considered largely positive media coverage of Meghan became decidedly more negative following the royal wedding in May 2018, and a slew of negative commentary in tabloid publications, both implicitly and explicitly racist, was routinely interlinked with Brexit discourse. Following Megxit, this hostility deepened, seemingly putting an end to the mythical construction of a progressive Britain once and for all.

At one level, tabloid news publications were responsible. They have a peculiar role in relation to the British royal family in that they are able to participate in what is known as the royal rota (the list of media outlets who get a turn at exclusive stories and photographs) while able to generate substantial misleading content by relying on leaks, false claims that made-up information came from unnamed 'royal insiders', and unethical access to information. This was revealed in 2007, when *News of the World* royal editor Clive Goodman was convicted of illegal interception of phone messages, later resulting in the 2011 Leveson Inquiry into the culture and ethics of the British press (Robinson, 2011). Tabloid publications skirt very close to the definition of fake news and disinformation, as we demonstrated in Chapter Four. By relying on sensationalism that invokes an emotive rather than a critical response, and by utilising adversity and 'side taking', tabloid journalism encourages hostility and vigilantism towards individuals who are positioned as folk devil (Hebdige, 1979).

In adopting that mode, the opportunity was missed for critically engaging with the issues around why the Duke and Duchess found their roles as working royals constraining, as well as the issues experienced as an archaic institution and its bureaucracy of courtiers struggled to incorporate new participants in senior roles, or why some members of the public felt threatened by a mixed-race royal who presented herself as an empowered, capable and socially conscious woman. Furthermore, there were limited opportunities to unpack critically some of the key logic underlying claims that historical issues experienced by royal wives a generation earlier were repeating themselves in an institution, sections of which perhaps had not modernised at all (Sussex Official, 2019), nor to understand the health and mental health risks experienced by public figures who are under persistent media scrutiny and often misleading or false reporting. Instead, the tabloid reporting approach was to condemn the independence of a woman or, indeed, a couple taking the agency to forge a meaningful life for themselves. As is long recognised, when a woman is publicly perceived to be 'taking charge' of her own life it is seen as an inappropriate replication of a traditionally masculine act (Butler, 1990). In a social setting that continues to be marked by patriarchal sentiment, the Duchess of Sussex was depicted as deviant and unbecoming for a 'royal' woman, revealing the extent to which trust in the royal family operates not by the capacity to remain relevant to politics, but in its capacity to be perceived as a residue of the past.

It therefore comes as little surprise that within news and social media discourse in relation to Megxit, the Duchess was depicted as a selfish person who showed a lack of consideration for how this decision would affect the royal family, and the British monarchy as a whole. It became routine for UK newspapers during this time to publish sensationalist headlines such as 'Megxit bombshell', 'royal countdown to chaos', 'the Sandringham showdown' and 'Monarchy in crisis' – word choices that position Harry and Meghan's decision in adversarial and hostile terms. Additionally, much of the coverage during this time focussed on how the royal family was undergoing 'crisis talks', 'civil war' and even a 'bitter Palace battle that raged through the night' (Ahmed, 2020). The depiction of two women at odds – the Duchesses of Cambridge and Sussex – drew on soap opera-style female adversity. Here, the Queen was routinely constructed as the family protector, who, according to the *Daily Mirror*, 'fights to save monarchy' (Myers, 2020). Conversely, she was also portrayed as a helpless agent who is being forced to gracefully accept Harry and Meghan's decision, as imbued within headlines such as 'her Majesty reluctantly gives in to young royals' and 'Queen to Harry: I want you to stay ... but you're free to go'. It was also revealed that, due to prohibitive practices placed by Buckingham Palace on working royals not to antagonise the media, the Duchess was not permitted to refute any false claims circulating about her in the media, although did so once the decision to cease being working royals was made. Both Meghan and Harry took legal action to stymie disinformation campaigns, with filed paperwork noting that false reports caused them 'tremendous emotional distress' (BBC News, 2020; Reuters Institute for the Study of Journalism, 2021).

While the disinformation and misleading stories in the tabloids drew on the distorted discourse of sensationalist royal reporting and could be remedied through legal action, it had the problematic wider effect of generating a public adversity that led to the toleration of substantially false, misleading and often ludicrous fake news campaigns. That is, the more the Duchess of Sussex was depicted by the tabloid press as the 'evil woman' wielding public relations and legal processes to shape her image, the more members of the public began to accept and believe fabricated accounts about her. These included stories about the Duchess' relationship with her mother, her baby shower, and purchases and renovations for the Sussexes' home at Frogmore Cottage. More alarmingly, they included conspiracy theories and disinformation campaigns that she had faked her pregnancy (Ruiz, 2020), that she threw a cup of tea that did not taste right at a staff member while on tour in Australia and screamed at the governor-general's staff after demanding that they bake banana bread in the middle of the night (Hawkings, 2021).

It was also claimed that her history as a student, actor and social activist was false, and she was in fact a 'yacht girl' (a euphemism for sex worker) – the sole evidence being a photograph of the Duchess posing on a yacht (RoyalFoibles, 2020). Corrective biographies, press statements and interviews are seen by this audience segment not as corrections or fact but as untrustworthy accounts. In this example, we see a significant case of the relationship between public distrust and fake news. Distrust in a public figure serves as the key ingredient that establishes fake news, disinformation and misinformation as credible and trustworthy on its own. In the case of the Duke and Duchess of Sussex, the routine practice of sensationalist reporting of royals who are less likely than others to upset the tenuous constitutional arrangements by berating the media, are unwilling or unable to alienate bad actors in the press, and only very rarely take legal action to curtail untruthful stories, created ideal conditions for substantial public distrust such that outrightly fake and conspiratorial news, including the ludicrous claim of perpetrating a fake pregnancy and a fake baby, could be read as credible accounts. Just as with Brexit, in which fake news was enabled after the generation of distrust of the complex bureaucratic, political and governance arrangements of European Union membership and protocols, the case of Megxit became one in which widespread conspiracy and public hostility flourished and has been sustained over time due to the ill-feeling towards the Duchess of Sussex, often in ways which deny the critical insights we might gain by trying to make sense of that ill-feeling in the context of gender and race.

Conclusion

While the fate of two royal family members who have become distrusted and the subject of substantial fake news is not a matter of democracy (where Brexit was), it is demonstrative of the key relationship between audiences positioned not as citizens but as consumers, the wider crisis over trust in anything that is said by anyone (including particularly, but not limited to, governance institutions), and the use of distrust to create credibility among certain audience segments who consume fake news and disinformation – not because it is sensible or rational or even interesting, but because it gains credibility when it is about figures, topics or persons that are positioned to be perceived as untrustworthy. Where the Megxit example matters for democracy, however, is in the potential impact of any fake news on any public figures, and whether or not there is a risk that cultures of distrust that breed disinformation will reduce the interest and likelihood of good people to want to enter public life in any form or setting.

It also demonstrates the wider problem of trust for the communication necessary to maintain and build democratic institutions, practices and ethics throughout social life. Without the trust of its audiences, the news cannot fulfil its democratic duties. Public confidence in political institutions is an essential component of meaningful electoral engagement. While mistrust can lead people to become more mobilised on account of genuine concerns about poor government and dubious mainstream media content, distrustful citizens have also been found to disproportionately vote for populist candidates or disengage from politics altogether (Hooghe, 2018). While questions of media credibility and reliability are certainly not new, the growing influence of digital media platforms as gateways to political information has played a significant role how people make sense of the world (and how they share this information with others). The wide reach of social media content, including informal discussions between friends, editorial content, and brand advertising, creates a digital environment where all content is presented as equal, which has arguably dissolved the hierarchy of information sharing that is central to more traditional news formats. As highlighted throughout this book, it is amid these conditions that fake news finds its audience.

In this chapter, we have begun to shed light on how fake news exacerbates an already pervasive mistrust of the news media, and of formal institutions more generally – a phenomenon dubbed the 'crisis of trust' (Flew, 2019). The democratic consequences of a sharply divided, polarised, and distrustful populace are exemplified by 2016's Brexit outcome and the sensationalism of Megxit in 2020, including the ensuing public vilification of the Sussexes and insidious spread of disinformation about the couple. As both events show, widespread mistrust in expertise, mainstream media content, and traditional elites lays fertile ground for the brand of post-truth politics that continuously enables misinformation and disinformation to thrive with consequences for democracy, tolerance, and social progress. With fake news continuing to gain traction and facilitate alarming levels of political and social division, citizens are faced with an increased degree of responsibility to exercise scepticism towards information they encounter, particularly in digital spaces. In turn, media organisations must consider the higher expectations for public accountability being directed, not just towards news organisations, but towards public institutions, political figures and digital platforms. There is indeed a growing call for news media professionals to exercise greater transparency with respect to their news-making practices (Chadha & Koliska, 2015; Curry & Stroud,

2019), which is already resulting in more substantive efforts to involve audiences in the news production process (Belair-Gagnon, Nelson, & Lewis, 2018). In the following chapter, we begin to unpack these kinds of initiatives, as well as other strategies – both current and proposed – to combat the negative effects of fake news. These include media and digital literacy programmes, formal and informal fact-checking practices, pedagogical frameworks within formal journalism education, and regulation/legislation aimed at stemming the flow of misinformation and disinformation.

Chapter Nine

Remedying Disinformation: Communication Practice in a World of Fake News

Introduction

Fake news in its contemporary form has been a subject of investigation and public anxiety, particularly since 2016. That does not mean, however, that the public, scholars, legislators and key media stakeholders have not been active in seeking remedies, prevention frameworks, intervention tactics and both regulatory and pedagogical solutions to disinformation and the circulation of fake and misleading content. Rather, while condemnation of fake news has dominated public and policy dialogue on media, digital communication and politics during recent years, solution-seeking has become a substantial element of that discourse, indicating a clear cultural desire to prevent, restrain or curtail the circulation of fake news. Much of the time, this is driven by concerns over its impact on democratic and electoral practices, alongside anxieties regarding the broader function of truth claims and the credibility of persons, science and social facts.

A tacit aspect of the discourse of remedy is the competition between different practices, assumptions that place regulation or education above each other, mechanisms that rely either on intensive and large-scale human intervention or non-human artificial decision-making such as moderation bots to 'clean up' disinformation. While a distinction between pedagogical and regulatory approaches can be drawn, there has been little regard for the assessing and addressing the ways in which different remedies might be understood to compete, intersect, support or impede one another. Jennifer Lagarde and Darren Hudgins (2018) provide a very useful list of potential responses and solutions to fake news in their book *Fact vs. Fiction*. Acknowledging 2016 as a pivotal year in which fake news emerged as a key social and public issue, they rightly argue that there is no foolproof system of ensuring news credibility, since no news story can every fully encompass what is real or truthful. Their approach, instead, is to note the necessity of a combination of education (providing lesson plans for capabilities in evaluating credibility) and a recommendation that readers and viewers make good use of fact-checking tools such as snopes.com and other online resources. Inquiries by legislative bodies

Fake News in Digital Cultures: Technology, Populism and Digital Misinformation, 125–137
Copyright © 2022 by Rob Cover, Ashleigh Haw and Jay Daniel Thompson
Published under exclusive licence by Emerald Publishing Limited
doi:10.1108/978-1-80117-876-120221009

around the world, however, have taken a broadly different approach, focussing unsurprisingly on the capabilities of regulation and platform responsibility. For instance, the UK Parliament's House of Commons Digital, Culture, Media and Sport Committee (2019) published its inquiry into disinformation in 2019, which focussed on the polarising effect of fake news and its role in reinforcing extreme views and the democratic value of a plurality of information. While the committee found that digital literacy should be a fourth pillar of education alongside the more traditional reading, writing and mathematics, its *core* recommendations were that regulation of social media platforms through legal provisions, a compulsory code of ethics, platform liability for harmful content, and the establishment of an independent regulator should be the principal mechanisms to prevent the circulation of disinformation and misleading content.

What does it mean, however, to frame actions and solutions as 'remedies' to a problem that, as we have described it throughout this book, is grounded in cultural forms? Is there a risk that we perceive fake news in the same way we need to think about the concomitant COVID-19 – a virus that is alien to human life, the spread of which we try to stop through careful measures of distancing, control, tracing, eradication and ultimately vaccination? Can we vaccinate ourselves against fake news? Should we further develop remedial practices that treat the problem, such as fact-checking? Can we stop the spread of fake news by disrupting its communicative flow? Or might we catch it at the sources and prevent each burst of fake news' infection of the media and information ecology?

In this chapter, we address a number of the remedies that have been put forward as antidotes to fake news. In our concluding chapter, we will then discuss the significant need for any solution or intervention, particularly those of a regulatory nature, to be underpinned by what is presently absent in most remedial discourse: an ethical approach that ensures the remedy does not destroy or curtail the relational benefits and utility of the present media ecology. We are drawing on a selection of advancements and responses to fake news to demonstrate how they emerge through the social and cultural underpinnings that drive contemporary media discourses. We thereby discuss in turn (i) the rise of fact-checking organisations, (ii) the cultural practices of informal fact-checking, (iii) perceptions of the continuing role of journalists as arbiters of credibility, (iv) developments in legislation and regulation that seek to stem or criminalise fake news, (v) platform collaborations and self-regulation, and (vi) media literacy, digital literacy education and other pedagogies. At stake here is not assessing what will and will not work, but formulating an understanding as to how counter-practices contra fake news are driven by a culture of engagement with solution-seeking, albeit solutions that are yet to be assessed for their compatibility with one another and for the ethics that must underpin any intervention into emergent media and cultural practices.

The Rise of Fact-checking Organisations and Agencies

Professional fact-checking entails verifying the accuracy of public statements by assessing them against the available, factual information. A 2021 study in the United States describes the aims of online fact-checkers as: '(1) helping users come to an informed viewpoint and an accurate understanding of a claim; and (2) stopping the spread of false claims' (Park, Park, Kang, & Cha, 2021). While fact-checking does not aim to prevent the circulation of fake news, it is widely perceived as a mechanism that, on the one hand, prompts a social adjustment to media practices in order to cope with and thereby incorporate fake news into contemporary cultural practices with harm minimisation and, on the other hand, stems the spread and impact of false or misleading content.

Professional fact-checking activities take a number of forms. These include reviewing the content posted to social media platforms, and tagging inappropriate material appropriately. On Facebook, for example, posts can be tagged as False, Altered, Partly False or Missing Context, depending on its level of factual inaccuracy as determined through moderation (Facebook Journalism Project, 2021). Many professional fact-checking organisations have become widely known and publicly recognised, including as Black Dot Research (Singapore), Full Fact (UK), and Snopes (USA). The latter had its inception in 1994, and encourages members of the public to contact them with topics that they would like fact-checked. These topics, and the content presented as an evaluation of the facts, are published on the *Snopes* website. Topics are of a diverse range, including in 2021 fact-checked content on whether or not shoe manufacturer *Converse* had replaced its 'all star' logo with a Satanic symbol (the answer is no), whether athlete Oxana Chusovitina has truly competed in eight Olympic Games (the answer is yes), and whether US politician Marco Rubio mistook a reporter named Germán Dam for an actual location in Venezuela (the answer is mixed: Rubio admitted to a typo by failing to capitalise the surname). Arguably, these and similar fact-checks are valuable for journalists checking the veracity of a story or lead, and for everyday users interested in the truth of an outlandish claim encountered in a fake news piece.

More recently, the International Fact Checking Network (IFCN) was established in September 2015 by the Poynter Institute (a media-focussed organisation based in Florida, US) to promote 'best practices and exchanges' in the field of fact-checking (Poynter, 2021). The IFCN's initiatives include a Code of Principles that it has designed for fact-checkers, an annual fact-checking conference, as well as articles published on its website that examine different issues relating to fact-checking. There has also been the introduction of an informal 'fact-checking' holiday on 2 April each year (Tardáguila & Örsek, 2019). What this points to is not simply that there has been the introduction of fact-checking either by a number of well-funded organisations seeking to ensure the veracity of communication or those who have been able to monetise fact-checking as a service. Nor does it indicate the outsourcing of fact-checking responsibilities that were previously part of a media outlet's staff or responsibilities combined with writing and journalism. Rather, the rise of institutions governing fact-checking organisations indicates that fact-checking itself has become an industry, employing large numbers of people to undertake fact-checking as specialised work (Bell, 2019) with codes of practice that help ensure quality. As the work of fact-checkers within media outlets has diminished either due to downsizing of payroll or shifting journalist responsibilities, a sector within the media and communication industry rises – not merely in response to fake news but evidently pushed further as a result of the social and political concerns that fake news has established. In one respect, it is not necessarily the practice of fact-checking but the presence of a fact-checking industry that makes a difference for the broader cultural perception of news and content. There is evidence, for example, that suggests the public exposure to the concept of fact-checking may 'lower the perceived accuracy of, and agreement with, communicative untruthfulness' (Hameleers, 2020, p. 4).

Nonetheless, fact-checking has its limitations. For example, one study points out that 'a large portion of political talk involves unverifiable statements or opinions outside the realm of fact-checking' (Walter & Salovich, 2021, p.5). In that respect, the presence of a fact-checking industry that, for reasons of overwhelming work, fails to flag a statement made by a politician may be unwittingly interpreted by readers as evidence that the statement is factually sound, when that may not be the case. Fact-checking is also not an entirely neutral or objective process, as bias is never completely avoidable (Park, Park, Kang, & Cha, 2021) and often subject to partisan selectivity (Shin & Thorson, 2017, p. 234). Thus, while formal fact-checking is notable as a cultural response to fake news, an industry and a practice, it is not a magic bullet in the struggle against disinformation and misleading content.

Informal Fact-checking Practices Among Everyday Users

Alongside agencies dedicated to fact-checking has been the active fostering of informal, collaborative and crowd-sourced activity of developing and checking factual content. Wikipedia is a good example of the collaborative framework that draws on large numbers of users to ensure factual content and to provide a cultural remedy to fake news. While sometimes derided as a platform of misinformation on the basis that anyone can contribute to or edit it, the reality is that a combination of editorial processes and the scale of very large numbers of contributors operating through debate is effective in producing factual entries. Studies have suggested that while Wikipedia contains errors, like any encyclopaedia, the factuality of assessed entries are indistinguishable from any published or traditional encyclopaedia (Shachaf & Hara, 2010, p. 358). Although Wikipedia is sometimes considered to be too pedestrian a source, enough studies have indicated that like most encyclopaedias it is not intended to be the final authority on a topic but can provide enough at-a-glance basic facts that lead readers to more in-depth resources (Cohen & Olson, 2010, pp. 32–33). In that respect, it contributes to a public 'commons' of factual knowledge that is available to any person to use to undertake broadly reliable fact-checking.

From the production and content delivery side, there are many examples of content producers actively drawing on a wide readership to undertake fact-checking. One example is the site Factinate. While the site appears to draw a readership through sensationalist click-bait, targeted advertising on social media, it purports to serve as a general knowledge site providing lists of facts that can be searched and used by journalists and other content producers and readers more generally (Factinate, 2021a). For example, a Factinate advertisement appearing on social media in June 2021 encouraged viewers to click with the surprising phrase

'Is Queen Elizabeth really as cold-blooded as they say?'. This leads to a site with approximately 100 pages of text comprised of numbered paragraphs with facts about the British royal family. None answer the click-bait question, and most are written in inaccurate, sensationalist language such as 'brutal' reactions, 'shocking' interviews, 'disgusted' responses to family matters, and so on (Factinate, 2021b). Sources are cited, many being Wikipedia and other, less reliable sites such as tabloid publications. As a source, it cannot be broadly assessed as valuable or factual. However, what is indicative of the cultural emergence of fact-checking as a practice and an artefact is the self-acknowledgment that errors and omissions are possible by encouraging users to contact directly to correct factual mistakes:

> At Factinate, we're dedicated to getting things right. We want our readers to trust us. Our editors are instructed to fact check thoroughly, including finding at least three references for each fact. However, despite our best efforts, we sometimes miss the mark. When we do, we depend on our loyal, helpful readers to point out how we can do better. Please let us know if a fact we've published is inaccurate …. (Factinate, 2021a)

We draw attention to this example not to consider the utility of the site in countering fake news, but in the fact that even a site dedicated to monetising sensationalism participates in a discourse of seeking support from the multitude to (ostensibly) make information more factual.

In both of these examples, we see 'collective intelligence' at play. The concept of collective intelligence was developed to describe a global shift away from 'expert' systems that supported authoritative institutions, and a concurrent shift towards meaning-making that is produced by the multitude of everyday internet users through online exchange and debate. For Rheingold (2003), the figure of the 'smart mob' is the product of the empowerment of open flows across networked links, dependent on active participation and, ultimately, a shared ethos – in this case an ethos of factuality, preserving and sharing factual content, and a shared opposition to circulation of false, incomplete or misleading information.

Wikipedia's decentralised governance framework is, for example, understood to produce more thorough factual accounts that are made available to all people under a principle of commons resourcing (Forte, Larco, & Bruckman, 2009), and readers are understood to be motivated through a non-transactional approach to providing, editing or refuting knowledge claims for a greater good (Yang & Lei, 2010). Likewise, the problematic Factinate site exemplifies the appeal to collective intelligence to participate in the production and correction of fact, even though this advertising-heavy site takes advantage of that labour unlike Wikipedia. The idea of collective intelligence, then, has sponsored an approach to fact-checking and fact-provision in an informal way that operates alongside fake news and, in some cases, provides resources that help counter it. As an emergent cultural practice, it utilises a commons approach to solution-seeking that places responsibility for the media and information ecology on its users rather than on platforms, governments or others.

The Continuing Role of Journalism

We now turn to the continuing role of journalists in approaches to remedy fake news. While journalism has often been discussed as a fourth estate of formal government, it has simultaneously been coded as having a wider governance role in the context of pastoral care (care of democracy, care of the people). We discussed the increasing neoliberalisation of news media and the reconfiguration of the media audience as an individual consumer in Chapter Eight. Here, we would like to extend that criticism by pointing to some of the ways in which the spectre of pastoral care has been invoked in perceptions of journalism itself as a remedy to fake news.

Pastoral care is a residual cultural concept that frames governance and institutional actor as having an obligation to 'shepherd' a flock unable to protect themselves. Typically perceived as a Christian ministry motif of feeding, shielding and guiding the flock – both as spiritual metaphor and material need – it is a framework of relationality that shifted during the European mediaeval era from the institution of the church into contemporary bourgeois morality (Porter, 1996) and the disciplinary and biopolitical governance systems extending into the present era. Pastoral frameworks of governance focus on shaping the utility of the individual and the health of the population (Fassin, 2009) through a range of practices, attitudes, norms, manners of leadership and guidance, monitoring and manipulation (Lazzarato, 2011). As Foucault (2007) noted in his analysis of power formations, pastoral care is a deployment of power that is operationalised across multiple spheres of governance, communication and interpersonal relations in a way which simultaneously constrains and cares for people in everyday life. It normalises through the promotion of the self-regulation of subjects by making some discourses or ways of making sense of the world available, and making others unavailable – not for malevolent purposes but for what is perceived to be the care of the flock.

One strand in the discourse of remedying fake news is to discuss traditional journalism through the framework of pastoral care. For example, the eSafety Commissioner in Australia advises that while fake news circulates, if something is reported by multiple journalists, it is likely to be truthful and factual (eSafety Commissioner, 2021). This draws on the idea of journalism as playing a benevolent role in the pastoral care, in that they news practices have the intention of care for their readership, the people, democratic practices and so on. To utilise the concept of journalism as based in pastoral care is to ignore the neoliberalised practices of constructing a news readership as consumers rather than as an audience as we discussed in Chapter Eight, and the monetisation of sensationalism as we discussed in Chapter Four. In both cases, aspects of contemporary journalism are ordinarily treated as suspect. Once journalism is placed within the lens of a remedial discourse contra fake news, it re-interpreted and re-framed as a practice of pastoral care. We are, of course, in agreement with aspects of journalism and news routines as having pastoral elements for the good of a wider population and democratic processes, and most journalists working for credible outlets perceive their roles in this way. At the same time, however, pastoral power disguises its capacity to regulate, the motivations for that regulation and the insidiousness of the systems of administration and governance it often upholds. In this context, the idea that journalism presents a remedy to fake news is one which may effectively undo the critical and dissenting position that questions pastoralism and its power operations.

The effectiveness of traditional journalism to operate as an effective antidote to fake news is itself suspect, since there is ample evidence that adherents of misinformation are untrusting of traditional media institutions (Haw, 2021; Klein, Clutton, & Dunn, 2019). Here, again, a pastoral motif returns in which subjects are called upon to place greater trust in the figure of the journalist as 'pastor'. Scholars, practioners and policymakers have been advocating for more consideration of role of trust in efforts to address fake news. For example, a recent report from the Knight Commission on Trust, Media and Democracy (2019) advocated for news media organisations to adopt 'radical transparency' by disclosing 'the context for every facet of their operations, ranging from business infrastructure to editorial decision-making to community engagement' (p. 78). By offering this level of transparency, they argue that journalism professionals can begin to address some of the underlying causes of mistrust of media organisations, thereby restoring a pastoral role. While the future of journalism in its present forms is unknown and difficult to predict, we argue that the call for transparency in media production should also be read as a call for the critique of pastoral power and an opening up of ethical dialogue on how to cohabit the media ecology in ways that allow both factuality and a dissolution of uneven power roles.

The Regulatory Environment

Regulatory responses to disinformation have emerged in many international jurisdictions since the mid-2010s. These take two forms: legislation enacted by various parliaments and congresses around the world, and both legislative and administrative pressure on platforms to adopt mandatory practices of removal of disinformation. In both cases, these have developed in the context of broader investigations and inquiries into the role of major digital platforms, expectations on them to play a role in the quality of information flows and the protection of their users, their capacity to compete with traditional news and the impact on traditional news outlet's profits, and concerns around very high profit margins that, due to international reach, escape taxation in many jurisdictions. The various inquiries, legislative debates and statutory solutions have, therefore, provided a conceptual framework in which disinformation is tightly linked with social media, and in which solutions to disinformation are understood as warranting a censorious approach, albeit one conducted primarily by social media platforms themselves.

It is beyond the scope of this book to provide a systematic analysis of every piece of legislation enacted in relation to disinformation or the various inquiries hosted by legislatures in many jurisdictions across the world. Rather, we will refer to two examples of legislation to demonstrate the nuances in approach while retaining an underlying regimentation of discourse. Harking back to our discussion in Chapter Five on deepfake videos as a key form of disinformation produced in the complex setting of creative interactivity, we note here that the State of California sought in 2019 to make it illegal to circulate doctored video content, images and audio when they relate to a politician in the lead-up to an election (Paul, 2019). Importantly, the legislation notes that deepfake disinformation is only prohibited if there is 'actual malice' behind its production or distribution, and the law cannot apply to any content that discloses that it is not a true recording or depiction if it uses the statement 'This _____ [insert content name] has been manipulated' (California Legislative Information, 2019). In the context of the US political and social framing of free speech, the legislation actively protects perpetrators who may be producing false or misleading information without ill-intent, including of course for purposes of satire or humour. Here the focus is not on regulating content that is perceived to have the potential to mislead a public, but on the extent to which a perpetrator was driven to mislead for the purposes that are not in the public interest.

In Singapore, the Protection from Online Falsehoods and Manipulation Act was passed in 2019, criminalising the communication of false statements, particularly where they relate to security, health, public safety and electoral politics. The Act empowers the Singapore government to enforce corrections, to oblige social media platforms and websites to provide links to fact-checked statements, to censor social media content or websites, and to apply criminal charges and penalties to platforms that circulate falsehoods. Singapore's Prime Minister Lee Hsien Loong stated that the legislation is to be seen as a key part of the defence against fake news, alongside public education (Al Jazeera, 2019). Having been used successfully to force social media platforms to issue a correction to a false claim of a 'Singapore strain' of COVID-19 to all Singaporean users in May 2021, the legislation remains controversial by having not determined clearly how false claims will be identified and whether the burden of proof that content is false should fall upon the Singapore government or the content creator (Kurohi, 2020). In this context, the legislation is therefore to be considered regulatory and enabling the penalisation of social media as the responsible party to operate under government direction in specific instances, although its capacity to provide guidelines to determine what constitutes misinformation is less clear.

Arguably, a regulatory approach to fake news may provide greater issues for the democratic flow of information, a point we address in more detail in the final chapter. It should be noted here, however, that there is some early evidence that authoritarian regimes are well-positioned to take advantage of fake news laws to censor anti-government information is growing (The Economist, 2021), and this rests on a singular problem we addressed in Chapter Two – whether or not it is possible to adequate define a piece of content as fake news, and how to determine with certainty that content is misinformation. The grey area in which definitional concerns find themselves leaves regulation open to abuse. It also results in continued concerns that creative, satirical work, humour that relies on news models, and other content that is untrue and *may* be read as fake news without necessarily being harmful will be subject to censorship in ways which will reduce the democratic potential of all communication. While the Californian Act focuses on the intention of the perpetrator and the Singaporean act is concerned with correction and take-downs, both operate with a regimentary discourse of intervention to remove fake news that has already been produced, rather than a focus on its prevention or on intervening with perpetrators at the source.

Platform Collaborations

While much of the discourse on regulation is focussed on legislation that mandates platform intervention and moderation, another form regulation takes is the voluntary participation by social media platforms in policing and censoring misleading content. This has been encouraged in the Australian context. In February 2021, the Australian Commonwealth Government passed the News Media and Digital Platforms Mandatory Bargaining Code Act, which required major social media platforms to pay Australian news outlets for any content it makes available on the platforms (Parliament of Australia, 2021). The legislation regulating social media's operations in Australia was produced in the context of a three-year public debate and inquiry by the Australian Competition and Consumer Commission into social media. While not ordinarily under the purview of the ACCC, the inquiry included recommendations related to the perceived role of social media in the circulation of disinformation and misinformation. A key recommendation that garnered substantial public interest was the establishment of a voluntary code of conduct for the management of disinformation and news quality (Dearman & Pyburne, 2021). The combined pressure of the news bargaining legislation, the inquiry and public interest resulted in the development of the Australian Code of Practice on Disinformation and Misinformation that commits its signatories to deploying safeguards to protect Australians from the harms of online disinformation and misinformation by adopting scalable measures to reduce their spread and visibility. The code, written by the not-for-profit industry association DIGI, was adopted by Twitter, Google, Facebook, Microsoft, Redbubble, TikTok, Adobe and Apple (DIGI, 2021). By self-regulating, the platforms have indicated their interest in participating in the regulation of fake news through identification, removal, censorship and banning mechanisms.

While there has been some public concern expressed as to whether or not the public can rely on or trust social media platforms to self-manage disinformation (Braue, 2021), one of the benefits of the code is that it encourages a more transparent management of fake news handling, thereby avoiding accusations of unwarranted censorship. It also encourages the partnering between the code's signatories and researchers and fact-checkers in order to collaborate more effectively and efficiently. As with our points about the role of collective intelligence in our discussion above on informal fact-checking practices, the collaborative nature of the voluntary code does thereby rely on a wider network of participants, albeit institutional ones, to actively intervene in fake news. However, much like the compulsory regulatory frameworks found in legislation, it does not have the capacity to seek to do more than intervene in extant cases of disinformation and misinformation and to ban or remove persistent perpetrators. The reliance by some platforms on human moderators and others on artificial decision-making and machine learning is yet to reveal effectiveness in regulating fake news.

Finally, it should be noted that voluntary industry codes of self-censorship are not always able to keep up with developments in public, social and cultural attitudes and understandings. For example, the 1930 Motion Picture Production Code of the United States provided guidelines to the Hollywood film industry on what should and should not be censored. The code provided both general principles on maintaining moral standards and specific items that could not be depicted on film. Notably, the code proscribed the banning of representations of homosexuality as a 'sex perversion' and the depiction of miscegenation, that is, relationships between white persons and persons of colour (Miller, 1994). Only three decades after it came into use, however, public attitudes to many of the depictions forbidden by the code had changed, and it was abandoned in 1968 in favour of the now familiar contemporary ratings system (Gilbert, 2013). In many ways, what the MPAA experience demonstrates is the difficult in aligning voluntary censorship with public attitudes when the regulatory practice is codified. Whether we can expect public attitudes to misleading content to change, or shifts in how misinformation and disinformation are defined, that would make the code less useful or relevant is unknown in advance, although we might expect a hardening of public interest in responding more readily to fake news over time.

Digital Literacy and Media Pedagogies

Finally, we turn here to a brief discussion of current directions in digital literacy and media pedagogies to highlight the last of the core remedies to fake news circulating in public sphere discourse: education and future generations. Educational frameworks relating to fake news are often associated with the plethora of media literacy and digital literacy programmes set up within and outside education institutions globally. Calls for increased media literacy through providing training on the recognition of fake stories and misinformation in schools are increasingly seen as a valuable corrective to the current emergence of fake news (Keller, 2016), although it operates within an untried assumption that audiences are, on the whole, not fully capable of recognising fake news and disinformation, rather than acknowledging the multifaced frameworks through which fake news might be appealing to particular audiences.

The term 'digital literacy' is used to describe the awareness and ability of online media users to access, manage and evaluate digital resources, participating in both communication and creativity, and constructing social action through those engagements (Koltay, 2011). Digital literacy programmes that are designed to stem fake news are typically focussed on the development of skills to detect factually incorrect information encountered through online platforms (e.g., Nordic Policy Centre, 2021). This focus on online materials distinguishes digital literacy from media literacy, the latter of which can also encompass media use in offline settings. The use of educational and literacy practices as a presumed remedy to fake news is witnessed significantly in recent calls to expand media and digital literacy education addressing the issue of fake news to disciplines beyond media and communication, arguably because fake news has become so ubiquitous that its conceptualisation, effects and consequences should be taught across all school and university subjects in order to increase understanding of the frameworks by which contemporary communication operates (Freberg & Kim, 2018; Mutsvairo & Bebawi, 2019).

Problematically, the concepts of media and digital literacy and educational programmes presume a flaw at the heart of the average audience member, positioned to be tricked into believing false information. The purveyor of fake news hoaxes, Paul Horner, noted that not only does fake news have a monetary value in the production of click-baited earnings from those who follow the links to determine the 'truth' of a story or confirm a particular kind of 'truth', fake news *works* precisely because in his view there is an audience available to be duped (Dewey, 2016). We disagree, of course, that audiences are inherently open to being duped by what they read. Throughout this book, we have addressed some of the different ways in which audiences of fake news can be understood, including the persuasive knowledge that audiences are broadly intelligent, discerning and actively engaged with content, meaning-making and analysis. It is therefore important to reiterate here that any claim that fake news is 'tricking' large numbers of members of the public into believing what is communicated only replicates outdated, pedestrian 'media effects' models that assume media content itself universally shapes behaviours, attitudes, voting patterns and viewpoints across an inherently passive audience. Dating back to the 1930s, such approaches as the propaganda or hypodermic models of communication suggest for the greater part that the audience is not interactive with the text, does not actively interpret, analyse or create meanings around the text, and seeks no form of creative participation or redistribution of the text (Turner, 1993, pp. 206–208). Cultural studies approaches have argued for nearly half a century that audiences are empowered and active in the interpretation of meaning and the assessment of content (Bennett, 1983; Fiske, 1989; Hall, 1993; Morley, 1980; Radway, 1988). Audience members and audience communities use tactics to resist the intended outcomes of a text (de Certeau, 1984), suggesting that audiences are, on the whole, well-positioned to resist the intention of fake news to 'dupe' audiences.

Arguably, however, contemporary audiences are marked by the active cultivation of ignorance. By this, we don't mean a lack of knowledge or information for which individuals should be made responsible or shamed, but a culturally produced disposition that is conditioned by education systems (Gilson, 2011). These exist within neoliberal frameworks of transactional exchange and engagement within the instantaneity of a matrix of information that produces information overload (Papacharissi, 2015, p. 44). These factors point to the need not for a literacy that teaches better citizenship and recognition, but for a cultural pedagogy to educate the public on fake news the myriad forms it takes, how to detect it and avoid spreading.

While media, digital literacy and pedagogical approaches represent important mechanisms for aiding in the recognition of fake news, disinformation and misleading content (Friesem, 2019), we argue that the combined force of institutional and cultural pedagogies that seek to address fake news must focus on practical abilities *and* reflexive competencies, thereby fostering greater understanding of the contemporary setting of media and cultural production, digital networks and the means by which content becomes trusted. This involves asking more questions than can be answered, and opening the space for developing answers rather than presenting those proscriptions. Some of these questions include: what are the conditions for assessing the extent to which journalistic media produced 'factual news', what constitutes an ethically grounded rate of fact-checking within contemporary news routines, how do we address the use of 'fake news' as an accusation by politicians to disavow the role of quality, fact-checked news writers in public sphere debate, and in what ways can we utilise the public reviews of fake news to ensure the future of quality, ethical journalism?

Conclusion

In seeking, developing and assessing remedies and prevention tactics to curtail the circulation of fake news, one of the key issues that needs to be borne in mind is that by necessity, these supposed 'remedies' emerge from within the same cultural, discursive and conceptual frameworks as fake news itself. One of the perennial problems with attempts to regulate the flow of content or to use technological solutions to prevent it is that such mechanisms operate in a push-and-pull relationship between regulators and users. This push-and-pull struggle was seen from the 2000s with early (push) attempts to lock digital content from being shared or manipulated, for example, in Macromedia flash files, resulting in the (pushback) development and widespread circulation of programmes that would unlock those files. This is a struggle that operates in exactly the same way as digital rights management applications and the immediate hacking of those applications by users seeking to gain control over the protected content (Cover, 2006).

Users with enough intent will always develop and share ways to overcome regulation over content, its integrity and its distribution. In 2021, we have found that attempts by Facebook to use moderator bots to uncover and prevent disinformation spread by anti-vaccination lobbyists were circumvented in an unsophisticated but effective way: key terms were removed from the content and replaced with the inoccuous and euphemistic code words such as 'dinner party' that became recognisable to the target audiences but undetectable as disinformation by the bots – indeed, future-proofed as Facebook could not reasonably censor all instances of dialogue that refer to dinner parties (Collins & Zadrony, 2021). What this indicates is that across the multiple remedies and prevention practices at play, regulation might be meaningful in providing an indication of a government, administration or platform's policy and intent to curtail fake news, but such regulatory forms have a long history of being circumvented by users. Perhaps new developments in artificial decision-making and machine learning will enable intervention that can mimic the labour-intensive work of in-person moderation into the future, but such developments have not yet stemmed the intentional sharing of disinformation and other misleading content.

That, then, leaves us with the framework of the increasing use of fact-checking practices – both formal and informal as described above – underpinned by a wider media and digital literacy. Together, both are longer-term endeavours, reliant on training up a future generation on global scale to acquire, refine and sustain the skills in detecting non-credible content, in taking the time to fact-check personally, and in taking care not to share content that is non-credible. Whether that can be achieved at scale to take advantage of the collective intelligence models we describe above is, of course, yet to be seen. This may indicate that while regulation is not a magic bullet, it may need to be a part of the picture of remedy-seeking in the shorter term. This is why we turn, in the next chapter, to developing ways of perceiving the field of fake news and remedy-seeking through an ethical framework, whereby new, global, culturally embedded and socially mandated ethical practices that see fake news as a form of violence against humanity itself, and thereby underscore our communication activities.

Chapter Ten

Ethical Practices, Digital Citizenship and Communication Futures

Introduction

One of the key arguments we have been making in this book is that fake news, disinformation and misleading content are not social anomalies that can be eradicated, technological irregularities that can be remedied with automated surveillance and censorship, nor alien practices that are the work of a few bad actors with ill-intent. Rather, we have argued that fake news is constituted in contemporary culture, the product and outcome of the convergence of emergent social and cultural factors including the rise of interactivity and user-generated content production, the dissolution of the authority of former gate-keeping and agenda-setting institutions, the polysemic approach to truth and meaning that comes with living in a postmodern culture, and the embedding of sensationalist and conspiratorial discourses in the media and information ecology. Fake news is, as we have shown, also related to the development of new applications such as the deepfake, new and re-figured practices of marginalisation within populist social and political settings, and the reduction of trust in media discourses and institutions. In short, fake news is a key element at the very core of contemporary communication, one that cannot simply be outlawed or curtailed without changing or refiguring how media and communication operate in contemporary everyday life.

As we discussed in Chapter Nine, there are a number of attempted responses, remedies and fixes across policy, technology, pedagogy and journalistic practices. In most cases, however, these are quick fixes to enable the continuation of meaningful communication, news-sharing and all the institutional, governance and social processes that depend on them. Separately, they are not well-positioned to address the underlying cultural conditions that construct and enable fake news and disinformation. Nor can they help us apprehend fake news through refiguring social and communication processes towards a more workable, trustworthy future communication ecology. While it is hopeful that, working together, some of these may help to change the underlying cultural and conceptual practices, what is really needed is a powerful force that generates a groundswell of concern about disinformation and misinformation without dismantling the positive aspects of cultural forms of digital interactivity and postmodern polysemy, both

Fake News in Digital Cultures: Technology, Populism and Digital Misinformation, 139–152
Copyright © 2022 by Rob Cover, Ashleigh Haw and Jay Daniel Thompson
Published under exclusive licence by Emerald Publishing Limited
doi:10.1108/978-1-80117-876-120221010

of which are central to emerging social relations, new democratic practices and popular frameworks of critique. This means we need to consider an *ethical* rather than a *regulatory* means of responding to fake news, including in ways which do not simply replace one form of violence (i.e., fake news) with another (e.g., extensive regulation, regimentation, censorship or increasing the inequitable access to the means of communication).

In this conclusive chapter, we would like to address some of the ways in which social ethics underpin the drive towards an obligation for everyone to participate in more ethical communication which we frame as active participation in behaviours and deeds that seek to minimise what we consider to be the *pollution* of a media and information ecology by fake news, disinformation and misleading content. This can be perceived as a call for all who are involved in communication: whether media professional, creative practitioner or engaged reader, whether the purveyors of fake news or those unthinkingly circulating misinformation. In other words, there is an obligation that is upon everyone from the very start of communication and that underpins the responsibility to communicate in ways that minimise harm and violence to others, whether that is the violence of misrepresentation, the harms to democratic practices and institutions, or the injury to the institutions – however problematic – that govern social relations. We will begin with some notes on why regulatory forms such as censorship, legal and policy interventions ought to be seen as undesirable, albeit sometimes practical, responses to fake news when they operate without an underlying ethical framework. We follow this with a discussion on how fake news can be perceived as acts of violence towards persons, groups and an ideal of democracy and, drawing on Butler and Levinas' arguments on ethics, why we are obliged as social and communicative subjects to engage in the information and media ecology in ways which minimise violence to others – that is, by neither deliberately nor unwittingly sharing disinformation and misleading content. Finally, we address two aspects that must come into play if an ethical approach to fake news can be honed into an applied socio-cultural practice: the restoration of the pastoral care framework of journalism, and the adaptation of digital citizenship concepts into ones of digital cohabitation in order to produce a view of the audience or readership not only as an active or interactive one, but as a critical one.

This conclusion is not meant as proscriptive or an imperative – rather, it provides a few ways in which one might move forward through more cultural and critical thinking towards responding to fake news. Ultimately, it will be up to practitioners, journalists, communicators and everyday persons to utilise the best parts of democratic engagement to build a future world – Including a world of communication and a world that situates critical communication as the core activity of what makes human civilisation itself.

Beyond Regulation

As an issue, a practice, a suspicion and a mode of readership, fake news emerges from within cultural formations, and cannot be blamed on individual actors, technologies or practices *as if* it is something that can easily be removed or eradicated.

Given the embeddedness to contemporary culture of interactive and co-creative technologies and postmodern practices of pastiche, bricolage and hyperreality, fake news is much less a 'parasite' on contemporary communication and much more a phenomenon that is in a symbiotic relationship with culture. This means that eradication through regulatory practices that restrict communication is a potential violence to culture itself. For example, we could develop strict regulatory regimes in every jurisdiction around the world that outlaw the deliberate dressing up of false content – such as material that would be judged by a 'reasonable person' person as untruthful – as if it were real or recognised news, visual footage or other material purporting to be the 'truth'. We could extend that by criminalising the act of knowingly sharing that material – effectively 'making outlaws' of those who misinform others. The cultural damage, however, is potentially greater. On the one hand, there is perhaps value to sustainable relationality in marking fake news as injurious speech that must be stopped, censored or cut off, because it certainly does do injury to, say, a person misrepresented in a deepfake depicted as speaking words or performing acts they neither did nor would do. On the other hand, however, by installing a censorship regime – a regulatory framework which is almost certainly impossible to conduct – one not only restricts speech that has been determined to be offensive, but actively *produces* certain ways of speaking (Butler, 1997b, pp. 128–129). Censorship in this sense becomes a constraining condition on the future development of speech, content, communication, communicative practices and creativity. And that may preclude a more ethical way of communicating that emerges from the freedom to tell stories in particular ways.

This is aside from the more problematic issue of attempting to utilise a 'reasonable person' argument as a means of determining not what is fake and what is not (fact-checking agencies and other practices outlined in the previous chapter can do this), but *how* much fakeness is allowable and the extent of fakeness permissible before something is regulated. Any regulatory regime demands a juridical framework for assessing how much of a breach of a 'truthful' depiction is at stake. Will a convincing parody of Shirley Bassey recorded by a drag performer and circulating on YouTube be deemed fake news, because it was at risk of being misread as the 'real' Bassey? Will a deepfake of Tom Cruise be deemed defamatory if it can be read as an obvious satire? Who will help us judge the extensiveness of disinformation in a text that might be read in one way by some and in an alternative way by others? There has not yet been a practical mechanism for such judgements that is genuinely workable, including reliance on older liberal-humanist 'reasonable person' arguments that have underpinned much censorship legislation in Anglophone settings. In this context, regulation of injurious content through judgements that determine what should and should not be identified as disinformation is contrary to embedding ethical digital culture moving forward.

In contending that regulation is not a singular solution or 'magic bullet', we are not suggesting that we do not hold to account those who engage in the production and dissemination of disinformation, misinformation and false or misleading content, nor that the institutional frameworks of legislation, policy and rational determination are unworkable. Indeed, we are arguing that there are very strong reasons why we need to bolster many of the extant mechanisms that discourage users from seeking to advantage from disinformation, and that prompt other users to take greater care of the veracity of the content they share. Practices of penalisation and punishment are not necessarily to be fully excluded. However, in any approaches to regulation and institutional practices that seek to curtail or remedy fake news, we need to ensure that these are underpinned by an ethical framework that takes into account four things: the *contingency* of rational and liberal-humanist institutional frameworks, the need to remove practices that *prejudgment* of the perpetration of misinformation along ideological or identity grounds, the *embedding* of care for the wellbeing of all users as the grounding for any action, and the *fostering* of care for the media ecology in ways that encourage all participants to be active in preventing and removing the toxicity of disinformation. In keeping these ethical perspectives in mind, we are able to shift focus away from restriction, regulation, regimentation and censorship as the 'go to' mechanisms of remedy, and towards approaching ethical relationships that foster a cultural literacy that make the deliberate use of disinformation and fakery unthinkable (and do so without sacrificing creativity, parody, satire, entertainment and pleasure).

If the sustainability of the communication ecology as one of care, pleasure, mutual understanding and productive discourse is placed at the centre of any approach to apprehending disinformation and fake news, then the question of sustaining trust in that ecology is at the very core of what needs to be secured. But the securing of the ecology must be thought through in tenuous, careful terms. Security is often the response to fear and anxiety (Caluya, 2007), and certainly fake news has created widespread global anxiety. The cultural anxieties provoked by the emergence of fake news are, indeed, important and genuine because they encourage us to collectively question the capacity of the public sphere to provide knowledge, information, discourses, ways of speaking and meaningful debate that offer distinctive, sensible and workable approaches to entertainment, engagement, identity, belonging, electoral politics, state responsibility, financial equity and so on.

At the same time, however, when such anxieties are constructed around the furthering of security rather than fostering ethical engagement with one another, we see yet another mode of regulation and regimentation that may in itself be a violence. For Maurizio Lazzarato (2011, p. 57), the role of communication within assumptions of trust actively fosters a socio-cultural sense 'universal distrust' as its conceptual corollary. That is, in a setting in which we call upon communication actors, readers, professionals and everyday users to feel trust, we are effectively constructing and inviting distrust. Such distrust of communication content has, of course, been a key factor in public and scholarly feelings about the known bias inherent in corporate journalism, the distortions that emerge as a result of journalistic buddy-relationships with parliamentarians and public figures, and the concerns and questions that arise over the extent to which contemporary journalism can operate as a public resource for the fact-checking of utterances by those whom we may also not trust. Distrust of either recognised journalism or, more rightly today, fake news is not necessarily a justification for a securitisation of communication which, through regimentary practices, will only engender further distrust.

The compulsion to be distrusting enough to discern reality from fakery, and distinguish between misinformation and news, and the cultural anxieties currently being expressed over the quality of communication are not, then, arguments for increased regulation, securitisation or institutionalisation of communication regimes. What that distrust calls for is precisely what Lazzarato articulates as being at the core of questions of trust: not for the arrest of producers of fake news, nor mechanisms for better determining the distinction between news and fakery, nor indeed frameworks for a renewed media literacy. Rather, it calls for critical engagement with the broad cultural frameworks that enable fake news if trust is to be an aspect of the future of communication. And that very distrust and the demand for more trust obliges us towards a more ethical way of perceiving communication which, as we outline below, involves understanding communication as the core activity of all social engagement, sociality and relationality. Communication thus underpins the very sense of selfhood, identity and being. That, alone, demands an ethical rather than a regimentary response to what has become the biggest challenge to communication in the current era.

Fake News' Violence

An ethical perspective calls upon us to understand fake news, disinformation and misleading content as violent acts. In doing so, we can invoke an underlying responsiveness based in an ethical obligation not to do violence to others. By arguing that fake news disrupts a clean, benign and pastoral communicative flow of discourse, and that it complicates an ordinary subject's reliance on trust, relationality and dialogue for stable subjectivity, liveability and social participation, any act which makes or exploits vulnerabilities in either of those processes by deliberately or unwittingly circulating misleading information is unethical and poses the risk of violence towards others. By drawing on Judith Butler's (2004, 2009b) work on precarity, subjectivity and ethics, we are interested here in putting forward some of the ways in which we can perceive a cultural, ethical and social obligation not to disrupt precarious communication ecologies by polluting them with fake rudimentary news, disinformation and misinformation. This can help move us from a responsiveness based in anxiety, regulation or securitisation and towards one grounded in developing modes of thinking about the broad array of players in communication in ways which are non-violent.

To determine something as violent is not, of course, simple. As Judith Butler (2020) has shown, violence is a labile term, subject to persistent disputes over whether both physical and linguistic attacks can be considered violent, and with the common practice of states and institutions labelling non-violent dissent as acts of violence (pp. 1–2). The concept and application of violence are always figured 'within a field of discursive, social, and state power', which includes naming practices that are neither clear nor always used in ethical ways (pp. 5–6). As Butler (2009b) has demonstrated, any attempt to limit a concept of violence either to the physical blow or to structural violence of oppression conducted by the state risks failing to account for the kinds of violence that are 'linguistic, emotional, institution, and economic – those that undermine and expose life to harm or death, but do not take the literal form of a blow' (p. 137). We can expand this point to include acts that *may* be framed as violent the broad activities, engagements, structures and practices that not only expose individual subjects to harm, including the harm of bewilderment caused by disinformation, but also the impact such activities have on the social and political life of a body-politic, a population, a cluster, an audience and a humanity. This is to understand the continuation of the social and political relations of a group or population – who inevitably rely on a discernible quality of communication, information, knowledge and participation – as a matter of grievability, such that to harm that continuity is to perform or participate in an act of violence (pp. 24–25).

We are thinking here about understanding both deliberate and involuntary linguistic and communicative harms that put at risk the smooth functioning of social participation as a normative form of liveability as acts of violence, no matter whether that social participation occurs in online communication (including the act of reading newspapers, face-to-face communication, creating content, producing or editing videos and so on). These activities all involve social participation and all oblige, as we shall show, participation that is ethical and that calls upon us to engage without violence. Without foreclosing on the polysemy and future meanings of violence, then, to engage in communication in a violent way might include acts that deliberately mislead a reader into believing something that is verifiably untrue, acts of lying, acts of negligence such as sharing non-credible information to those who may believe it, and acts which fail to protect the wider sustainability of trust in, and reliability of, a media and digital communication framework.

How can we then say that fake news is violent? Without reiterating the arguments about the impact of fake news we have already covered in this book, we can state very briefly here that the deliberate or unwitting circulation of disinformation, misinformation and misleading content performs violent acts in at least three different ways. Firstly, fake news and disinformation performs an act of violence to their targets, usually in terms of deliberate or non-deliberate reputational damage and misrepresentation of acts, statements and views. For the most part, we have seen this applied both deliberately and unwittingly to politicians and to other public figures like Meghan, the Duchess of Sussex. Here, beliefs, actions, standpoints, experiences or attitudes are distorted or wholly fabricated.

Similarly, those whose faces and physical features are blended through deepfakes into believable and reputation-damaging pornography are not only misrepresented but potentially damaged permanently when careers are abruptly ended and the creative work they have engaged in is discredited in unwarranted ways. We can understand this as violent from a Kantian perspective: Immanuel Kant's philosophic framework for the respect of human subjects, originally foregrounded in the late eighteenth century, prescribes that we distinguish between people and objects. By interfering with the rational choices a person may make to control their image, reputation and veracity of their words is to treat that person as a 'thing' and not as a human subject (Kant, 1959, pp. 46–47). In deliberately misrepresenting an issue (in the form of disinformation) or carelessly circulating misinformation (by posting or sharing false content without adequately checking and verifying), one disrupts the dignity and agency of a human subject, institution or organisation of people, and treats them as an object by distorting their reputation or experience. While agency, of course, is a problematic and sometimes ungraspable concept, and it is not fully clear whether subjects who are grounded in communication methods and languages that precede them can fully have or experience agency, it remains the case that by denying a subject's sense of agency to control information about themselves is not only to breach certain liberal-humanist ideals of freedom but to perform a violence towards their dignity and self-efficacy. When a subject becomes available to be distorted for content, they are re-figured not as a subject who is vulnerable to being wounded by that content, but as a means or mechanism to achieve another end. That is an unethical violence.

We might also argue that such disinformation curtails the agency of other actors in communication processes. For example, those whose role in an act of communication is based in information-seeking have their agency stemmed when the toxicity and conflict in the media ecology makes it difficult to find, critically engage with and utilise information adequately. This is perhaps most clearly seen today in the context of the COVID-19 pandemic and the capacity to make informed, clear decisions about vaccination amidst so much contamination of the media ecology and health communication practices by anti-vaccination disinformation that discredits genuine, peer-reviewed research by unrecognised means. The phrase 'do your own research' began as a motif encouraging patients to take agency over their bodies by knowledge empowerment in order better to participate in health and medical shared decision-making (Kata, 2012), conforming to the idea that critical agency is grounded in knowledge and informed participation in decisions that affect the body. The phrase became a powerful mechanism by which to encourage stronger engagement with institutions such as medicine and health that have historically restricted participation by making monolithic the figure of the expert medical professional. However, the phrase was co-opted by the anti-vaccination lobby and immunisation deniers as weasel words, an anti-institutional meme and as a mechanism to encourage unwitting users not to spend time critically unpacking complex medico-biological information, but to be directed instead to specific sites which rely on pseudo-scientific language to make false claims, and often to monetise those claims (Vagg, 2017). Here, the imperative 'do your own research' as a means of discrediting credible research in favour of disinformation is an act of violence that disrupts the possibilities for its targets to make *genuinely* informed decisions about their bodies, health and wellbeing.

By suggesting that one engage in their 'own research' not only directs readers and viewers to non-credible health information, but pollutes the framework through which knowledge is gained critically by refiguring the meaning of research as uncritically 'looking things up' online and encouraging users to engage with information that affirms a pre-existing belief or attitude as fact. This is not to condemn those who do so, since the skills for research, verification, analysis and critical thinking are not democratically distributed among all users – a separate but urgent issue. Rather, we claim that anyone who pollutes the ecology with dangerous health disinformation, knowing that it will be taken by people as research who will then make *uninformed* decisions about their health, is inhibiting the agency of other people and perpetrating violence to their bodies *and* their capacity to engage in essential knowledge frameworks themselves.

Secondly, fake news does violence to the workings of democratic practices, including institutions, trust, electoral processes and the capacity to make a decision. We have discussed this aspect at length throughout this book, and there is nothing today that is controversial in arguing that disinformation and misinformation have the capacity to distort views, attitudes and ways of thinking, rendering it difficult to uphold either the reality or the myth of liberal-humanist democracy. We might add, however, that one aspect of the ethical concern here is that, again, disinformation and misinformation treat not only the subject of the fake news content but the intended audience as, in the Kantian sense, an object rather than a human subject of agency. Here, by duping (or unwittingly participating in the duping of) an audience, group, electorate, fan-base or other formation of community or citizenry into decisions or actions that would otherwise not be taken if an objectively perceived *normative* flow of factual information had been in place, the purveyors and unwitting circulators of fake news perpetrate violence against the decision-making capacities and agency of that group. The Brexit case, which we discussed in Chapter Eight, is a good example as to how confusing, misleading, non-factual, exaggerated and an otherwise problematic information ecology contributed to actions (voting) in ways that might not have happened had there been in place what we recognise as the more staid, normative factual flows of the past. The difficulty, of course, is who decides what is a normative factual information ecology, what it should look like, the limits on its meaning-making functions, and whether the imposition of mediasphere shaped and imaged by the decidability of a few is, in itself, a further kind of violence or regimentation.

Thirdly, there is the violence towards an ideal of democracy and democratic flows of communication itself. Both are ideals that are never realised since they are marked by the constraints of late-twentieth century liberal-humanism and neoliberalism, and acts of violence such as exclusion, imprisonment, marginalisation, dehumanisation and inequalities are insidiously perpetrated in the name of those ideals (Shinko, 2010, p. 725). Several strands of democratic thinking imagine a free-flowing communicative space in which participation is equitable, and in which both truth and the appreciation of a democratic ideal are imagined to underpin all utterances (Habermas, 1989). This principle has usually – and rightly – governed the rejection or critique of agenda-setting institutions and editorial practices (McCoy, 1993, p. 146; Philo, 1995, p. 176), and prompted the celebration of early interactivity, digital participation and user-generated content production as a more democratic framework for communication (Cover, 2004b) or, indeed, a disruptive one that was the hope for ushering in an unforeseen democracy of postmodernised communication. However, in the context of the cultural framework in which we find the simultaneous dissolution of institutional practices of truth and trust and the many ill-effects fake news and disinformation, permitting the free-flowing slippage of meaning and its impact on even gestures towards democratic ideals is also an act of violence.

Responding in Ethics to Fake News

If we begin by recognising that fake news, disinformation and misleading content are active in the production of violence perpetrated upon people, societies, institutions, ideals and justice, then in what ways can we perceive an ethics that obliges us to prevent the spread of fake news? Butler (2004) has put forward the case for an ethics of non-violence that is useful for weighing up the competing obligations for working against practices that perform or enact violence. Drawing on her work on vulnerability, and her readings of Emmanuel Levinas' approach to ethics based in obligatory responsiveness to 'the other', we can begin by recognising that those people, societies, institutions, ideals and the concept of justice are all vulnerable, precarious and thereby call upon us to engage with them in an obligatory mode of non-violence.

This is not, of course, to be read as an obligation to let any institution, person or practice persist without critique. Rather, it is to recognise that despite all the reasonable and ethical misgivings about certain older institutions, including those that regulate others and those that have historically perpetrated violence, they may well provide the remedies against fake news in such a way that is not unjust or creates inequities, *but only if* underpinned by an ethical framework. For Butler (2009b), looking to the core institutions of the nation-state as the solution to any form of violence and to rely on the nation-state for protection from violence through regimentation and regulatory ideals is very often to 'exchange one potential violence for another', even though this may be one of the few available choices in a specific, temporal and temporary context (p. 26).

Butler's approach thus provides some useful ways by which to address the ethical quandary at the core of how to address fake news without instilling a sovereign system of censorship, regulation and refusal. By drawing on her account of Levinasian ethics, we can perceive our obligation here not as something we pass on to existing regulatory institutions to handle on our behalf, nor as an appeal to older and often exclusionary concepts of a social contract to act with regimentary unity towards the ends of a nation-state. Rather, the obligation of practicing non-violence needs to be recognised as the underlying framework by which we come into subjectivity in the first place, preceding any communication or encounter with others and thereby the governing condition by which any communication takes place. In the case of our work on fake news, we might say that we are not obliged towards non-violence just because we are subjects who would like to communicate in a non-polluted media and information ecology, but because our very subjectivity itself *depends wholly on non-violent communication for survival*.

For Levinas (1969), we are obliged to respond without violence to the call of the other (the subject that is not ourself) by recognising that subject as worthy of non-violence. In doing so, the language of hospitality, recognition and non-violence is an act of 'calling into question of the I' (p. 171). That is, because our individual subjectivity is from the very beginning linguistically constituted by what it is not – the other – it exists *for* the other and is thus obligated towards the other (p. 261). Prior to communicating (sharing material online, creating deliberately misleading content or sharing information without checking its credibility and veracity first) we recognise that, as communicators, we are constituted by the otherness of the other with whom we communicate. In the communicative encounter with the other (which may be in real-time or occur in an unknowable future through the persistence of our utterances online), it is pre-conditioned through an obligation to thereby communicate without violence, including the three forms of violence we described above.

In the Levinasian and Butlerian ethical position, the act of recognising our shared vulnerability as corporeal and communicating creatures operates at the core of social connection. In recognising that the other may be vulnerable to the communication we perform, the needs of the other are figured as our own spiritual and ethical needs – one is obliged by virtue of being a subject 'to apprehend the Other's material needs and put those needs first' (Butler, 2006, p. 127). We are thus obliged to put the needs of the quality, credibility, veracity, form and potential meanings of our acts of communication in mind by recognising the vulnerability of those we may never meet and never know as others who may experience the impact of our communication, and thereby to ensure that communication occurs without violence. Such an ethics of non-violence, then, can be formed through an understanding that all humans are vulnerable in our exposure to language and to the encounter with one another, which arguably includes the non-physical encounter in forms of real-time and asynchronous communication. The other is vulnerable to the wounding of our words, and we are thereby obliged to do what we can to minimise that wounding, even if we cannot control the meaning, effect or reception of those words of communiques in advance. Through perceiving the commonality of vulnerability for ourselves and for the other whom we encounter, following Levinas, we are compelled to engage in relationality through responsibility and responsiveness to one another.

What Butler articulates is a means by which the human subject is conceived as being predicated on a primary vulnerability through dependence upon others – because from the very start we are corporeal, embodied creatures who cannot survive without that dependence on others, that participation in social engagement. This means, then, that our entire selfhood and identity is built on social relationality, not individuality. Re-reading Levinas, she proposes an ethical position through the notion that one has a *responsibility* to others that emerges in an act of *encounter* and *recognition* of the other, meaning a need to see past the ordinary frames of engagement – such as communicative norms and emergent practices – so that we can see the other as woundable (Butler, 2009b, p. 163). This ethics is not, for either Levinas or Butler, a simple injunction to *behave* in a particular way, but a requirement to engage in practices of deciding without pre-judging how those decisions will actually end (Butler, 2007, p. 187). In other words, an ethical approach does not resolve the ethical problem it raises, but opens the *possibility* for subjects to recognise the vulnerability of others through understanding it in terms of their own vulnerability and thereby initiating a struggle one must undertake with one's own violence (p. 181). It is therefore, as Angela McRobbie (2006) puts it, a discourse capable of 'intervening to challenge, interrupt and minimize aggressive retaliation' (p. 82), which we take to mean here a non-aggressive engagement in the information and media ecology that calls upon ourselves to reflect on our own violence in the encounter, whether our communication will be 'received' now or later.

Although this philosophic framework for sustaining a media and information ecology that is unpolluted and thereby non-violent is a complex one that operates as a goal and an ideal rather than a practical framework, it is not without a pragmatism that can form the basis of our literacy on communication, social participation and belonging. We are obliged not to create or share fake news because, as human subjects, we all share a primary vulnerability from the very beginning. This means that before we are even subjects, we are dependent not just on social care and participation, but on a communication, information and media ecology that permits us to be subjects in ways that call upon us not to be 'things' in the Kantian sense but to gain the full dignity and agency of subjectivity (Fukuyama, 2019, p. 51).

While our communication always risks violence, because we cannot ever know in advance how our texts and utterances' meanings will be activated or interpreted, we nevertheless are obliged to non-violent communication due to the shared constitution of ourselves in that media ecology to participate in it in a way which minimises the potential violence of our communication, whether that is a real-time encounter or asynchronous communication, or a communique that has been circulated to others unforeseen and never intended. We are, therefore, obliged from the beginning not to do violence to others that any act of deliberate creating disinformation would bring. And we are obliged not to do the violence to others that any careless circulation of misleading content might produce – that is, participate in misinformation, even unwittingly or circulate without care or concern about the veracity of the source or the credibility of information. Furthermore, in an ecology marked by the reach and permanency of what we post, we are obliged from the beginning to ensure non-violence towards others whom we will never meet and may not yet exist. This means doing everything in our power as individuals, as collectives, as members of platform spaces, as communities of readers, as institutions, as professionals and as both the creators and the outcome of communication itself, to ensure that our shared sociality and shared media and information ecology is not polluted by fake news.

To put this into pragmatic terms, the ethical commitment rests with the digital culture that is the lived everyday comprised of *all* users. That is, it would be a mistake to understand the obligation as an individual one or as a framework we can individually shirk off to elected officials, regulatory bodies, government institutions or platform hosts to manage on our behalf. Rather, this is an obligation that comes into play because we are social subjects and have no choice but to communicate. Ethics is not always something that can be applied practically without setting rules, and any epistemic system of rules risks undoing the democratic contingency on which all ethics must be based. In a very practical sense, however, we might consider one example as to how to be an ethical communicator in an everyday sense: sharing any post or any information calls upon us not to share content that purports to be factual without having been fact-checked, just to reinforce our egos that depend on the domination of our beliefs or that depend on winning an argument at the cost of veracity. The ethical obligation is instead to check the veracity and credibility of the information and its source. That does not demand that we must decide not to use it if it does not meet a particular, objectively given standard. Rather, what it obliges is that our communication of that content, or sharing and re-posting of that information, is done in such a way that we make clear to present and future readers – or intended and unintended targets – that it is not necessarily fact-checked and should be read critically rather than trustingly. This is where our obligation to increase the quality and experience of trust comes into play: by actively and always participating in the labour of determining the trustworthiness of a source and encouraging in each and every communication the pedagogical learning of new ways to determine trustworthiness so that our communicative acts can be trusted, just and ethical.

Conclusion

In this final section, we would like to make a few conclusive remarks about how and why an ethical approach to remedying fake news and to conceiving digital futures warrants thinking outside the normative frameworks of regulation and instead, underpinning any remedy with the ethics of non-violence described above. To put this into the context, then, of cohabitation in digital spaces, we argue here that in the 2020s, cohabitation of digital worlds is unchosen because it has become a normative requirement for participation in social and political life. As the key institution or ecology through which social and political knowledge, norms, discourses and frameworks of thinking or understanding circulate, and in which we participate not as witnesses or spectators but as co-creators of both content and meaning, there is an obligation to recognise and respect the unchosen form of this necessary way of being. We are, therefore, obliged ethically not only to do no violence (to others, to democratic processes or to the ideal of democracy itself – as we have argued above) but also not to make lives unliveable, which means in our digital context to make it difficult, complex or impossible for people to make informed decisions about their lives, their social participation and their political engagement through polluting the space with disinformation or carelessly circulating misleading content.

While the go-to framework or remedy tends towards regulation and, to a lesser extent, a less pernicious pedagogy and digital literacy, ensuring an ethical underpinning means that we are placed in the frame of a quandary that requires a complex set of decisions over *how* to respond to activities that toxicify the media and information ecology with disinformation. Within the approach towards responsiveness and recognition foregrounded here, ethics produces a quandary, a requirement persistently to question ones' actions and a situation that can reconstitute the subject anew in the encounter with the other. What the encounter with the other describes is a 'struggle over the claim of nonviolence without any judgment about how the struggle finally ends' (Butler, 2007, p. 187).

If we consider, for example, the case of President Trump's circulation of misleading content across several online spaces, we can see and describe these not only as having caused violence, but as violent acts in themselves. We are ethically responsible, on the one hand, towards and for Donald Trump, which means bringing his undesirable otherness into those shared ecologies (Levinas, 1969, p. 76). In welcoming here, however, we are not giving over the ecology to an alternative practice of domination or a struggle over whose meaning should dominate. Rather, such inclusivity is an act of welcome that in itself is an act of 'calling into question of the I' (p. 171) – because the subject is linguistically constituted by the other, we exist *for* the other and are thus obligated towards the other (Levinas, 1969, p. 261).

The obligations of inclusivity, hospitality and welcome, however, do not preclude the need to require the other to remove themselves from spaces in which harm is being done. The ban on President Trump by a number of social media sites was auspiced under liberal-humanist perceptions of the contract, mechanised rightly through claims that Trump's disinformation and other injurious speech was a breach of the terms of service, and undertaken publicly in order to protect the public and minimise harm.

At the practical, applied level, recognising the subject who has given up on the ethical relation warrants certain kinds of policy and policing, even when they fall into necessary regulatory frameworks. The actions can, therefore, include banning based on an assessment of the violence of disinformation, but must absolutely not occur because one disagrees with the kind of disinformation or his political stance (even when we do). It is an ethical approach that demands that even in banning a perpetrator we are bound to that perpetrator as a member of a community, someone who must be given a chance to participate and only removed when the clarity of communication remains persistently threatened. It is an obligation to be ethical towards the perpetrator and to be undone through remaining bound to them, even if that other must be removed. And it is a requirement to acknowledge that even if the removal creates peace or reduces vulnerability and harm, if a banning is to be ethical it must be perceived as a loss.

Thus, while censorship of a person spreading disinformation is not an ethical response in itself, it can be a form of practical justice when that disinformation is apprehended as doing violence to the ecology itself. Our ethical obligation, however, also obliges us (and the social network platforms and educators) to develop new and as-yet unforeseen ways to permit participation even of the perpetrator in ways which reduces the harm of future disinformation. That may be, as we indicated in Chapter Nine, a future culture in which digital literacy permitting the instant recognition of disinformation is at its core, rather than the violent decidability of regulation. The fact that the solution remains unknowable does not mean it is a critical exercise we can ignore.

We have tried in this book to come at the topics of fake news, disinformation and misinformation from a critical and cultural perspective in order to begin the process of finding new solutions to a problem that has had a broadly negative impact on the quality of communication, the liveability of ordinary users, trust in media practices and socially supportive institutions and future of the relationship between democracy, sociality and communication. We have addressed the many issues created by fake news in its present form and tried to locate those in social and cultural terms, and have investigated some of the practical remedies in the previous chapter as well as how we might begin to conceive an ethical approach in the present chapter. At the same time, however, we have been careful not to impose a set of injunctions – such as demanding the regulatory banning of fake news or suggesting a free-for-all – in order not to foreclose on the possibilities for the future. Fake news, disinformation and the circulation of misleading content are, as we have described, an ethical issue for the future of communication. And, given, the centrality of communication to our very subjectivity as human beings and as the mode through which we engage in social participation and belonging, it remains that what is at stake in trying to ensure a cleaner, more trustworthy, more respectful and less polluted media ecology, is in many ways the future of human subjectivity itself. Rather than understanding fake news as a problem we can eradicate, cut out or suppress, it is a serious social issue that emerges because we communicate in the context of our contemporary neoliberal, postmodernised, sensationalist and entertainment-seeking culture. How we address fake news is therefore inseparable from how we begin to address our global contemporary culture and how we perceive more just, more democratic ways of being into the future.

References

Abbas, T. (2004). After 9/11: British south Asian Muslims, Islamophobia, multiculturalism, and the state. *American Journal of Islamic Social Sciences, 21*(3), 26–38. doi: 10.35632/ajiss.v21i3.506

Abidin, C. (2018). *Internet celebrity: Understanding fame online.* Bingley: Emerald Publishing.

Ahlgren, M. (2021). 50+ Twitter statistics & facts for 2020. Retrieved from https://www.websitehostingrating.com/twitter-statistics/

Ahmed, S. (2004). *The cultural politics of emotion.* Edinburgh: Edinburgh University Press.

Ahmed, M. (2020). The 'Megxit' in British and American headlines: A critical discourse analysis. *Textual Turnings: An International Peer-Reviewed Journal in English Studies, 2*(1), 135–151. doi: 10.21608/ttaip.2020.133421

AHRC. (2020). *Where's all the data on COVID-19 racism?* Retrieved from https://humanrights.gov.au/about/news/opinions/wheres-all-data-covid-19-racism

Ajder, H., Patrini, G., Cavalli, F., & Cullen, L. (2019). *The state of deepfakes: Landscape, threats, and impact.* Retrieved from https://regmedia.co.uk/2019/10/08/deepfake_report.pdf

Al Jazeera. (2019). Singapore controversial 'fake news' law goes into effect. *Al Jazeera*, 2 October. Retrieved from https://www.aljazeera.com/news/2019/10/2/singapore-controversial-fake-news-law-goes-into-effect

Alba, D. (2020). Misinformation about George Floyd protests surges on social media. *New York Times*, 1 June. Retrieved from https://www.nytimes.com/2020/06/01/technology/george-floyd-misinformation-online.html

Albright, J. (2017). Welcome to the era of fake news. *Media and Communication, 5*(2), 87–89. doi: 10.17645/mac.v5i2.977

Alexander, B. (2017). *The new digital storytelling: Creating narratives with new media.* Santa Barbara, CA: Praeger.

Allcott, H., & Gentzkow, M. (2017). Social media and fake news in the 2016 election. *Journal of Economic Perspectives, 31*(2), 211–236. doi: 10.1257/jep.31.2.211

Allen, B., & Stevens, D. (2018). *Truth in advertising?: Lies in political advertising and how they affect the electorate.* London: Rowman & Littlefield.

Anderson, B. (1983). *Imagined communities: Reflections on the origins and spread of nationalism.* London: Verso.

Anderson, C. (2016). *White rage: The unspoken truth of our racial divide.* London: Bloomsbury.

Anderson, M., Barthel, M., Perrin, A., & Vogels, E. A. (2020). #BlackLivesMatter surges on Twitter after George Floyd's death. *Pew Research Center*. Retrieved from https://www.pewresearch.org/fact-tank/2020/06/10/blacklivesmatter-surges-on-twitter-after-george-floyds-death/

Andersen, K. G., Rambaut, A., Lipkin, W. I., Holmes, E. C., & Garry, R. F. (2020). The proximal origin of SARS-CoV-2. *National Medicine, 26*(4), 450–452. doi: 10.1038/s41591-020-0820-9

Andrejevic, M. (2002). The work of Being watched: Interactive media and the exploitation of self-disclosure. *Critical Studies in Media Communication, 19*(2), 230–248. doi: 10.1080/07393180216561

Angelides, S. (2005). The emergence of the paedophile in the late twentieth century. *Historical Studies, 36*(126), 272–295. doi: 10.1080/10314610508682924

Anselmi, M. (2018). *Populism: An introduction*. Abingdon: Routledge.

AP News. (2021). Transcript of Trump's speech at rally before US Capitol riot. *AP News*, 14 January. Retrieved from https://apnews.com/article/election-2020-joe-biden-donald-trump-capitol-siege-media-e79eb5164613d6718e9f4502eb471f27

Appadurai, A. (2003). Archive and aspiration. In J. Brouwer & A. Mulder (Eds.), *Information is alive* (pp. 14–25). Rotterdam: V2_Publishing and NAI Publishers.

Austin, E. W., & Pinkleton, B. R. (1999). The relation between media content evaluations and political disaffection. *Mass Communication and Society*, *2*(3–4), 105–122. doi: 10.1080/15205436.1999.9677867

Avnur, Y. (2020). What's wrong with the online echo chamber: A motivated reasoning Account. *Journal of Applied Philosophy*, *37*(4), 578–593. doi: 10.1111/japp.12426

Baigent, M., Leigh, R., & Lincoln, H. (1982). *The holy blood and the holy grail*. London: Jonathan Cape.

Barthel, M., & Mitchell, A. (2017). American's attitudes about the news media deeply divided along partisan lines. *Pew Research Center*. Retrieved from http://www.journalism.org/2017/05/10/americans-attitudes-about-the-news-media-deeply-divided-alongpartisan-lines/

Bartlett, A., Clarke, K., & Cover, R. (2019). *Flirting in the era of #MeToo: Negotiating intimacy*. Basingstoke: Palgrave Macmillan.

Baudrillard, J. (1988). Simulacra and simulations. In M. Poster (Ed.), *Jean Baudrillard: Selected writings* (pp. 166–184). Cambridge: Polity Press.

BBC News. (2020). Meghan felt 'unprotected' amid 'false' media claims, court documents suggest. *BBC News*, 2 July. Retrieved from https://www.bbc.com/news/uk-53258761

BBC News. (2021a). TikTok: GP posts videos to tackle vaccine fake news. *BBC News*, 22 January. Retrieved from https://www.bbc.com/news/av/uk-england-beds-bucks-herts-55741095

BBC News. (2021b). Pete Evans: Instagram ban for Australian chef over conspiracy theories. *BBC News*, 17 February. Retrieved from https://www.bbc.com/news/world-australia-56095218

Belair-Gagnon, V., Nelson, J. L., & Lewis, S. C. (2018). Audience engagement, reciprocity, and the pursuit of community connectedness in public media journalism. *Journalism Practice*, *13*(5), 558–575. doi: 10.1080/17512786.2018.1542975

Bell, C. (2018). The people who think 9/11 might have been an 'inside job'. *BBC News*, 1 February. Retrieved from https://www.bbc.com/news/blogs-trending-42195513

Bell, E. (2019). The fact-check industry. *Columbia Journalism Review*, Fall. Retrieved from https://www.cjr.org/special_report/fact-check-industry-twitter.php

Bellware, K. (2021). Cheer mom used deepfake nudes and threats to harass daughter's teammates, police say. *Washington Post*, 14 March. Retrieved from https://www.washingtonpost.com/nation/2021/03/13/cheer-mom-deepfake-teammates/

Benn, S. I. (1982). Individuality, autonomy and community. In E. Kamenka (Ed.), *Community as a social ideal* (pp. 43–62). London: Edward Arnold.

Bennett, T. (1983). Texts, readers, reading formations. *Literature and History*, *9*(2), 214–227.

Bennett, S. (2019). Values as tools of legitimation in EU and UK Brexit discourses. In V. Koller, S. Kopf, & M. Miglbauer (Eds.), *Discourses of Brexit* (pp. 17–31). New York, NY: Routledge.

Berkowitz, R. (2020). A game designer's analysis of QAnon. *Curioserinstitute*, 1 October. Retrieved from https://medium.com/curiouserinstitute/a-game-designers-analysis-of-qanon-580972548be5

Berlant, L. (2007). Slow death (sovereignty, obesity, lateral agency). *Critical Inquiry*, *33*(4), 754–780. doi: 10.1086/521568

Berners-Lee, T. (1999). Keynote talk to the *LCS 35th Anniversary celebrations*, Cambridge MA, 14 April. Retrieved from https://www.w3.org/1999/04/13-tbl.html

Bhatia, M. (2012). Migrant remarks on the nose. *Sydney Morning Herald*, 11 January. Retrieved from https://www.smh.com.au/politics/federal/migrant-remarks-on-the-nose-20120110-1ptfu.html

Biagi, S. (2014). *Media/impact: An introduction to mass media*. Boston, MA: Cengage Learning.

Blake, A. (2017). Kellyanne Conway says Donald Trump's team has 'alternative facts.' Which pretty much says it all. *The Washington Post*, 23 January. Retrieved from https://www.washingtonpost.com/news/the-fix/wp/2017/01/22/kellyanne-conway-says-donald-trumps-team-has-alternate-facts-which-pretty-much-says-it-all/

Blitz, M. J. (2018). Lies, line drawing, and deep fake news. *Oklahoma Law Review*, *71*(59), 59–116. Retrieved from https://papers.ssrn.com/sol3/papers.cfm?abstract_id=3328273

Boczkowski, P.J., Mitchelstein E., & Matassi, M. (2018). 'News comes across when I'm in a moment of leisure': Understanding the practices of incidental news consumption on social media. *New Media & Society, 20*(10), 3523–3539. doi: 10.1177/1461444817750396

Boler, M., & Davis, E. (2018). The affective politics of the 'post-truth' era: Feeling rules and networked subjectivity. *Emotion, Space & Society, 27*(1), 75–85. doi: 10.1016/j.emospa.2018.03.002

Borden, S. L., & Tew, C. (2007). The role of journalist and the performance of journalism: Ethical lessons from 'fake' news (seriously). *Journal of Mass Media Ethics, 22*(4), 300–314. doi: 10.1080/08900520701583586

Bourdieu, P. (1983). Forms of capital. In J. Richardson (Ed.), *Handbook of theory and research for the sociology of education* (pp. 241–258). New York, NY: Greenwood Press.

Bowler, S., & Karp, J. A. (2004). Politicians, scandals, and trust in government. *Political Behavior, 26*(3), 271–287. doi: 10.1023/B:POBE.0000043456.87303.3a

boyd, d. (2008). Facebook's privacy trainwreck: Exposure, invasion, and social convergence. *Convergence: The International Journal of Research into New Media Technologies, 14*(1), 13–20. doi: 10.1177/1354856507084416

Boyd-Barrett, O. (1995). Conceptualizing the 'Public Sphere'. In O. Boyd-Barrett & C. Newbold (Eds.), *Approaches to media: A reader* (pp. 230–234). London: Arnold.

Braue, D. (2021). Big tech giants embrace disinformation code. *InformationAge*, 23 February. Retrieved from https://ia.acs.org.au/article/2021/big-tech-giants-embrace-disinformation-code.html

Bregler, C., Covell, M., & Slaney, M. (1997). Video rewrite: Driving visual speech with audio. *Proceedings of the 24th annual conference on computer graphics and interactive techniques*. Retrieved from https://www2.eecs.berkeley.edu/Research/Projects/CS/vision/human/bregler-sig97.pdf

Brehm, J., & Rahn, W. M. (1997). Individual level evidence for the causes and consequences of social capital. *American Journal of Political Science, 41*(3), 999–1023. doi: 10.2307/2111684

Brett, J. (1992). *Robert Menzies' forgotten people*. Carlton, Vic: Melbourne University Press.

Britzky, H. (2017). Everything Trump has called 'FAKE NEWS'. *Axios*, 9 July. Retrieved from https://www.axios.com/everything-trump-has-called-fake-news-1513303959-6603329e-46b5-44ea-b6be-70d0b3bdb0ca.html

Brookes, E. (2020). Side-by-side headlines make it starkly clear: The tabloids had it in for Meghan. *Stuff*, 16 January. Retrieved from https://www.stuff.co.nz/life-style/life/118811544/sidebyside-headlines-make-it-starkly-clear-the-tabloids-had-it-in-for-meghan

Bruns, A. (2008). *Blogs, wikipedia, second life, and beyond: From production to produsage*. New York, NY: Peter Lang.

Bruns, A., Harrington, S., & Hurcombe, E. (2020). 'Corona? 5G? Or both?': Dynamics of COVID-19/5G conspiracy theories on Facebook. *Media International Australia, 177*(1), 12–29. doi: 10.1177/1329878X20946113

BSUH Maternity. (2021). What are our goals for gender inclusive perinatal care? *Facebook,* 9 February. Retrieved from https://www.facebook.com/BSUHMaternityServices/posts/what-are-our-goals-for-gender-inclusive-perinatal-carewe-want-to-ensure-that-our/3930010230396323/

Buckingham, D. (Ed.) (2008). *Youth, identity, and digital media.* Cambridge, MA: MIT Press.

Buffardi, L. E., & Campbell, W. K. (2008). Narcissism and social networking web sites. *Personality and Social Psychology Bulletin, 34*(10), 1303–1314. doi: 10.1177/0146167208320061

Burgess, J., & Green, J. (2009). *YouTube: Online video and participatory culture.* Cambridge: Polity.

Burkhardt, J. M. (2017). *Combating fake news in the digital age.* Chicago, IL: American Library Association.

Bush, G. W. (2001). President Bush addresses the nation. *The Washington Post,* 20 September. Retrieved from https://www.washingtonpost.com/wp-srv/nation/specials/attacked/transcripts/bushaddress_092001.html

Butler, J. (1990). *Gender trouble: Feminism and the subversion of identity.* London: Routledge.

Butler, J. (1997a). *The psychic life of power: Theories in subjection.* Stanford, CA: Stanford University Press.

Butler, J. (1997b). *Excitable speech: A politics of the performative.* London: Routledge.

Butler, J. (2004). *Precarious life.* London: Verso.

Butler, J. (2006). The desire to live: Spinoza's *Ethics* under pressure. In V. Kahn, N. Saccamano, & D. Coli (Eds.), *Politics and the passions 1500–1850* (pp. 111–130). Princeton, NJ: Princeton University Press.

Butler, J. (2007). Reply from Judith Butler to Mills and Jenkins. *Differences: A Journal of Feminist Cultural Studies, 18*(2), 180–195.

Butler, J. (2009a). Critique, dissent, disciplinarity. *Critical Inquiry, 35*(4), 773–795. doi: 10.1086/599590

Butler, J. (2009b). *Frames of war: When is life grievable?* London: Verso.

Butler, J. (2020). *The force of non-violence: An ethico-political bind.* London: Verso.

Butler, J., & Athanasiou, A. (2013). *Dispossession: The performative in the political.* Cambridge: Polity.

Butler, J., Gambetti, Z., & Sabsay L. (2016). Introduction. In J. Butler, Z. Gambetti & L. Sabsay (Eds.), *Vulnerability in resistance* (pp. 1–11). Durham: Duke University Press.

California Legislative Information. (2019). *AB-730 Elections: Deceptive audio or visual media.* Retrieved from https://leginfo.legislature.ca.gov/faces/billTextClient.xhtml?bill_id=201920200AB730

Caluya, G. (2007). The architectural nervous system: Home, fear, insecurity. *M/C Journal, 10*(4). doi: 10.5204/mcj.2689

Cappella, J., & Jamieson, K. H. (1997). *Spiral of cynicism: The press and the public good.* New York, NY: Oxford University Press.

Carey, J. (1988). *Communication as culture: Essays on media and society.* London: Routledge.

Carey, K. (2017). *Fake news: How propaganda influenced the 2016 election, a historical comparison to 1930's Germany.* Snow Hill, MD: Marzenhale Publishing.

Carland, S. (2020). We know racism and recessions go together. Australia must prepare to stop a racism spike here. *The Conversation,* 14 May. Retrieved from https://theconversation.com/we-know-racism-and-recessions-go-together-australia-must-prepare-to-stop-a-racism-spike-here-138215

Carmen. (2019). Meghan Markle Sex Tape Allegedly Being Shopped! WATCH THIS!. *Carmen,* 2 April. Retrieved from https://b95forlife.iheart.com/featured/carmen/content/2019-04-01-meghan-markle-sex-tape-allegedly-being-shopped-watch-this/

Carroll, L. (2015). Fact-checking Trump's claim that thousands in New Jersey cheered when World Trade Center tumbled. *Politifact*, 22 November. Retrieved from https://www. politifact.com/truth-o-meter/statements/2015/nov/22/donald-trump/fact-checking-trumps-claim-thousands-new-jersey-ch

Castells, M. (2010). *The rise of the network society* (2nd ed.). Chichester: Wiley-Blackwell.

Castells, M. (2012). *Networks of outrage and hope: Social movements in the internet age.* Cambridge: Polity Press.

CBS News. (2019). Doctored Nancy Pelosi video highlights threat of 'deepfake' tech. *CBS News*, 24 May. Retrieved from https://www.cbsnews.com/news/doctored-nancy-pelosi-video-highlights-threat-of-deepfake-tech-2019-05-25/

Chadha, K., & Koliska, M. (2015). Newsrooms and transparency in the digital age. *Journalism Practice*, 9(2), 215–229. doi: 10.1080/17512786.2014.924737

Chakhoyan, D. (2018). Deep fakes could threaten democracy. What are they and what can be done? *World Economic Forum*. Retrieved from https://www.weforum.org/agenda/2018/11/deep-fakes-may-destroy-democracy-can-they-be-stopped/

Chilton, L. (2021). Piers Morgan storms off *Good Morning Britain* after Alex Beresford condemns him for 'trashing' Meghan Markle. *The Independent*, 9 March. Retrieved from https://www.independent.co.uk/arts-entertainment/tv/news/piers-morgan-gmb-meghan-markle-alex-beresford-b1814352.html

Cillizza, C. (2017). Sean Spicer held a press conference. He didn't take questions. Or tell the whole truth. *The Washington Post*, 21 January. Retrieved from https://www.washingtonpost.com/news/the-fix/wp/2017/01/21/sean-spicer-held-a-press-conference-he-didnt-take-questions-or-tell-the-whole-truth/

Clancy, L., & Yelin, H. (2020). 'Meghan's manifesto': Meghan Markle and the co-option of feminism. *Celebrity Studies*, 11(3), 372–377. doi: 10.1080/19392397.2018.1541541

Cohen, A. P. (1985). *The symbolic construction of community*. London: Ellis Horwood & Tavistock Publications.

Cohen, M. L., & Olson, K. C. (2010). *Legal research in a nutshell*. Detroit, MI: Gale.

Collins, E. (2016). Trump ad uses footage from Morocco, not Mexican border. *Politico*, 4 January. Retrieved from https://www.politico.com/story/2016/01/donald-trump-ad-footage-border-morocco-217332

Collins, B. (2018). Russia-linked account pushed fake Hillary Clinton sex video. *NBC News*, 11 April. Retrieved from https://www.nbcnews.com/tech/security/russia-linked-account-pushed-fake-hillary-clinton-sex-video-n864871

Collins, B., & Zadrony, B. (2021). Anti-vaccine groups changing into 'dance parties' on Facebook to avoid detection. *NBC News*, 22 July. Retrieved from https://www.nbcnews.com/tech/tech-news/anti-vaccine-groups-changing-dance-parties-facebook-avoid-detection-rcna1480?fbclid=IwAR1o1fDOb%E2%80%A6

Colwell, A. (2021). TikTok's fake news problem. *Spectator*, 28 March. Retrieved from https://www.spectator.com.au/2021/03/tiktoks-fake-news-problem/

Cook, J., van der Linden, S., Lewandowsky, S., & Ecker, U. (2020). Coronavirus, 'plandemic' and the seven traits of conspiratorial thinking. *The Conversation*, 16 May. Retrieved from https://theconversation.com/coronavirus-plandemic-and-the-seven-traits-of-conspiratorial-thinking-138483

Corner, J. (2017). Fake news, post-truth and media–political change. *Media, Culture and Society*, 39(7), 1100–1107. doi: 10.1177/0163443717726743

Cover, R. (2004a). Bodies, movements and desires: Lesbian/gay subjectivity and the stereotype. *Continuum: Journal of Media & Cultural Studies*, 18(1), 81–98. doi: 10.1080/1030431032000181012

Cover, R. (2004b). Interactivity: Reconceiving the audience in the struggle for textual 'control'. *Australian Journal of Communication*, 31(1), 107–120. Retrieved from https://www.academia.edu/655909/Interactivity_Reconceiving_the_audience_in_the_struggle_for_textualcontrolof_narrative_and_distribution

Cover, R. (2006). Audience inter/active: Interactive media, narrative control and reconceiving audience history. *New Media & Society, 8*(1), 213–232. doi: 10.1177/1461444806059922

Cover, R. (2010). More Than a watcher: *Buffy* fans, amateur music videos, romantic slash and intermedia. In P. Attinello, J. K. Halhard, & V. Knights (Eds.), *Music, sound and silence in Buffy the Vampire Slayer* (pp. 131–148). London: Ashgate.

Cover, R. (2012). Performing and undoing identity online: Social networking, identity theories and the incompatibility of online profiles and friendship regimes. *Convergence: The International Journal of Research Into New Media Technologies, 18*(2), 177–193. doi: 10.1177/1354856511433684

Cover, R. (2013). Community print media: Perceiving minority community in multicultural South Australia. *Continuum: Journal of Media and Cultural Studies, 27*(1), 110–123. doi: 10.1080/10304312.2013.736951

Cover, R. (2015). Mobility, belonging and bodies: Understanding discourses of anxiety towards temporary migrants in Australia. *Continuum: Journal of Media & Cultural Studies, 29*(1), 32–44. doi: 10.1080/10304312.2014.968523

Cover, R. (2016). *Digital identities: Creating and communicating the online self.* London: Elsevier.

Cover, R. (2020). Vulnerability and the discourse of 'forgotten people': Populism, population and cultural change. *Continuum: Journal of Media & Cultural Studies, 34*(5), 749–762. doi: 10.1080/10304312.2020.1798875

Cravey, A. J. (2021). Building collective power amidst white supremacist backlash. *Gender, place and culture: A journal of feminist geography.* Online First. doi: 10.1080/0966369X.2021.1887092

Creed, B. (1993). *The Monstrous-feminine: Film, feminism, psychoanalysis.* London: Routledge.

Creed, B. (2003). *Media matrix: Sexing the new reality.* St. Leonards, NSW: Allen & Unwin.

Curry, A. L., & Stroud, N. J. (2019). The effects of journalistic transparency on credibility. Assessments and engagement intentions. *Journalism, 22*(4), 901–918. doi: 10.1177/1464884919850387

Daddow, O. (2013). Margaret Thatcher, Tony Blair and the Eurosceptic tradition in Britain. *The British Journal of Politics and International Relations, 15*(2), 210–227. doi: 10.1111/j.1467-856X.2012.00534

Dahlgren, P., & Sparks, C. (1992). *Journalism and popular culture.* London: Sage.

Daniels, J. (2018). The algorithmic rise of the 'alt-right'. *Contexts, 17*(1), 60–65. doi: 10.1177/1536504218766547

Dans, E. (2021). Visualizing the echo chamber. *Forbes*, 19 March. Retrieved from https://www.forbes.com/sites/enriquedans/2021/03/19/visualizing-the-echochamber/?sh=417a6caa4167

Das, M. (2020). Social construction of stigma and its implications: Observations from COVID-19. *Social Sciences and Humanities Open.* doi: 10.2139/ssrn.3599764

Davidson, W. B., & Cotter, P. R. (1989). Sense of community and political participation. *Journal of Community Psychology, 17*(2), 119–125. doi: 10.1002/1520-6629

Davis, M. (2019a). A new, online culture war? The communication world of Breitbart.com. *Communication Research and Practice, 5*(3), 241–254. doi: 10.1080/22041451.2018.1558790

Davis, M. (2019b). Globalist war against humanity shifts into high gear': Online anti-vaccination websites and 'anti-public' discourse. *Public Understanding of Science, 28*(3), 357–371. doi: 10.1177/0963662518817187

de Certeau, M. (1984). *The practice of everyday life.* Berkeley, CA: University of California Press.

de Haldevang, M. (2018). Russian trolls and bots are flooding Twitter with Ford-Kavanaugh disinformation. *Quartz*, 3 December. Retrieved from https://qz.com/1409102/russian-trolls-and-bots-are-flooding-twitterwith-ford-kavanaugh-disinformation/

Dean, J. (1998). *Aliens in America: Conspiracy cultures from outerspace to cyberspace.* London: Cornell University Press.

Dearman, P., & Pyburne, P. (2021). *Bills Digest No. 48, 2020-21*, 15 February. Retrieved from https://www.aph.gov.au/Parliamentary_Business/Bills_Legislation/bd/bd2021a/21bd048#_Toc64377246

Debord, G. (1994). *The society of the spectacle.* New York, NY: Zone.

Debussman, B., Jr. (2021). Deepfake is the future of content creation. *BBC News*, 8 March. Retrieved from https://www.bbc.com/news/business-56278411

Del Vicario, M., Bessi, A., Zollo, F., Petroni, F., Scala, A. Caldarelli, G., ... Quattrociocchi, W. (2016). The spreading of misinformation online. *Proceedings of the National Academy of Sciences, 113*(3), 554–559. doi: 10.1073/pnas.1517441113

Depoux, A., Martin, S., Karafillakis, E., Preet, R., Wilder-Smith, A., & Larson, H. (2020). The pandemic of social media panic travels faster than the COVID-19 outbreak. *Journal of Travel Medicine, 27*(3), 1–2. doi: 10.1093/jtm/taaa031

Dery, M. (1993). Culture jamming: Hacking, slashing and sniping in the empire of signs. *Open Magazine.* Retrieved from http://markdery.com/?page_id=154

Dewey, C. (2016). Facebook fake-news writer: 'I think Donald Trump is in the White House because of me'. *Washington Post*, 17 November. Retrieved from https://www.washingtonpost.com/news/the-intersect/wp/2016/11/17/facebook-fake-news-writer-i-think-donald-trump-is-in-the-white-house-because-of-me/?utm_term=.42ceafd555c6

DIGI. (2021). *Disinformation Code.* Retrieved from https://digi.org.au/disinformation-code/

Dobre, C. (2012). *Furries: Enacting animal anthropomorphism.* Plymouth: University of Plymouth Press.

Dobson-Lohman, E., & Potcovaru, A. M. (2020). Fake news content shaping the COVID-19 pandemic fear: Virus anxiety, emotional contagion, and responsible media reporting. *Analysis and Metaphysics, 19*, 94–100. doi: 10.22381/AM19202011

Donegan, J., & Evans, R. (2001). Running amok: The Normanton race riots of 1888 and the genesis of white Australia. *Journal of Australian Studies, 25*(71), 83–98. doi: 10.1080/14443050109387723

Donelly, B. (2017). Senate inquiry to investigate the 'future of journalism' in Australia. *The Age*, 10 May. Retrieved from http://www.theage.com.au/

Dorlin, E. (2016). Bare subjectivity: Faces, veils, and masks in the contemporary allegories of western citizenship.' In J. Butler, Z Gambetti, & L. Sabsay (Eds.), *Vulnerability in resistance* (pp. 236–255). London: Duke University Press.

Douglas, K. M., Uscinski, J. E., Sutton, R. M., Cichocka, A., Nefes, T., Ang, C. S., & Deravi, F. (2019). Understanding conspiracy theories. *Political Psychology, 40*(3–5), 3–35. doi: 10.1111/pops.12568

Dreher, T. (2010). Speaking up or being heard? Community media interventions and the politics of listening. *Media, Culture & Society, 32*(1), 85–103. doi: 10.1177/0163443709350099

Dreher, T. (2020). Racism and media: A response from Australia during the global pandemic, *Ethnic and Racial Studies, 43*(13), 2363–2371. doi: 10.1080/01419870.2020.1784452

Duggan, L. (2003). *The twilight of equality? Neoliberalism, cultural politics and the attack on democracy.* Boston, MA: Beacon Press.

Dyer, R. (1993). *The matter of images: Essays on representations.* London: Routledge.

Eager, T. W., & Musso, C. (2001). Why did the World Trade Centre collapse? Science, engineering, and speculation. *JOM, 53*(12). Retrieved from https://www.tms.org/pubs/journals/JOM/0112/Eagar/Eagar-0112.html

Edelman Trust Barometer. (2019). *2019 Edelman trust barometer global report.* Retrieved from https://www.edelman.com/sites/g/files/aatuss191/files/2019-03/2019_Edelman_Trust_Barometer_Global_Report.pdf?utm_source=website&utm_medium=global_report&utm_campaign=downloads

Edwards, L., Occhipinti, S., & Ryan, S. (2000). Food and immigration: The indigestion trope contests the sophistication narrative. *Journal of Intercultural Studies, 21*(3), 297–308. doi: 10.1080/07256860020007458

Egelhofer, J. L., & Lecheler, S. (2019). Fake news as a two-dimensional phenomenon: A framework and research agenda. *Annals of the International Communication Association, 43*(2), 97–116. doi: 10.1080/23808985.2019.1602782

Ellison, N. B., Steinfeld, C., & Lampe, C. (2007). The benefits of Facebook 'friends': Social capital and college students' use of online social network sites. *Journal of Computer-Mediated Communication, 12*(4), 1143–1168. doi: 10.1111/j.1083-6101.2007.00367.x

Elvestad, E., Phillips, A., & Feuerstein, M. (2018). Can trust in traditional news media explain cross-national differences in news exposure of young people online? A comparative study of Israel, Norway and the United Kingdom. *Digital Journalism, 6*(2), 216–235. doi: 10.1080/21670811.2017.1332484

Eribon, D. (2004). *Insult and the gay self* [M. Lucey, trans.]. Durham, NC: Duke University Press.

eSafety Commissioner. (2021). *Fake News*. Retrieved from https://www.esafety.gov.au/young-people/fake-news

Facebook Journalism Project. (2021). What publishers need to know about fact-checking on Facebook. *Facebook Journalism Project*, 15 June. Retrieved from https://www.facebook.com/journalismproject/programs/third-party-fact-checking/publisher-faqs

Factinate. (2021a). *About – Factinate*. Retrieved from https://www.factinate.com/about/

Factinate. (2021b). *Revealing Facts About Elizabeth II, The Abiding Queen*. Retrieved from https://www.factinate.com/people/42-royal-facts-queen-elizabeth-ii/

Farhall, K., Carson, A., Wright, S., Gibbons, A., & Lukamto, W. (2019). Political elites' use of fake news discourse across communications platforms. *International Journal of Communication, 13*(23), 4353–4375. Retrieved from https://ijoc.org/index.php/ijoc/article/view/10677/2787

Fassin, D. (2009). Another politics of life is possible. *Theory, Culture & Society, 26*(6), 44–60. doi: 10.1177/0263276409106349

Fassin, D. (2021). Of plots and men: The heuristics of conspiracy theories. *Current Anthropology, 62*(2), 128–137. doi: 10.1086/713829

Filiciak, M. (2003). Hyperidentities: Postmodern identity patterns in massively multiplayer online role-playing games. In M. J. P. Wolf & B. Perron (Eds.), *The video game theory reader* (pp. 87–101). London: Routledge.

Fink, K. (2019). The biggest challenge facing journalism: A lack of trust. *Journalism, 20*(1), 40–43. doi: 10.1177/1464884918807069

Fischer, F. (1986). *Kaiserreich to third reich: Elements of continuity in German history 1871–1945*. London: Routledge.

Fisher, C. (2016). The trouble with 'trust' in news media. *Communication Research and Practice, 2*(4), 451–465. doi: 10.1080/22041451.2016.1261251

Fisher, C. (2018). What is meant by 'trust' in news media? In K. Otto & A. Köhler (Eds.), *Trust in media and journalism* (pp. 19–38). Berlin: Springer.

Fiske, J. (1989). *Understanding popular culture*. London: Unwin Hyman.

Fiske, J. (1992). Popularity and the politics of information. In P. Dahlgren & C. Sparks (Eds.), *Journalism and popular culture* (pp. 45–63). London: Sage.

Fiske, J. (1996). *Media matters: Everyday culture and political change*. Minneapolis: University of Minnesota Press.

Fletcher, R., & Nielsen, R. K. (2017). People don't trust news media – and this is key to the global misinformation debate. In H. Derakhshan & C. Wardle (Eds.), *Understanding and addressing the disinformation ecosystem* (pp. 13–17). Philadelphia, PA: Annenberg School for Communication at the University of Pennsylvania.

Fletcher, R., & Nielsen, R. K. (2018). Are people incidentally exposed to news on social media? A comparative analysis. *New Media & Society, 20*(7), 2450–2468. doi: 10.1177/1461444817724170

Fletcher, R., & Park, S. (2017). The impact of trust in the news media on online news consumption and participation. *Digital Journalism, 5*(10), 1281–1299. doi: 10.1080/21670811.2017.1279979

Flew, T. (2005). *New media: An introduction* (2nd ed.). Oxford: Oxford University Press.

Flew, T. (2019). Digital communication, the crisis of trust, and the post-global. *Communication Research and Practice, 5*(1), 4–22. doi: 10.1080/22041451.2019.1561394

Flew, T., Dulleck, U., Park, S., Fisher, C., & Isler, O. (2020). *Trust and mistrust in Australian news media*. Brisbane, QLD: The BEST Centre, Queensland University of Technology.

Forgey, Q., & Din, B. (2021). Biden and Harris condemn anti-Asian violence as investigation into Atlanta shootings continues. *Politico*, 19 March. Retrieved from https://www.politico.com/news/2021/03/19/georgia-lawmaker-biden-shooting-investigation-477158

Forrest, J., Blair, K., & Dunn, K. (2020). Racist attitudes, out-groups and the Australian experience. *Australian Journal of Social Issues, 56*(1), 78–93. doi: 10.1002/ajs4.112

Forte, A., Larco, V., & Bruckman, A. (2009). Decentralization in Wikipedia governance. *Journal of Management Information Systems, 26*(1), 49–72. doi: 10.2753/MIS0742-1222260103

Foucault, M. (1970). *The order of things*. London: Tavistock.

Foucault, M. (1976). *The will to knowledge. The history of sexuality* (Vol. 1). [R. Hurley, trans.]. London: Penguin Books.

Foucault, M. (1980). *Power/knowledge: Selected interviews & other writings 1972–1977* [C. Gordon et al., trans.]. New York, NY: Pantheon.

Foucault, M. (2007). *Security, territory, population: Lectures at the Collège de France, 1977–78* [G. Burchell, trans.]. Hampshire: Palgrave Macmillan.

Foucault, M. (2008). *The birth of biopolitics: Lectures at the Collège de France, 1978–79* [G. Burchell, trans.]. Hampshire: Palgrave Macmillan.

Fozdar, F., Spittles, B., & Hartley, L. K. (2014). Australia Day, flags on cars and Australian nationalism. *Journal of Sociology, 51*(2), 317–336. doi: 10.1177/1440783314524846

Freberg, K., & Kim, C. M. (2018). Social media education: Industry leader recommendations for curriculum and faculty competencies. *Journalism & Mass Communication Educator, 73*(4), 379–391. doi: 10.1177/1077695817725414

Friesem, Y. (2019). Teaching truth, lies, and accuracy in the digital age: Media literacy as project-based learning. *Journalism & Mass Communication Educator, 74*(2), 185–198. doi: 10.1177/1077695819829962

Frostensen, S. (2017). A crowd scientist says Trump's inauguration attendance was pretty average. *Vox*, 24 January. Retrieved from https://www.vox.com/policy-and-politics/2017/1/24/14354036/crowds-presidential-inaugurations-trump-average

Fukuyama, F. (2019). *Identity: Contemporary identity politics and the struggle for recognition*. London: Profile Books.

Gabbatt, A. (2021). 'From hearsay to hard evidence': Are UFOs about to go mainstream? *The Guardian*, 29 May. Retrieved from https://www.theguardian.com/world/2021/may/29/ufos-uap-america-pentagon-report

Gaber, I. (2017). Did the BBC fail its Brexit balancing act? In J. Mair, T. Clark, N. Fowler, R. Snoddy, & R. Tait (Eds.), *Brexit, Trump, and the media* (pp. 45–48). Bury St Edmunds: Abramis Academic.

Gaber, I., & Fisher, C. (2021). 'Strategic lying': The case of Brexit and the 2019 UK election. *The International Journal of Press/Politics*. doi: 10.1177/1940161221994100

Gamson J. (1998). *Freaks talk back: Tabloid talk shows and sexual nonconformity*. Chicago, IL: Chicago University Press.

Garrett, R. K. (2009). Echo chambers online? Politically motivated selective exposure among Internet news users. *Journal of Computer-Mediated Communication, 14*(2), 265–285. doi: 10.1111/j.1083-6101.2009.01440.x

Georgacopoulos, C., & Poche, T. (2020). *Fake news, disinformation and the George Floyd protests.* Retrieved from https://faculty.lsu.edu/fakenews/about/protestfakenews.php

Gerstner, E. (2020). Face/Off: Deepfake 'face swaps' and privacy laws. *Defense Council Journal, 1*(January), 1–14. Retrieved from https://www.iadclaw.org/assets/1/17/Face_Off_-_DeepFake_Face_Swaps_and_Privacy_Laws.pdf?4179

Gilbert, N. (2013). *Better left unsaid: Victorian novels, Hays Code films, and the benefits of censorship.* Stanford, CA: Stanford University Press.

Gilbey, R. (2019). A 'deep fake' app will make us film stars – but will we regret our narcissism? *The Guardian*, 5 September. Retrieved from https://www.theguardian.com/technology/2019/sep/04/a-deep-fake-app-will-make-us-film-stars-but-will-we-regret-our-narcissism

Gillespie, E. (2020). 'Pastel QAnon': The female lifestyle bloggers and influencers spreading conspiracy theories through Instagram. *The Feed*, 30 September. Retrieved from https://www.sbs.com.au/news/the-feed/pastel-qanon-the-female-lifestyle-bloggers-and-influencers-spreading-conspiracy-theories-through-instagram

Gilroy, P. (2004). *After empire: Melancholia or convivial culture?* London: Routledge.

Gilson, E. (2011). Vulnerability, ignorance, and oppression. *Hypatia, 26*(2), 308–332. doi: 10.1111/j.1527-2001.2010.01158.x

Glynn, K. (2000). *Tabloid culture: Trash taste, popular power, and the transformation of American television.* Durham, NC: Duke University Press.

Grčar, M., Cherepnalkoski, D., Mozetič, I., & Novak, P. K. (2017). Stance and influence of Twitter users regarding the Brexit referendum. *Computational Social Networks, 4*(1), 1–25. doi: 10.1186/s40649-017-0042-6

Green, L. (2008). Is it meaningless to talk about 'the internet'? *Australian Journal of Communication, 35*(3), 1–14. Retrieved from https://ro.ecu.edu.au/cgi/viewcontent.cgi?article=1825&context=ecuworks

Greenspan, R. E. (2020). QAnon builds on centuries of anti-Semitic conspiracy theories that put Jewish people at risk. *Insider*, 25 October. Retrieved from https://www.insider.com/qanon-conspiracy-theory-anti-semitism-jewish-racist-believe-save-children-2020-10

Habermas, J. (1989). *The structural transformation of the public sphere* [T. Burger, trans.]. Cambridge: Polity Press.

Hall, S. (1979). The great moving right show. *Marxism Today*, January, 14–20.

Hall, S. (1993). Encoding/decoding. In S. During (Ed.), *The cultural studies reader* (pp. 90–103). London: Routledge.

Hameleers, M. (2020). Separating truth from lies: Comparing the effects of news media literacy interventions and fact-checkers in response to political misinformation in the US and Netherlands. *Information, Communication & Society.* doi: 10.1080/1369118X.2020.1764603

Hamilton, J. T., & Morgan, F. (2016). Bridging the content gap in low-income communities. In M. Lloyd & L. A. Friedland (Eds.), *The communication crisis in America, and how to fix it* (pp. 183–197). New York, NY: Palgrave Macmillan.

Hanitzsch, T., Van Dalen, A., & Steindl, N. (2018). Caught in the nexus: A comparative and longitudinal analysis of public trust in the press. *The International Journal of Press/Politics, 23*(1), 3–23. doi: 10.1177/1940161217740695

Hänska, M., & Bauchowitz, S. (2017). Tweeting for Brexit: How social media influenced the referendum. In J. Mair, T. Clark, N. Fowler, R. Snoddy, & R. Tait (Eds.), *Brexit, Trump, and the media* (pp. 31–35). Bury St Edmunds: Abramis Academic Publishing.

Harcup, T., & O'Neill, D. (2017). What is news? News values revisited (again). *Journalism Studies, 18*(12), 1470–1488. doi: 10.1080/1461670X.2016.1150193

Harrison, J. (2018). Fake news has always existed, but quality journalism has a history of survival. *The Conversation*, 3 May. Retrieved from http://theconversation.com/fake-news-has-always-existed-but-quality-journalism-has-a-history-of-survival-95615

Hartnett, S.J., & Stengrim, L. (2004). 'The whole operation of deception': Reconstructing President Bush's rhetoric of weapons of mass destruction. *Cultural Studies, Critical Methodologies, 4*(2), 152–197. doi: 10.1177/1532708603262787

Harvey, J. (2021). Doctor laughs out loud at tinfoil hat-worthy suspicion about vaccines. *HuffPost*, 3 May. Retrieved from https://www.huffpost.com/entry/coronavirus-vaccine-tracking-devices_n_608a3633e4b0ccb91c2dd0e2

Hashim, H., Mohamad Salleh, M. A., & Mohamad, E. (2015). Usage analysis of visual digital (DVFx) special effects on short films and genre. *Malaysian Journal of Communication, 31*(2), 99–115. Retrieved from https://www.researchgate.net/publication/292354949_Usage_analysis_of_visual_digital_DVFX_special_effects_on_short_films_and_genre

Hatterstone, S. (2020). Piers Morgan: 'Do I genuinely feel a pathological hatred of vegan sausage rolls? No'. *The Guardian*, 12 October. Retrieved from https://www.theguardian.com/lifeandstyle/2020/oct/12/piers-morgan-what-does-trump-smell-like-expensive-aftershave-and-a-whiff-of-hairspray

Haw, A. L. (2020). What drives political news engagement in digital spaces? Reimagining 'echo chambers' in a polarised and hybridised media ecology. *Communication Research and Practice, 6*(1), 38–54. doi: 10.1080/22041451.2020.1732002

Haw, A. L. (2021). Constructions of 'fake news' among Australian political news audiences: A critical discourse perspective. *Journal of Language and Politics*, Online First. doi: 10.1075/jlp.21028.haw

Hawkings, C. J. (2021). What is believed to have happened on Harry and Meghan's Australia tour. *Project Fangirl*, 4 April. Retrieved from https://cjhawkings.com/australia-tour-meghan-harry/

Hebdige, D. (1979). *Subculture: The meaning of style*. London: Methuen.

Heckler, N., & Ronquillo, J. C. (2019). Racist fake news in United States' history: Lessons for public administration. *Public Integrity, 21*(5), 477–490. doi: 10.1080/10999922.2019.1626696

Hegarty, B., Marshall, D., Rasmussen, M. L., Aggleton, P., & Cover, R. (2018). Heterosexuality and race in the Australian same-sex marriage postal survey. *Australian Feminist Studies, 33*(97), 400–416. doi: 10.1080/08164649.2018.1536441

Henningham, J. (1993). The Press. In S. Cunningham & G. Turner (Eds.), *The media in Australia: Industries, texts, audiences* (pp. 59–71). St. Leonards: Allen & Unwin.

Hoadley, C. M., Xu, H., Lee, J. J., & Rosson, M. B. (2010). Privacy as information access and illusory control: The case of the Facebook news feed privacy outcry. *Electronic Commerce Research and Applications, 9*(1), 50–60. doi: 10.1016/j.elerap.2009.05.001

Hochschild, A. (2016). *Strangers in their own land: Anger and mourning on the American right*. New York, NY: New Press.

Hollingworth, J. (2002). The yellow peril: Race, national identity and the Chinese in Australia. *Agora, 37*(3), 64–68. doi: 10.1177/1440783315593182

Holmes, D. (2019). A culture defined by rage. *Medium*, 9 February. Retrieved from https://medium.com/@dvdhlms3/a-culture-defined-by-rage-b5dcd623a876

Hooghe, M. (2018). Trust and elections. In E. M. Uslaner (Ed.), *The Oxford handbook of social and political trust* (pp. 617–632). Oxford: Oxford University Press.

Hoppe, T. (2018). 'Spanish flu': When infectious disease names blur origins and stigmatize those infected. *American Journal of Public Health, 108*(11), 1462–1464. doi: 10.2105/AJPH.2018.304645

House of Commons Digital, Culture, Media and Sport Committee. (2019). *Disinformation and 'fake news': Final report*. London: House of Commons and UK Parliament.

Howard, P. N., Woolley, S., & Calo, R. (2018). Algorithms, bots, and political communication in the US 2016 election: The challenge of automated political communication for election law and administration. *Journal of Information Technology & Politics, 15*(2), 81–93. doi: 10.1080/19331681.2018.1448735

Hughes, S. (2017). American monsters: Tabloid media and the satanic panic, 1970–2000. *Journal of American Studies, 51*(3), 691–719. doi: 10.1017/S0021875816001298

Humprecht, E. (2019). Where 'fake news' flourishes: A comparison across four Western democracies. *Information, Communication & Society, 22*(13), 1973–1988. doi: 10.1080/1369118X.2018.1474241

Huxley, J. (1927). The tissue-culture king. *Amazing Stories,* 2(5). Retrieved from https://archive.org/stream/AmazingStoriesVolume02Number05/AmazingStoriesVolume02Number05_djvu.txt

Inglehart, R. F., & Morris, P. (2016). Trump, Brexit, and the rise of populism: Economic have-nots and cultural backlash. *Harvard Kennedy School Working Paper Series 26.* Retrieved from https://papers.ssrn.com/sol3/papers.cfm?abstract_id=2818659

Ireton, C., & Posetti, J. (2018). *Journalism, 'fake news' and disinformation.* Paris: UNESCO

Jack, C. (2019). Wicked content. *Communication, Culture and Critique, 12*(4), 435–454. doi: 10.1093/ccc/tcz043

Jaiswal, J., LoSchiavo, C., & Perlman, D. C. (2020). Disinformation, misinformation and inequality-driven mistrust in the time of COVID-19: Lessons unlearned from AIDS denialism. *AIDS and Behaviour, 24*(10), 2776–2780. doi: 10.1007/s10461-020-02925-y

Jameson, F. (1985). Postmodernism and consumer society. In H. Foster (Ed.), *Postmodern culture* (pp. 111–125). London: Pluto Press.

Jameson, F. (1988). Cognitive mapping. In C. Nelson & L. Grossberg (Eds.), *Marxism and the interpretation of culture* (pp. 347–360). Chicago, IL: University of Illinois Press.

Jameson, F. (1991). *Postmodernism, or the cultural logic of late capitalism.* Durham, NC: Duke University Press.

Jamieson, A. (2017). 'You are fake news': Trump attacks CNN and BuzzFeed at press conference. *The Guardian,* 12 January. Retrieved from https://www.theguardian.com/us-news/2017/jan/11/trump-attacks-cnn-buzzfeed-at-press-conference

Jamieson, K. H. (2015). Implications of the demise of 'fact' in political discourse. *Proceedings of the American Philosophical Society, 159*(1), 66–84. Retrieved from https://www.jstor.org/stable/24640171

Jane, E. A. (2015). Flaming? What flaming? The pitfalls and potentials of researching online hostility. *Ethics and Information Technology, 17*(1), 65–87. doi: 10.1007/s10676-015-9362-0

Jenkins, H. (2008). *Convergence culture. Where old and new media collide.* New York, NY: NYU Press.

Jeung, R. (2020). *Incidents of Coronavirus discrimination: A report for A3PCON and CAA.* Retrieved from https://www.asianpacificpolicyandplanningcouncil.org/stop-aapi-hate/

Johnson, A. (1909). Review of *The repeal of the Missouri compromise: Its origin and authorship* by P. O. Ray. *The American Historical Review, 14*(4), 835–836. doi: 10.2307/1837085

Johnson, T. J., & Kaye, B. K. (2013). The dark side of the boon? Credibility, selective exposure and the proliferation of online sources of political information. *Computers in Human Behavior, 29*(4), 1862–1871. doi: 10.1016/j.chb.2013.02.011

Kandel, S. (2021). Who was Jason Langhans? Details on Tooradin House Party Mysterious Death. *Heightzone,* 13 April. Retrieved from https://heightzone.com/who-was-jason-langhans-details-on-tooradin-house-party-mysterious-death/

Kant, I. (1959). *Foundations of the metaphysics of morals* [L. W. Beck, trans.]. Indianapolis, IN: Bobbs-Merrill.

Karpf, D. (2019). On digital disinformation and democratic myths. *Social Science Research Council MediaWell.* Retrieved from https://mediawell.ssrc.org/expert-reflections/on-digital-disinformation-and-democratic-myths/

Karr, C. (2019). Enforcing California's 'deepfake' ban could prove challenging. *Epoch Times*, 18 October. Retrieved from https://www.theepochtimes.com/enforcing-californias-deepfake-ban-could-prove-challenging_3115476.html

Kata, A. (2012). Anti-vaccine activists, Web 2.0, and the postmodern paradigm: An overview of tactics and tropes used online by the anti-vaccination movement. *Vaccine, 30*(25), 3778–3789. doi: 10.1016/j.vaccine.2011.11.112

Katz, E. (1959). Mass communication research and the study of popular culture: An editorial note on a possible future for this journal. *Studies in Public Communication, 2*, 1–6. Retrieved from http://repository.upenn.edu/asc_papers/165

Kaye, B. K., & Johnson, T. J. (2002). Online and in the know: Uses and gratifications of the web for political information. *Journal of Broadcasting and Electronic Media, 46*(1), 54–71. doi: 10.1207/s15506878jobem4601_4

Keller, J. (2016). Meet the professor calling out the fake and misleading news sites clogging your Facebook feed. *Pacific Standard Magazine*, 16 November. Retrieved from https://psmag.com/news/meet-the-professor-calling-out-the-fake-and-misleading-news-sites-clogging-your-facebook-feed

Kent, M. (2012). From neuron to social context: Restoring resilience as a capacity for good survival. In M. Under (Ed.), *The social ecology of resilience: A handbook of theory and practice* (pp. 111–125). New York, NY: Springer.

Kim, S. W., & Sue, K. P. (2020). Using Psychoneuroimmunity against COVID-19. *Brain, Behavior, and Immunity*. doi: 10.1016/j.bbi.2020.03.025

Klein, C., Clutton, P., & Dunn, A. G. (2019). Pathways to conspiracy: The social and linguistic precursors of involvement in Reddit's conspiracy theory forum. *PloS One, 14*(11). doi: 10.1371/journal.pone.022509

Knight Commission on Trust, Media and Democracy. (2019). *Crisis in democracy: Renewing trust in America*. Retrieved from https://knightfoundation.org/reports/crisis-in-democracy-renewing-trust-in-america/

Knobloch, S., Carpentier, F. D., & Zillmann, D. (2003). Effects of salience dimensions of informational utility on selective exposure to online news. *Journalism and Mass Communication Quarterly, 80*(1), 91–108. doi: 10.1177/107769900308000107

Knott, M. (2021). Fringe, feasible or false? The COVID-19 Wuhan lab leak theory gets a second look. *Sydney Morning Herald*, 23 May. Retrieved from https://www.smh.com.au/world/north-america/fringe-feasible-or-false-the-covid-19-wuhan-lab-leak-theory-gets-a-second-look-20210521-p57tts.html

Kohring, M., & Matthes, J. (2007). Trust in news media: Development and validation of a multidimensional scale. *Communication Research, 34*(2), 231–252. doi: 10.1177/0093650206298071

Koltay, T. (2011). The media and the literacies: Media literacy, information literacy, digital literacy. *Media, Culture & Society, 33*(2), 211–221. doi: 10.1177/0163443710393382

Kurohi, R. (2021). Pofma curtails constitutional right to free speech, SDP argues in apex court appeal. *The Straits Times*, 18 September. Retrieved from https://www.straitstimes.com/politics/pofma-curtails-constitutional-right-to-free-speech-sdp-argues-in-apex-court-appeal

Kwanda, F. A., & Lin, T. T. (2020). Fake news practices in Indonesian newsrooms during and after the Palu earthquake: A hierarchy-of-influences approach. *Information, Communication & Society, 23*(6), 849–866. doi: 10.1080/1369118X.2020.1759669

Kwon, Y. J., & Kwon, K.-N. (2015). Consuming the objectified self: The quest for authentic self. *Asian Social Science, 11*(2), 301–312. doi: 10.5539/ass.v11n2p301

LaChine, J. (2017). *'Coming soon to a neighborhood near you…' The very real effects and great human costs of fake news: A critical discourse analysis of Breitbart News Network's representation of Muslim and Syrian refugees in the weeks leading up to the 2016 presidential election*. Masters Dissertation, Uppsala University, Sweden.

Ladd, J. M. (2012). *Why Americans hate the media and how it matters.* Princeton, NJ: Princeton University Press.

LaFrance, A. (2020). The prophecies of Q. *The Atlantic.* June. Retrieved from https://www.theatlantic.com/magazine/archive/2020/06/qanon-nothing-can-stop-what-is-coming/610567/

Lagarde, J., & Hudgins, D. (2018). *Fact vs. fiction: Teaching critical thinking skills in the age of fake news.* Portland, OR: International Society for Technology in Education.

Lau, R. R., & Redlawsk, D. P. (2001). Advantages and disadvantages of cognitive heuristics in political decision making. *American Journal of Political Science, 45*(4), 951–971. doi: 10.2307/2669334

Lazarsfeld, P. F., Berelson, B., & Gaudet, H. (1944). *The people's choice.* New York, NY: Columbia University Press.

Lazer, D. M. J., Baum, M. A., Benkler, Y., Berinsky, A. J., Greenhill, K. M., Menczer, F., … Zittrain, J. L. (2018). The science of fake news. *Science, 359*(6380), 1094–1096. doi: 10.1126/science.aao2998

Lazzarato, M. (2009). Neoliberalism in action: Inequality, insecurity and the reconstitution of the social. *Theory, Culture & Society, 26*(6), 109–133. doi: 10.1177/0263276409350283

Lazzarato, M. (2011). *The making of indebted man: An essay on the neoliberal condition* [J. D. Jordan, trans.]. South Pasadena, CA: Semiotext(e).

Lazzarato, M. (2013). *Governing by debt* [J. D. Jordan, trans.]. South Pasadena, CA: Semiotext(e).

Lee, M. Y. H. (2015). Donald Trump's false comments connecting Mexican immigrants and crime. *The Washington Post,* 8 July. Retrieved from https://www.washingtonpost.com/news/fact-checker/wp/2015/07/08/donaldtrumps-false-comments-connecting-mexican-immigrants-and-crime

Lee, M. Y. (2016). Trump's false claim that the murder rate is the 'highest it's been in 45 years'. *The Washington Post,* 3 November. Retrieved from https://www.washingtonpost.com/news/fact-checker/wp/2016/11/03/trumps-false-claim-that-the-murder-rate-is-the-highest-its-been-in-45-years/

Lenters, M. (2021). Deepfakes: Danger to democracy or creativity for all? *Innovatin Origins,* 30 March. Retrieved from https://innovationorigins.com/deepfakes-danger-to-democracy-or-creativity-for-all/

Lenthang, M. (2021). Atlanta shooting and the legacy of misogyny and racism against Asian women. *ABC News,* 22 March. Retrieved from https://abcnews.go.com/US/atlanta-shooting-legacy-misogyny-racism-asian-women/story?id=76533776

LePrince-Ringuet, D. (2018). Iran has its own fake news farms, but they're complete amateurs. *Wired,* 25 October. Retrieved from https://www.wired.co.uk/article/iran-fake-news

Lerbaek, T. O., & Olsen, B. E. V. (2020). *Fake news on Twitter related to the refugee crisis 2016: An exploratory case study.* Kristiansand, Norway: University of Agder.

Lessig, L. (2008). *Remix: Making art and commerce thrive in the hybrid economy.* London: Bloomsbury Academic.

Levinas, E. (1969). *Totality and infinity* [A. Lingis, trans.]. Pittsburgh, PA: Duquesne University Press.

Lewis, J. D., & Weigert, A. (1985). Trust as a social reality. *Social Forces, 63*(4), 967–985. doi: 10.1093/sf/63.4.967

Lingis, A. (1994). *Foreign bodies.* New York: Routledge.

Liu, H. (2008). Social network profiles as taste performances. *Journal of Computer-Mediated Communication, 13*(1), 252–275. doi: 10.1111/j.1083-6101.2007.00395.x

Lloyd, M. (2007). Radical democratic activism and the politics of resignification. *Constellations, 14*(1), 129–146. Retrieved from https://www.academia.edu/5312037/Radical_Democratic_Activism_and_the_Politics_of_Resignification

Locke, J. (1988). *Two treatises of government*. Cambridge: Cambridge University Press.

Lopez-Smith, I. (2017). *Centralising citizenship for media reform: Local news audiences of Brexit*. Lund: Lund University.

Lovink, G., & Rossiter, N. (2018). *Organization after social media*. Brooklyn, NY: Minor Compositions.

Lumsden, K., Goode, J., & Black, A. (2019). 'I will not be thrown out of the country because I'm an immigrant': Eastern European migrants' responses to hate crime in a semi-rural context in the wake of Brexit. *Sociological Research Online, 24*(2), 167–184. doi: 10.1177/1360780418811967

Lumsden, K., & Morgan, H. (2017). Media framing of trolling and online abuse: silencing strategies, symbolic violence, and victim blaming. *Feminist Media Studies, 17*(6), 926–940. doi: 10.1080/14680777.2017.1316755

MacKenzie, A., & Bhatt, I. (2020). Lies, bullshit and fake news: Some epistemological concerns. *Post-digital Science and Education, 2*(1), 9–13. doi: 10.1007/s42438-018-0025-4

Maddocks, S. (2020). 'A Deepfake porn plot intended to silence me': Exploring continuities between pornographic and 'political' deep fakes. *Porn Studies, 7*(4), 415–423. doi: 10.1080/23268743.2020.1757499

Mail Online. (2017). This one's a bit dirty, Harry! Prince's girlfriend Meghan Markle is seen performing sex act in a CAR during premiere episode of 90210 in newly resurfaced scene. *Daily Mail*, 13 March. Retrieved from https://www.dailymail.co.uk/tvshow-biz/article-4308208/Meghan-Markle-seen-performing-sex-act-CAR-90210.html

Maley, J. (2017). Insult machines like Milo Yiannopolous haven't lost free speech, just their bully pulpit. *Sydney Morning Herald*, 24 February. Retrieved from https://www.smh.com.au/opinion/insultmachines-like-milo-yiannopolous-havent-lost-free-speech-just-their-bully-pulpit-20170223-gujlcp.html

Mara, W. (2019). *Fake News – Global Citizens: Modern Media*. Ann Arbor, MI: Cherry Lake Publishing.

Maras, M. H., & Alexandrou, A. (2019). Determining authenticity of video evidence in the age of artificial intelligence and in the wake of Deepfake videos. *The International Journal of Evidence & Proof, 23*(3), 255–262. doi: 10.1177/1365712718807226

Marshall, H., & Drieschova, A. (2018). Post-truth politics in the UK's Brexit referendum. *New Perspectives, 26*(3), 89–105. doi: 10.1177/2336825X1802600305

Martine, T., & De Maeyer, J. (2019). Networks of reference: Rethinking objectivity theory in journalism. *Communication Theory, 29*(1), 1–23. doi: 10.1093/ct/qty020

Mason, L. E., Krutka, D., & Stoddard, J. (2018). Media literacy, democracy, and the challenge of fake news. *Journal of Media Literacy Education, 10*(2), 1–10. doi: 10.23860/JMLE-2018-10-2-1

McCoy, T. S. (1993). *Voices of difference: Studies in critical philosophy and mass communication*. Cresskill, NJ: Hampton Press.

McGuiness, P. P. (2021). Want to be part of the fashionable set? Don't join the 'freethinkers'. *The Age*, 19 June. Retrieved from https://www.theage.com.au/national/want-to-be-part-of-the-fashionable-set-don-t-join-the-freethinkers-20210618-p58270.html

McIntosh, J. (2020). Introduction: The Trump era as a linguistic emergency. In J. McIntosh & N. Mendoza-Denton (Eds.), *Language in the Trump era: Scandals and emergencies* (pp. 1–43). Cambridge: Cambridge University Press.

McMillan, S. (2002). A four-part model of cyber-interactivity: Some cyber-places are more interactive than others. *New Media & Society, 4*(2), 271–291. doi: 10.1177/146144480200400208

McNair, B. (2017). *Fake news: Falsehood, fabrication and fantasy in journalism*. London: Routledge.

McNair, B. (2018). *Fake news: Falsehood, fabrication and fantasy in journalism*. London: Routledge.

McRobbie, A. (2006). Vulnerability, violence and (cosmopolitan) ethics: Butler's *Precarious Life. The British Journal of Sociology, 57*(1), 69–86.

McRobbie, A. (2020). *Feminism and the politics of resilience: Essays on gender, media and the end of welfare*. Cambridge: Polity.

Menzies, R. (1942). The forgotten people. *Speech*, 22 May. Retrieved from http://www.liberals.net/theforgottenpeople.htm

Mercado, M. (2020). *Disinformation and hate speech harm BIPOC*. Los Angeles, CA: The National Hispanic Media Coalition. Retrieved from https://www.nhmc.org/wp-content/uploads/2020/09/Disinformation-and-Hate-Speech-Harm-BIPOC-NHMC.pdf

Metzger, M. J., Hartsell, E. H., & Flanagin, A. J. (2015). Cognitive dissonance or credibility? A comparison of two theoretical explanations for selective exposure to partisan news. *Communication Research, 47*(1), 3–28. doi: 10.1177/0093650215613136

Mikkelson, D. (2020). *Did CNN fake footage of 'Palestinians dancing in the street' after the terrorist attack on the USA?* Retrieved from https://www.snopes.com/fact-check/false-footaging/

Mill, J. S. (1972). *Utilitarianism, on liberty, and considerations on representative government*. London: J.M. Dent & Sons.

Miller, F. (1994). *Censored Hollywood*. Atlanta: Turner Publishing.

Miller, C. (2020). Coronavirus: Far-right spreads Covid-19 'infodemic' on Facebook. *BBC News*, 4 May. Retrieved from https://www.bbc.com/news/technology-52490430

Miller, D., & Sinanan, J. (2014). *Webcam*. Cambridge: Polity Press.

Milner, A. (1996). *Literature, culture and society*. St. Leonards, NSW: Allen & Unwin.

Miranda, C. (2001). Terror Australis: Bin Laden groups in our suburbs. *Daily Telegraph*, 12 October, pp. 1, 4.

Mitchell, A., & Oliphant, J. B. (2020). Americans immersed in COVID-19 news: Most think media are doing fairly well covering it. *Pew Research Center*. Retrieved from https://www.journalism.org/2020/03/18/americansimmersed-in-covid-19-news-most-think-media-are-doing-fairly-wellcovering-it/

Moffitt, B. (2017). Populism in Australia and New Zealand. In C. R. Kaltwasser, P. Taggart, P. O. Espejo, & P. Ostiguy (Eds.), *The Oxford handbook of populism* (online). Oxford: Oxford University Press. doi: 10.1093/oxfordhb/9780198803560.013.3

Moore, M., & Ramsay, G. (2017). *UK media coverage of the 2016 EU referendum campaign*. London: Centre for the Study of Media, Communication and Power, Kings College London. Retrieved from https://www.kcl.ac.uk/policy-institute/assets/cmcp/uk-media-coverage-of-the-2016-eu-referendum-campaign.pdf

Morgan, G. (2016). *Global Islamophobia: Muslims and moral panic in the West*. London: Routledge.

Morley, D. (1980). *The 'Nationwide' audience*. London: British Film Institute.

Morrissey, L. (2017). Alternative facts do exist: Belief, lies and politics. *The Conversation*, 5 October. Retrieved from https://theconversation.com/alternative-facts-do-exist-beliefs-lies-and-politics-84692

Mudde, C., & Kaltwasser, C. R. (2017). *Populism: A very short introduction*. Oxford: Oxford University Press.

Muller, D. (2014). *Journalism ethics for the digital age*. Melbourne: Scribe Publications.

Mutsvairo, B., & Bebawi, S. (2019). Journalism educators, regulatory realities, and pedagogical predicaments of the 'fake news' era: A comparative perspective on the Middle East and Africa. *Journalism & Mass Communication Educator, 74*(2), 143–157. doi: 10.1177/1077695819833552

Mutz, D. C., & Reeves, B. (2005). The new videomalaise: Effects of televised incivility on political trust. *American Political Science Review, 99*(1), 1–15. doi: 10.1017/S0003055405051452

Myers, R. (2020). Queen fights to save monarchy in royal crisis talks after Harry and Meghan news. *The Daily Mirror*, 9 January. Retrieved from https://www.mirror.co.uk/news/uk-news/queen-fights-save-monarchy-royal-21250128

Naruniec, J., Helminger, L., Schroers, C., & Weber, R. M. (2020). High-resolution neural face swapping for visual effects. *Eurographics Symposium on Rendering, 39*(4). Retrieved from https://studios.disneyresearch.com/wp-content/uploads/2020/06/High-Resolution-Neural-Face-Swapping-for-Visual-Effects.pdf

National LGBTI Health Alliance. (2020). *Snapshot of mental health and suicide prevention statistics for LGBTI people.* Retrieved from https://d3n8a8pro7vhmx.cloudfront.net/lgbtihealth/pages/549/attachments/original/1595492235/2020-Snapshot_mental_health_%281%29.pdf?1595492235

Naylor, B. (2021). Read Trump's Jan 6 Speech, a key part of impeachment Trial. *NPR*. Retrieved from https://www.npr.org/2021/02/10/966396848/read-trumps-jan-6-speech-a-key-part-of-impeachment-trial

Nelson, C., & Grossberg, L. (1988). *Marxism and the interpretation of culture.* Chicago, IL: University of Illinois Press.

New York Times. (2020). Going rogue: Prince Harry and Meghan caught the palace off guard. *New York Times*, 10 January. Retrieved from https://www.nytimes.com/2020/01/09/world/europe/duchess-sussex-prince.html?action=click&module=RelatedLinks&pgtype=Article

Newman, N., Fletcher, R., Kalogeropoulos, A., Levy, D. A. L., & Nielsen, R. K. (2018). *Reuters Institute digital news report 2018.* Oxford: Reuters Institute for the Study of Journalism.

Newman, N., Fletcher, R., Schulz, A., Andi, S., & Nielsen, R. (2020). *Reuters Institute digital news report 2020.* Oxford: Reuters Institute for the Study of Journalism.

Nickerson, R. S. (1998). Confirmation bias: A ubiquitous phenomenon in many guises. *Review of General Psychology, 2*(2), 175–220. doi: 10.1037/1089-2680.2.2.175

Nielsen, R. K., & Graves, L. (2017). *'News you don't believe': Audience perspectives on fake news.* Oxford: Reuters Institute for the Study of Journalism.

Nieva, R. (2021). QAnon channels delete their own YouTube videos to evade punishment. *CNet*, 13 May. Retrieved from https://www.cnet.com/features/qanon-channels-are-deleting-their-own-youtube-videos-to-evade-punishment/

Noel, T. K. (2020). Conflating culture with COVID-19: Xenophobic repercussions of a global pandemic. *Social Sciences and Humanities Open.* doi: 10.1016/j.ssaho.2020.100044

Nordic Policy Centre. (2021). Media literacy education in Finland. *Nordic Policy Centre.* Retrieved from https://www.nordicpolicycentre.org.au/media_literacy_education_in_finland

Nuckols, B. (2017). Inaugural crowds sure to be huge _ but how huge? *Associated Press – The big story*, 18 January. Retrieved from https://web.archive.org/web/20170213034009/http://bigstory.ap.org/article/7afad98b7d78423cbb5140fe810e3480/when-it-comes-inaugural-crowds-does-size-matter

OfCom. (2020). *Half of UK adults exposed to false claims about Coronavirus.* Retrieved from https://www.ofcom.org.uk/about-ofcom/latest/featuresand-news/half-of-uk-adults-exposed-to-false-claims-about-coronavirus

Ognyanova, K. (2016). Researching community information needs. In M. Lloyd & L. A. Friedland (Eds.), *The communication crisis in America, and how to fix it* (pp. 31–46). New York, NY: Palgrave Macmillan.

Ognyanova, K., Lazer, D., Robertson, R. E., & Wilson, C. (2020). Misinformation in action: Fake news exposure is linked to lower trust in media, higher trust in government when your side is in power. *Harvard Kennedy School Misinformation Review, 1*(4), 1–19. doi: 10.37016/mr-2020-024

Ogonowski, A., Montandon, A., Botha, E., & Reyneke, M. (2014). Should new online stores invest in social presence elements? The effect of social presence on initial trust formation. *Journal of Retailing and Consumer Services, 21*(4), 482–491. doi: 10.1016/j.jretconser.2014.03.004

Ohman, C. (2020). Introducing the pervert's dilemma: A contribution to the critique of deepfake pornography. *Ethics and Information Technology, 22*(2), 133–140. doi: 10.1007/s10676-019-09522-1

Oremus, W. (2016). Only you can stop the spread of fake news. *Slate,* 13 December. Retrieved from http://www.slate.com/articles/technology/technology/2016/12/intro-ducing_this_is_fake_slate_s_tool_for_stopping_fake_news_on_facebook.html

Pacepa, I. M., & Rychlak, R. J. (2013). *Disinformation: Former spy chief reveals secret strategies for undermining freedom, attacking religion, and promoting terrorism.* Montgomery, AL: WND Books.

Papacharissi, Z. (2015). *Affective publics: Sentiment, technology, and politics.* Oxford: Oxford University Press.

Pariser, E. (2011). *The filter bubble: What the Internet is hiding from you.* New York, NY: Penguin.

Park, S., Fisher, C., Fuller, G., & Lee, J. (2018). *Digital news report: Australia 2018.* Canberra, ACT: News and Media Research Centre, University of Canberra.

Park, S., Park, J. Y., Kang, J.-H., & Cha, M. (2021). The presence of unexpected biases in online fact-checking. *Harvard Kennedy School Misinformation Review,* 27 January. Retrieved from https://misinforeview.hks.harvard.edu/article/the-presence-of-unex-pected-biases-in-online-fact-checking/

Parliament of Australia. (2021). *Treasury Laws Amendment (News Media and Digital Platforms Mandatory Bargaining Code) Bill 2021.* Retrieved from https://parlinfo.aph.gov.au/parlInfo/download/legislation/bills/r6652_aspassed/toc_pdf/20177b01.pdf;fileType=application%2Fpdf

Pate, U. A., & Idris, H. (2017). How journalists survived to report: Professionalism and risk management in the reporting of terror groups and violent extremism in North East Nigeria. In U. Carlsson & R. Pöyhtäri (Eds.), *The assault on journalism: Building knowledge to protect freedom of expression* (pp. 159–170). Göteborg: Nordicom University.

Paul, K. (2019). California makes 'deepfake' videos illegal, but law may be hard to enforce. *The Guardian,* 8 October. Retrieved from https://www.theguardian.com/us-news/2019/oct/07/california-makes-deepfake-videos-illegal-but-law-may-be-hard-to-enforce

Paul, K. (2020). TikTok: False posts about US election reach hundreds of thousands. *The Guardian,* 6 November. Retrieved from https://www.theguardian.com/technol-ogy/2020/nov/05/tiktok-us-election-misinformation

Pennycook, G., Cannon, T., & Rand, D. G. (2018). Prior exposure increases perceived accuracy of fake news. *Journal of Experimental Psychology, 147*(12), 1865–1880. doi: 10.1037/xge0000465

Perry, D. K. (1996). *Theory and research in mass communicaiton: Contexts and conse-quences.* Mahwah, NJ: Lawrence Erlbaum.

Person, B., Sy, F., Holton, K., Govert, B., & Liang, A. (2004). Fear and stigma: The epi-demic within the SARS outbreak. *Emerging Infectious Diseases, 10*(2), 358–363. doi: 10.3201/eid1002.030750

Pettegrew, J. (1995). A post-modernist moment: 1980s commercial culture and the found-ing of MTV. In G. Dines & J. M. Humez (Eds.), *Gender, race and class in media* (pp. 488–498). Thousand Oaks, CA: Sage.

Phillips, R., & Rankin, R. (2003). Australia: State Labor government and media attack Anti-Discrimination Board. *World Socialist Website,* 30 May. Retrieved from https://www.wsws.org/en/articles/2003/05/anti-m30.html

Philo, G. (1993). Getting the message: Audience research in the Glasgow University Media Group. In J. Eldridge (Ed.), *Getting the message: News, truth and power* (pp. 254–270). London: Routledge.

Philo, G. (1995). The media in a class society. In G. Philo (Ed.), *Glasgow media group reader, Volume 2: Industry, economy, war and politics* (pp. 176–183). London: Routledge.

Plummer, K. (1995). *Telling sexual stories: Power, change and social worlds*. London: Routledge.

Polletta, F., & Callahan, J. (2017). Deep stories, nostalgia narratives, and fake news: Storytelling in the Trump era. *American Journal of Cultural Sociology*, 5(3), 392–408. doi: 10.1057/s41290-017-0037-7

Polonski, V. (2016). Social media voices in the UK's EU referendum. *Medium*, 15 May. Retrieved from https://medium.com/@slavacm/social-media-voices-in-theuks-eu-referendum-brexitor-bremain-what-does-the-internet-say-about-ebbd7b27cf0f#.wtk0mbjfq

Porter, R. (1996). Is Foucault useful for understanding eighteenth and nineteenth century sexuality? In N. R. Keddie (Ed.), *Debating gender, debating sexuality* (pp. 247–267). London: New York University Press.

Povinelli, E. A. (2012). *Economies of abandonment: Social belonging and endurance in late liberalism*. Durham, NC: Duke University Press.

Poynter. (2021). *The international fact checking network*. Retrieved from https://www.poynter.org/ifcn/

Poynting, S., Noble, G., Tabar, P., & Collins, J. (2004). *Bin Laden in the suburbs: Criminalising the Arab other*. Sydney, NSW: Sydney Institute of Criminology.

Prochazka, F., & Schweiger, W. (2019). How to measure generalized trust in news media? An adaptation and test of scales. *Communication Methods and Measures*, 13(1), 26–42. doi: 10.1080/19312458.2018.1506021

Pulver, A. (2018). Nicolas Cage expresses 'frustration' with Cage rage internet meme. *The Guardian*, 19 September. Retrieved from https://www.theguardian.com/film/2018/sep/19/nicolas-cage-rage-internet-meme-mandy

Putnam, R. D. (1993). *Making democracy work: Civic traditions in modern Italy*. Princeton, NJ: Princeton University Press.

Radway, J. (1988). Reception study: Ethnography and the problems of dispersed audiences and nomadic subjects. *Cultural Studies*, 2(4), 359–376. doi: 10.1080/09502388800490231

Randell-Moon, H. (2017). Thieves like us: The British monarchy, celebrity, and settler colonialism. *Celebrity Studies*, 8(3), 393–408. doi: 10.1080/19392397.2017.1299019

Rattner, N. (2021). Trump's election lies were among his most popular tweets. *CBNC*, 13 January. Retrieved from https://www.cnbc.com/2021/01/13/trump-tweets-legacy-of-lies-misinformation-distrust.html

Repo, J., & Yrjölä, R. (2015). We're all princesses now: Sex, class, and neoliberal governmentality in the rise of middle-class monarchy. *European Journal of Cultural Studies*, 18(6), 471–760. doi: 10.1177/1367549415572320

Reuters Institute for the Study of Journalism. (2021). *Timeline: Prince Harry and Meghan – and 'Megxit'*. Retrieved from https://www.reuters.com/article/us-britain-royals-meghan-timeline-idUSKBN2AX18V

Rheingold, H. (2003). *Smart mobs: The next social revolution*. Cambridge, MA: Basic Books.

Ricoeur, P. (1970). *Freud and philosophy: An essay on interpretation* [D. Savage, trans.]. London: Yale University Press.

Rizmal, Z. (2021). Family of Jason Langhans pleads for justice after teenager's death following party assault. *ABC News*, 15 April. Retrieved from https://www.abc.net.au/news/2021-04-15/jason-langhans-family-appeals-for-justice/100070984

Robertson, A. (2018). I'm using AI to face-swap Elon Musk and Jeff Bezos, and I'm really bad at it. *The Verge*, 11 February. Retrieved from https://www.theverge.com/2018/2/11/16992986/fakeapp-deepfakes-ai-face-swapping

Robinson, J. (2018). The Legal Nightmare that is FakeApp. *Medium*, 6 February. Retrieved from https://medium.com/@astukari/the-legal-nightmare-that-is-fakeapp-321afc0565e3

Robinson, J. (2011). NoW phone-hacking scandal: News Corp's 'rogue reporter' defence unravels. *The Guardian*, 18 January. Retrieved from https://www.theguardian.com/media/2011/jan/17/phone-hacking-news-of-the-world?CMP=twt_fd

Rosello, M. (1998). *Declining the stereotype: Ethnicity and representation in French cultures:* Hanover, NH: University Press of New England.

Rothschild, M. (2021). *The storm is upon us: How QAnon became a movement, cult, and conspiracy theory of everything.* London: Melville House.

RoyalFoibles. (2020). Who Meghan was before Harry, and who she wasn't. *RoyalFoibles*, 16 June. Retrieved from https://www.royalfoibles.com/who-meghan-was-before-harry-and-who-she-wasnt/

Ruiz, M. (2020). 'Megxit' doesn't mean what you think it means. *Vanity Fair*, 17 January. Retrieved from https://www.vanityfair.com/style/2020/01/meghan-markle-megxit-problem

Rzymski, P., & Nowicki, M. (2020). COVID-19-related prejudice toward Asian medical students: A consequence of SARS-CoV-2 fears in Poland. *Journal of Infection and Public Health, 13*(6), 873–876. doi: 10.1016/j.jiph.2020.04.013

Salazar, P.-J. (2018). The alt-right as a community of discourse. *Javnost – The Public, 25* (1–2), 135–143. doi: 10.1080/13183222.2018.1423947

Samier, E. A. (2014). *Secrecy and tradecraft in educational administration: The covert side of educational life.* London: Routledge.

Schäfer, C., & Schadauer, A. (2018). Online fake news, hateful posts against refugees, and a surge in xenophobia and hate crimes in Austria. In G. Dell'Orto & I. Wetzstein (Eds.), *Refugee news, refugee politics: Journalism, public opinion and policymaking in Europe* (pp. 109–116). New York, NY: Routledge.

Sebastian, M., & Bruney, G. (2020). Years after being debunked, interest in Pizzagate is rising a Again. *Esquire*, 24 July. Retrieved from https://www.esquire.com/news-politics/news/a51268/what-is-pizzagate/

Senft, T. (2008). *Cam girls: Celebrity and community in the age of social networks.* New York, NY: Peter Lang.

Sengul, K. (2019). Critical discourse analysis in political communication research: A case study of right-wing populist discourse in Australia. *Communication Research and Practice, 5*(4), 376–392. doi: 10.1080/22041451.2019.1695082

Sengul, K. (2020). Never let a good crisis go to waste: Pauline Hanson's exploitation of COVID-19 on Facebook. *Media International Australia, 178*(1), 101–105. doi: 10.1177/1329878X20953521

Shachaf, P., & Hara, N. (2010). Beyond vandalism: Wikipedia trolls. *Journal of Information Science, 36*(3), 357–370. doi: 10.1177/0165551510365390

Shephard, A. (2021). The conservative media really wants you to think the capitol riot is the left's fault. *New Republic*, 9 January. Retrieved from https://newrepublic.com/article/160845/conservative-media-really-wants-think-capitol-riot-lefts-fault

Shimizu, K. (2020). 2019-nCoV, fake news, and racism. *The Lancet, 395*(10225), 685–686. doi: 10.1016/S0140-6736(20)30357-3

Shin, J., & Thorson, K. (2017). Partisan selective sharing: The biased diffusion of fact-checking messages on social media. *Journal of Communication, 67*(2), 233–255. doi: 10.1111/jcom.12284

Shinko, R. E. (2010). Ethics after liberalism: Why (autonomous) bodies matter. *Millennium – Journal of International Studies, 38*(3), 723–745. doi: 10.1177/0305829810366474

Silverman, C. (2016). How the bizarre conspiracy theory behind 'pizzagate' was spread. *Buzzfeed*, 6 December. Retrieved from https://www.buzzfeed.com/craigsilverman/fever-swamp-election

Silverman, C., & Alexander, L. (2016). How teens in the Balkans Are duping Trump supporters with fake news. *BuzzFeed News*, 3 November. Retrieved from https://www.buzzfeednews.com/article/craigsilverman/how-macedonia-became-a-global-hub-for-pro-trump-misinfo

Simic, Z. (2016). Struggle street – Poverty porn? In M. Arrow, J. Baker, & C. Monagle (Eds.), *Small screens: Essays on contemporary Australian television* (pp. 171–187). Melbourne, Vic: Monash University Publishing.

Singer, J. B. (2003). Who are these guys? The online challenge to the notion of journalistic professionalism. *Journalism, 4*(2), 139–163. doi: 10.1177/1464884903004002021

Singer, M. (2018). Why are women overwhelmingly cast as the villains on reality TV? *Sydney Morning Herald*, 7 February. Retrieved from https://www.smh.com.au/entertainment/celebrity/why-are-women-overwhelmingly-cast-as-the-villains-on-reality-tv-20180206-h0uknr.html

Singh Grewal, D. (2016). Conspiracy theories in a networked world. *Critical Review, 28*(1), 24–43. doi: 10.1080/08913811.2016.1167404

Slavtcheva-Petkova, V. (2016). Are newspapers' online discussion boards democratic tools or conspiracy theories' engines? A case study on an Eastern European 'media war'. *Journalism & Mass Communication Quarterly, 93*(4), 1115–1134. doi: 10.1177/1077699015610880

Smith-Shomade, B. E. (2004). Narrowcasting in the new world information order: A space for the audience? *Television & New Media, 5*(1), 69–81. doi: 10.1177/1527476403259746

Speed, E., & Mannion, R. (2017). The rise of post-truth populism in pluralist liberal democracies: Challenges for health policy. *International Journal of Health Policy and Management, 6*(5), 249–251. doi: 10.15171/IJHPM.2017.19

Spring, M. (2020). Coronavirus: The human cost of virus misinformation. *BBC News*, 27 May. Retrieved from https://www.bbc.com/news/stories-52731624

Stanton, Z. (2020). You're living in the golden age of conspiracy theories. *Politico*, 17 June. Retrieved from https://www.politico.com/news/magazine/2020/06/17/conspiracy-theories-pandemic-trump-2020-election-coronavirus-326530

Stawicki, S. P., Firstenberg, M. S., & Papadimos, T. J. (2020). The growing role of social media in international health security: The good, the bad, and the ugly. In A. Masys, R. Izurieta, & M. R. Ortiz (Eds.), *Global health security: Advanced sciences and technologies for security applications* (pp. 341–347). Cham: Springer.

Stefanone, M. A., Vollmer, M., & Covert, J. M. (2019). In news we trust? Examining credibility and sharing behaviors of fake news. *In Proceedings of the 10th international conference on social media and society* (pp. 136–147). doi: 10.1145/3328529.3328554

Sterrett, D., Malato, M., Benz, J., Kantor, L., Tompson, T., Rosenstiel, T., … Loker, K. (2019). Who shared it?: Deciding what news to trust on social media, *Digital Journalism, 7*(6), 783–801. doi: 10.1080/21670811.2019.1623702

Stratton, J. (1998). *Race daze: Australia in identity crisis*. London: Pluto.

Subedar, A. (2018). The godfather of fake news. *BBC News*, 27 November. Retrieved from https://www.bbc.co.uk/news/resources/idt-sh/the_godfather_of_fake_news

Sunstein, C. (2001). *Echo chambers: Bush vs. Gore, impeachment, and beyond*. Princeton, NJ: Princeton University Press.

Sussex Official. (2019). *Statement by His Royal Highness Prince Harry, Duke of Sussex.* Retrieved from https://sussexofficial.uk/

Swart, J., & Broersma, M. (2021). The trust gap: Young people's tactics for assessing the reliability of political news. *The International Journal of Press/Politics.* doi: 19401612211006696

Szostek, J. (2018). Nothing is true? The credibility of news and conflicting narratives during 'information war' in Ukraine. *The International Journal of Press/Politics, 23*(1), 116–135. doi: 10.1177/1940161217743258

Taber, C. S., & Lodge, M. (2006). Motivated skepticism in the evaluation of political beliefs. *American Journal of Political Science, 50*(3), 755–769. doi: 10.1111/j.1540-5907.2006.00214.x

Tan, C. (2020). COVID-19 has prompted a spike in racist attacks. We need to start tracking them better. *ABC News*, 9 May. Retrieved from https://www.abc.net.au/news/2020-05-09/coronavirus-covid-19-racist-attacks-data-collection-strategy/12229162?nw=0

Tandoc, E. C., & Takahashi, B. (2017). Log in if you survived: collective coping on social media in the aftermath of Typhoon Haiyan in the Philippines. *New Media and Society, 19*(11), 1778–1793. doi: 10.1177/1461444816642755

Tandoc, E. C., Lim, Z. W., & Ling, R. (2018). Defining 'fake news'. *Digital Journalism*, *6*(2), 137–153. doi: 10.1080/21670811.2017.1360143

Tardáguila, C., & Örsek, B. (2019). How the world celebrated the third International Fact-Checking Day. *Poynter*, 9 April. Retrieved from https://www.poynter.org/fact-checking/2019/how-the-world-celebrated-the-third-international-fact-checking-day/

Tavernise, S., & Oppel, R. A. (2020). Spit on, yelled at, attacked: Chinese-Americans fear for their safety. *The New York Times*, 23 March. Retrieved from https://www.nytimes.com/2020/03/23/us/chinese-coronavirus-racist-attacks.html

Taylor, A. (2016). A Twitter hoax briefly convinced some that Queen Elizabeth II was dead. *The Washington Post*, 31 December. Retrieved from https://www.washingtonpost.com/news/worldviews/wp/2016/12/30/a-twitter-hoax-briefly-convinced-britain-that-queen-elizabeth-ii-was-dead/

Taylor, R. (2021). Midwives told to stop using terms like 'mothers', 'breastfeeding' and 'maternal'. The Daily Mirror, 10 February. Retrieved from https://www.mirror.co.uk/news/uk-news/midwives-told-stop-using-terms-23473645

Terranova, T. (2009). Another life: The nature of political economy in Foucault's genealogy of biopolitics. *Theory, Culture & Society*, *26*(6), 234–262. doi: 10.1177/0263276409352193

The Economist. (2021). Censorious governments are abusing 'fake news' laws. *The Economist*, 11 February. Retrieved from https://www.economist.com/international/2021/02/11/censorious-governments-are-abusing-fake-news-laws

Thompson, J. D., & Cover, R. (2021). Digital hostility, internet pile-ons, and shaming: A case study. *Convergence: The International Journal of Research into New Media Technologies*, Online First. doi: 10.1177/13548565211030461

Thompson, J. D., & Muller, D. (2021). Freedom of speech is not freedom from ethics: the 2019 Israel Folau media controversy as a case study. *Media International Australia*, Online First. doi: 10.1177/1329878X21992890

Tong, S., Van Der Heide, B., Langwell, L., & Walther, J. B. (2008). Too much of a good thing? The relationship between number of friends and interpersonal impressions on Facebook. *Journal of Computer-Mediated Communication*, *13*(3), 531–549. doi: 10.1111/j.1083-6101.2008.00409.x

Towers-Clark, C. (2019). Mona Lisa and Nancy Pelosi: The implications of deepfakes. *Forbes*, 31 May. Retrieved from https://www.forbes.com/sites/charlestowersclark/2019/05/31/mona-lisa-and-nancy-pelosi-the-implications-of-deepfakes/?sh=336ed8214357

Tsfati, Y., & Cappella, J. N. (2003). Do people watch what they do not trust?: Exploring the association between news media skepticism and exposure. *Communication Research*, *30*(5), 504–529. doi: 10.1177/0093650203253371

Tsfati, Y., & Cappella, J. N. (2005). Why do people watch news they do not trust? The need for cognition as a moderator in the association between news media skepticism and exposure. *Media Psychology*, *7*(3), 251–271. doi: 10.1207/S1532785XMEP0703_2

Tucker, J., Guess, A., Barbera, P., Vaccari, C., Siegel, A., Sanovich, S., ... Nyhan, B. (2018). Social media, political polarization, and political disinformation: A review of the scientific literature'. *SSRN Working Paper Series*. doi: 10.2139/ssrn.3144139

Turner, V. (1969). *The ritual process: Structure and anti-structure*. Chicago, IL: Aldine Publishing.

Turner, G. (1993). Media texts and messages. In S. Cunningham & G. Turner (Eds.), *The media in Australia: Industries, texts, audiences* (pp. 205–266). St. Leonards: Allen & Unwin.

Turner, G. (2012). Online gate is open but talkback bulls are a long way from bolting. *The Australian*, 15 October. Retrieved from http://www.theaustralian.com.au/media/

Urry, J. (2007). *Mobilities*. Cambridge: Polity.

Uscinski, J. E., Enders, A. M., Klofstad, C., Seelig, M., Funchion, J., Everett, C., ... Murthi, M. (2020). Why do people believe COVID-19 conspiracy theories? *Harvard Kennedy School Misinformation Review*, *1*(3), 1–12. doi: 10.37016/mr-2020-015

Uslaner, E. (2002). *The moral foundations of trust*. Cambridge: Cambridge University Press.

Vagg, M. (2017). Please don't do your own research on immunisation; you'll get it wrong. *The Conversation*, 6 March. Retrieved from https://theconversation.com/please-dont-do-your-own-research-on-immunisation-youll-get-it-wrong-74091

van der Meer, T. G. L. A., Verhoeven, P., Beentjes, J. W. J., & Vliegenthart, R. (2017). Disrupting gatekeeping practices: Journalists' source selection in times of crisis. *Journalism*, *18*(9), 1107–1124. doi: 10.1177/1464884916648095

van der Nagel, E. (2020). Verifying images: Deepfakes, control, and consent. *Porn Studies*, *7*(4), 424–429. doi: 10.1080/23268743.2020.1741434

Van Zoonen, L. (2012). I-pistemology: Changing truth claims in popular and political culture. *European Journal of Communication*, *27*(1), 56–67. doi: 10.1177/0267323112438808

Vargo, C. J., Guo, L., & Amazeen, M. A. (2018). The agenda-setting power of fake news: A big data analysis of the online media landscape from 2014 to 2016. *New Media & Society*, *20*(5), 2028–2049. doi: 10.1177/1461444817712086

Virdee, S., & McGeever, B. (2018). Racism, crisis, Brexit. *Ethnic & Racial Studies*, *41*(10), 1802–1819. doi: 10.1080/01419870.2017.1361544

Vittert, L. (2019). Are conspiracy theories on the rise in the US? *The Conversation*, 18 September. Retrieved from https://theconversation.com/are-conspiracy-theories-on-the-rise-in-the-us-121968

Waisbord, S. (2018a). The elective affinity between post-truth communication and populist politics. *Communication Research and Practice*, *4*(1), 17–34. doi: 10.1080/22041451.2018.1428928

Waisbord, S. (2018b). Truth is what happens to news: On journalism, fake news and post-truth. *Journalism Studies*, *19*(13), 1866–1878. doi: 10.1080/1461670X.2018.1492881

Walter, N., & Salovich, N. A. (2021). Unchecked vs. Uncheckable: How opinion-based claims can impede corrections of misinformation. *Mass Communication and Society*. doi: 10.1080/15205436.2020.1864406

Wang, C. (2019). Deepfakes, revenge porn and the impact on women. *Forbes*, 1 November. Retrieved from https://www.forbes.com/sites/chenxiwang/2019/11/01/deepfakes-revenge-porn-and-the-impact-on-women/?sh=6092fe8a1f53

Warner, M. (1999). *The trouble with normal: Sex, politics, and the ethics of queer life*. New York, NY: The Free Press.

Weidhase, N. (2021). The feminist politics of Meghan Markle: Brexit, femininity and the nation in crisis. *European Journal of Cultural Studies*. doi: 10.1177/1367549420980010

Wenger, E. (1998). *Communities of practice: Learning, meaning, and identity*. Cambridge: Cambridge University Press.

Westerlund, M. (2019). The emergence of deepfake technology: A review. *Technology Innovation Management Review*, *9*(11), 39–52. doi: 0.22215/timreview/1282

Whatukthinks. (2016a). *How likely or unlikely do you think it is that Turkey will join the EU in the next 10 years?* Retrieved from https://whatukthinks.org/eu/questions/how-likely-or-unlikely-do-you-think-it-isthat-turkey-will-join-the-eu-in-the-next-10-years/

Whatukthinks. (2016b). *Is it true or false that Britain sends £350 million a week to the European Union?* Retrieved from https://whatukthinks.org/eu/questions/is-it-true-or-false-that-britain-sends-350-million-a-week-to-the-european-union/

Williams, R. (1977). *Marxism and literature*. Oxford: Oxford University Press.

Williams, R. (1990). The technology and the society. In D. Bennett (Ed.), *Popular fiction: Technology, ideology, production, reading* (pp. 9–22). London: Routledge.

Williams, A. E. (2012). Trust or bust?: Questioning the relationship between media trust and news attention. *Journal of Broadcasting & Electronic Media*, *56*(1), 116–131. doi: 10.1080/08838151.2011.651186

Wilson, C. C., & Gutierrez, F. (1985). *Minorities and media: Diversity and the end of mass communication*. Beverly Hills, CA: Sage.

Winchester, L. (2015). BBC reporter tweets 'Queen has DIED' during macabre 'rehearsal' for monarch's death. *Express*, 3 June. Retrieved from https://www.express.co.uk/news/royal/581915/Queen-hospital-unwell-Buckingham-Palace-BBC-tweet

Winter, S., & Krämer, N. (2012). Selecting science information in web 2.0: How source cues, message sidedness, and need for cognition influence users' exposure to blog posts. *Journal of Computer-Mediated Communication, 18*(1), 80–96. doi: 10.1111/j.1083-6101.2012.01596

Wisker, Z. L. (2020). The effect of fake news in marketing halal food: A moderating role of religiosity. *Journal of Islamic Marketing, 12*(3), 558–575. doi: 10.1108/JIMA-09-2020-0276

World Health Organization. (2020). *Novel Coronavirus (2019-nCoV) situation report 13*. Retrieved from https://www.who.int/docs/default-source/coronaviruse/situation-reports/20200202-sitrep-13-ncov-v3.pdf

Wu, C., Qian, Y., & Wilkes, R. (2020). Anti-Asian discrimination and the Asian-white mental health gap during COVID-19. *Ethnic and Racial Studies, 44*(5), 1–7. doi: 10.1080/01419870.2020.1851739

Yang, H.-L., & Lai, C.-Y. (2010). Motivations of Wikipedia content contributors. *Computers in Human Behavior, 26*(6), 1377–1383. doi: 10.1016/j.chb.2010.04.011

Yerlikaya, T., & Aslan, S. T. (2020). Social media and fake news in the post-truth era. *Insight Turkey, 22*(2), 177–196. doi: 10.25253/99.2020222.11

Zarocostas, J. (2020). How to fight an infodemic. *The Lancet, 395*(10225), 676. doi: 10.1016/S0140-6736(20)30461-X

Zaryan, S. (2017). *Truth and trust: How audiences are making sense of fake news*. Lund: Lund University.

Zizek, S. (2002). *Welcome to the desert of the real! Five essays on September 11 and related dates*. London: Verso.

Zuckerberg, M. (2016). Message to Facebook users, 16 November. Private communique.

Zwickl, S., Wong, A. F. Q., Dowers, E., Leemaqz, S. Y. L., Bretherton, I., Cook, T., & Cheung, A. S. (2021). Factors associated with suicide attempts among Australian transgender adults. *BMC Psychiatry, 21*(1), 1–9. doi: 10.1186/s12888-021-03084-7

Zylinska, J. (2004). Guns n' rappers: Moral panics and the ethics of cultural studies. *Culture Machine, 6*. Retrieved from https://culturemachine.net/deconstruction-is-in-cultural-studies/guns-n-rappers/

Index

www.ingramcontent.com/pod-product-compliance
Lightning Source LLC
Chambersburg PA
CBHW070336270326
41926CB00017B/3883